Joseph Kleitsch is the most perverse person I've ever met. Artistically and personally. He's the despair of the art dealer, the bane of the reviewer. He can't be labeled, classified, pigeon-holed or otherwise definitely and securely rubber-stamped, which is to his credit, but a source of pathetic bewilderment to his followers. . . . Kleitsch's artistic appetite . . . happen[s] to be remarkably discriminating, active, vastly and diversely absorbing! . . . Because of his perversity, which spells diversity, he gives infinite joy.

—Sonia Wolfson, April 19, 1931[1]

FOREWORDS
Joan Irvine Smith
James Irvine Swinden
Jean Stern

INTRODUCTION
William H. Gerdts

Patricia Trenton

Joseph Kleitsch
A Kaleidoscope of Color

THE IRVINE MUSEUM ❦ IRVINE, CALIFORNIA

©2007 The Irvine Museum
18881 Von Karman Avenue
Irvine, California 92612
www.irvinemuseum.org

Library of Congress Control Number 2007936651
ISBN 978-0-9714092-8-6 (cloth)
    978-0-9714092-9-3 (paper)

Edited and indexed by Jean Patterson
Designed by Lilli Colton
Printed in China through Overseas Printing Company

All measurements are in inches; height precedes width.

COVER: Joseph Kleitsch, *Red and Green* (detail), 1923.
Oil on canvas, 36 x 40". The Irvine Museum.
PAGE 2: Joseph Kleitsch, *Mission San Juan Capistrano* (detail),
1924. Oil on canvas, 24 x 30". The Joan Irvine Smith Collection.

Table of Contents

President's Foreword *by Joan Irvine Smith* ❧ 9
Vice-President's Foreword *by James Irvine Swinden* ❧ 13
Director's Foreword *by Jean Stern* ❧ 17
Preface and Acknowledgments *by Patricia Trenton* ❧ 21
Introduction *by William H. Gerdts* ❧ 29

CHAPTER I Kleitsch's World: The Emerging Artist, 1882–1902 ❧ 45
CHAPTER II The Survival Years: The Formative Period, 1902–1912 ❧ 49
  Cincinnati—Over-the-Rhine, 1902–1903 ❧ 49
  Denver—"The Mile-High City," 1904–1907 ❧ 52
  Hutchinson, Kansas—A Brief Encounter, 1907 ❧ 56
  Mexico City—Pre-Revolution, 1907–1909 ❧ 56
  Mexico City—The Progressive Era under President Madero, 1911–1912 ❧ 62
CHAPTER III Chicago in the 1910s: From Transition to Maturity, 1912–1920 ❧ 69
CHAPTER IV Southern California: Coming of Age, 1920–1931 ❧ 97
  Influences from Abroad—Tour of Europe, 1926–1927 ❧ 152
CHAPTER V An Art of Urgency: A Sense of Time and Place, 1928–1930 ❧ 189
EPILOGUE A Tribute, 1930–1931 ❧ 211

Notes ❧ 231
Appendix ❧ 257
Selected Bibliography ❧ 265
Index ❧ 273

GOVERNOR ARNOLD SCHWARZENEGGER

August 1, 2007

Dear friends,

I am both honored and delighted to have the opportunity to introduce *Joseph Kleitsch: A Kaleidoscope of Color*. For me, this exhibition is striking on a number of different levels. Joseph Kleitsch was an important painter – and chronicler – of California as it came into the twentieth century, and his work even today serves as a window into a time that was full of promise.

I think it's also safe to say that he was someone for whom California and America represented the best that the world has to offer. Like me, he came to the United States from Europe to gain a better life and success doing what he loved. A look through the pages of this book proves that he succeeded at both.

At the same time, though, he gave thought to the wider world around him. I appreciate his concerns for maintaining the most beautiful and unique aspects of California at a time when "conservation" was not the widely known term it is today. His paintings themselves are a terrific recognition of the beautiful natural environment of Laguna Beach as he saw it decades ago.

I congratulate Joan Irvine Smith, president of The Irvine Museum; James Irvine Swinden, vice president; and Director Jean Stern and his staff for organizing and touring this magnificent exhibition. As always, I am inspired by the work of my fellow Californians.

Sincerely,

Arnold Schwarzenegger

President's Foreword

The Board of Directors and staff of The Irvine Museum take great pride and pleasure in presenting this illustrious book on the art and life of Joseph Kleitsch (1882–1931), authored by Dr. Patricia Trenton. The mission of The Irvine Museum is to preserve and display California art of the Impressionist period, and it is our goal to present these magnificent works of art not only to our constituents in California, but also to people throughout the United States and the world over. The paintings that comprise *Joseph Kleitsch: A Kaleidoscope of Color* reflect the highest standards of American art. Furthermore, those that focus on landscapes encapsulate the unique qualities of California Impressionism by combining great beauty with historical significance and, most of all, a deep reverence for nature.

Landscape painting is a time-honored tradition that is inseparable from the spirit of American art. In the early 1800s, at the time of the Industrial Revolution, a group of dedicated landscape painters called the Hudson River School ventured into what was then the "wilderness" of the Hudson River Valley. Lamenting the destruction of their natural environment, they painted virgin and unspoiled countryside. These artists were in awe of the beauty and grandeur of nature and developed a popular and long-lived style that centered on landscape as primary subject. In a very real sense, they were the environmental activists of their day.

In California, a similar group of spiritually aware painters working in the early 1900s recorded the beauty of nature. William Wendt (1865–1946) believed that nature was a manifestation of God and viewed himself as nature's faithful interpreter. His feelings for the land were so profound that only rarely did he include people or animals in his landscapes. Maurice Braun (1877–1941) was affiliated with the Theosophical Society, whose tenets included transcendentalism and the belief that every natural object has a spiritual presence.

Joseph Kleitsch was also one of the leaders of this nascent environmental movement. Painfully aware that the idyllic environment of Laguna Beach was passing, he set out to paint the locales that were most at risk. In chapter five of this book, Dr. Trenton states: "Through his actions and paintings, Kleitsch was recognized as an early preservationist by his peers and by art critics. His recognition of Laguna's imminent transition from village to urban center prompted his efforts to record and preserve its unique lifestyle. In his quest to preserve the past, Kleitsch dedicated almost a decade to faithfully recording and interpreting the rural nature

Joseph Kleitsch, *Bougainvillea, Mission San Juan Capistrano*, 1924. Oil on canvas, 30 x 24". Private Collection, courtesy of The Irvine Museum.

of Old Laguna. In a series of lyrical pictures, he delineated the character of its village buildings and streets, its shores and coastline, and its distant mountains."

With the coming of the 1930s, art no longer paid homage to nature, and artists turned to the cities and the material attributes of the modern age for inspiration. It is said that art mirrors society and that when we supplanted our regard for nature, we placed our trust in technology and undervalued the importance of our natural environment. Now, the perils of ignoring the environment have become painfully clear to people the world over.

The splendor of nature fascinated artists in the past and compelled them to create beautiful paintings. Today, with the renaissance of the glorification of nature in art, that spirit is motivating enlightened people in the same way that it energized artists of nearly a hundred years ago. Their common bond is a deep reverence for nature, and their common goal is to preserve the environment. No statement is more eloquent than the silent testament of these magnificent paintings. Each generation, in its turn, is the steward of the land, water, and air. Our time is now. I sincerely hope that the message these paintings impart will inspire us all to action in this most pressing obligation.

Joan Irvine Smith
President
The Irvine Museum

Joseph Kleitsch, *Enchantment* (detail), 1922. Oil on canvas, 22 x 18 ¼". The Joan Irvine Smith Collection.

Vice-President's Foreword

Joseph Kleitsch: A Kaleidoscope of Color by Dr. Patricia Trenton is a beautiful and informative book on an important member of the California art community in the early twentieth century. A quick glance at the images in this book surely shows that Kleitsch's paintings reflect the highest quality of American art. Indeed, he was an accomplished Impressionist, with unparalleled mastery of elegant line and brilliant color.

Moreover, when we look at these paintings by Kleitsch, we rejoice in seeing life in an isolated, idyllic community, resplendent with aspects of a bygone day: small houses in large lots, unpaved streets, and trees and flowers everywhere. In many ways, old Laguna Beach was characteristic of the ideal small American town.

Originally home to Native Americans who gathered their food from the abundantly lush hillsides and ocean, Laguna Beach was subsequently settled by homesteaders (responsible for the eucalyptus trees that now flourish there), merchants, shopkeepers, celebrities, and artists.

In the late 1800s, Laguna became a resort area with its own "tent city" in the tourist season. Not long afterward, its first hotel was built, and soon the flourishing seaside village became a destination for the social elite. Among Laguna's earliest celebrity visitors, one could count Madame Helena Modjeska, Rudolph Valentino, Charlie Chaplin, Mary Pickford, Errol Flynn, Harold Lloyd, and John Steinbeck, to name but a few.

At about this time, Norman St. Clair (1875–1963) came to Laguna Beach and became the first professional artist to paint the surf, hillsides, and lagoons that ringed the picturesque village. Soon, other noteworthy artists joined him, including Edgar Payne (1883–1947), William Wendt (1865–1946), Gardner Symons (1862–1930), and Frank Cuprien (1871–1946); by 1916, about half of Laguna's 300 year-round residents were artists. Two years later, Payne led his colleagues to form the Laguna Beach Art Association and forever established Laguna's place in the history of California art. This artistic tradition continues to this day through no less than three major art festivals and the world-famous Pageant of the Masters.

In 1920, Kleitsch became a full-time resident of Laguna Beach and joined the art association. A chronicler of everyday life, Kleitsch has left us with a rich pictorial history of life in one of California's most picturesque settings. Through his remarkable paintings, he has preserved forever the natural beauty of a little

Joseph Kleitsch, *The Old Post Office* (*Laguna Beach*) (detail), 1922–23. Oil on canvas, 40 x 34". Laguna Art Museum Collection. Gift of the Estate of Joseph Kleitsch in memory of his wife Edna.

Eden on the Southern California coast that over the years has been compromised by the desire to build a more affluent society, though not necessarily a better one. Kleitsch's paintings should inspire us to examine our past and to explore ways in which to reconcile the preservation of nature's gifts and the remaining beauty of our world with the inevitable advancement of humankind.

James Irvine Swinden
Vice-President
The Irvine Museum

Joseph Kleitsch, *Laguna Road* (detail), 1924. Oil on canvas, 36 x 40". Collection of the City of Laguna Beach.

Director's Foreword

It is with great pride and pleasure that The Irvine Museum presents this wonderfully written and richly illustrated book, *Joseph Kleitsch: A Kaleidoscope of Color* by Dr. Patricia Trenton.

When The Irvine Museum opened, nearly fifteen years ago, Joan Irvine Smith, our founder and president, expressed her vision that the museum publish a series of monographs documenting the art and life of each important California artist during the period 1890–1930. This monograph on Joseph Kleitsch (1882–1931) takes its place alongside our previous books on Guy Rose (1867–1925), Paul de Longpré (1855–1911), and Albert R. Valentien (1862–1925).

In addition, The Irvine Museum has co-published with the Laguna Art Museum a monograph on Colin Campbell Cooper (1856–1937), written by Dr. Deborah Solon, and a forthcoming monograph on William Wendt (1865–1946), by Dr. Will South.

As of this writing, our museum has three more books currently in the research and pre-production stages, including one on Arthur Beaumont (1890–1978), the celebrated California watercolor painter who became the official artist of the U.S. Navy. The brilliant and absorbing text was written by Geoffrey Beaumont, son of the artist. The second book is on John Frost (1890–1937), the remarkable California Impressionist who was stricken with tuberculosis early in life and died at age forty-seven. The Frost book is being prepared by noted California historians Phil Kovinick and Marian Yoshiki-Kovinick. The third book is the Guy Rose Catalogue Raisonné, compiled over the last fifteen years by Roy C. Rose, grand-nephew of the artist and recognized authority on the works of Guy Rose. A catalogue raisonné is an illustrated compilation of all known works by an artist, and as such, is notoriously time consuming.

In the coming years, The Irvine Museum plans to publish definitive books on Maurice Braun (1877–1941), Sam Hyde Harris (1889–1977), and Arthur G. Rider (1886–1975). Learned authorities on each of these artists have expressed a desire to write the relevant texts.

Our museum's exhibitions and publications programs are just two of the many ways we fulfill our commitment to education and preservation of California's cultural heritage. We reach a large number of people who come to exhibitions, both here in Irvine and in various traveling exhibitions that tour

Joseph Kleitsch, *Jeweled Hills* (detail), c. 1922.
Oil on canvas, 26 x 24". Collection of Lenoir Josey.

California and the rest of the country. For those who cannot come to Irvine, we have a long-standing policy, indeed from the first day we opened our doors, that if any non-profit school, library, or other public institution writes a request on its letterhead, the museum will send them a complete set of its books in hardbound editions. To date, I would estimate that we have distributed nearly 2,000 sets of free books to qualifying institutions.

Of course, this newly published volume on Joseph Kleitsch will be included in the sets of Irvine Museum books in the program discussed above. Now, I invite you to read and enjoy this magnificent book, and to discover our heritage of superb paintings that make up the history of California art.

(Mr.) Jean Stern
Executive Director
The Irvine Museum

Joseph Kleitsch, *Cloister, Mission San Juan Capistrano* (detail), c. 1924. Oil on canvas, 17 x 20". Private Collection, courtesy of The Irvine Museum.

Preface and Acknowledgments

The artist Joseph Kleitsch was unique in many respects. An immigrant from Central Europe, he quickly embraced an American way of life, particularly those freedoms that allowed him to express himself without constraint at his easel and to participate in community activities with verve and flamboyance.

Kleitsch had early success as a portraitist, initially in Europe and then in the adopted country that he genuinely loved and admired. His achievement manifested itself in many commissions that demonstrate his extraordinary ability to capture not only the appearance of his subject but also the individual's character, personality, mood, and even passion. An outstanding example of Kleitsch's genius is his portrait of Isador Berger (1917) in which the prominent violinist is portrayed as being completely immersed in the performance of a sonata or rhapsody.

While Kleitsch continued to paint portraits throughout his career, until his premature death in 1931, he was also able to demonstrate his unique talents as a prominent California plein-air painter in such works as *The Old Post Office* (1922–23). And as an early disciple of the preservationist movement, he worked feverishly to record on canvas the character of Old Laguna Beach before it was completely overrun and destroyed by the rampant land boom and development of the Roaring Twenties.

In Southern California, a dramatic change occurred in Kleitsch's art. His palette lightened, his brushstroke became more vigorous, color-laden, and arbitrary, and his focus on portraiture less primary. Kleitsch painted a prodigious number of Old Laguna scenes, some exuberantly baroque still lifes and profusely decorative genre scenes in dazzling color and light, and those expressive impressionistic images of land and sea as seen in *Laguna Cove* (1925). Color and decorative patterning emerged as essential to Kleitsch's compositions. They are clearly evident in the California pictures that seem to partake of the spirit of Hungarian painting. Kleitsch displayed the same love of vivid chromatic effects and the same impassioned lyricism that is evident in Hungarian decorative arts.

In Kleitsch's later years his career blossomed, and he earned a reputation as one of the outstanding California plein-air painters of his day. However, the Great Depression, his untimely death, the forced disposition of his estate, and changing tastes all contributed to a waning interest in his art over almost half a century.

The early 1980s found collectors again drawn to the work of the

Joseph Kleitsch, *Portrait of Isador Berger* (*Rhapsody*) (detail), 1917. Oil on canvas, 40 x 30". Collection of Dr. and Mrs. Edward H. Boseker, courtesy of George Stern Fine Arts.

California plein-air artists. In 1990 *California Light: 1900–1930*, the Laguna Art Museum's scholarly publication and exhibition of nine plein-air painters, generated significant renewed interest in this group of artists. Many of the California painters of this period were rediscovered, among them Joseph Kleitsch. As the principal author of the book, as well as co-curator of that exhibition, I chose to write the essay on Kleitsch. Much of my initial research on the painter took place over a four-year period under the auspices of the Laguna Art Museum. In the years following the exhibition, I continued my research on the artist and finally decided that he deserved a comprehensive monograph. After discovering many of his outstanding paintings, I became even more convinced that Kleitsch was an exceptional artist, unique among California painters. Although his versatility was well recognized by the critics of his time, the evolution of his art was not a linear development like that of California Impressionist Guy Rose (1867–1925). Kleitsch's restless nature resulted in frequent changes of direction as he explored numerous creative avenues. To my mind this made him a more interesting and exciting artist than most plein-air painters of his time.

My goal has been to integrate him into the mainstream of American art history, believing that this would have happened in his short lifetime had not his dealer, Earl Stendahl, had a too-narrow business perspective on Kleitsch's future and insufficient financial resources to offer him national exposure.

It is most appropriate at this time to express my deep gratitude to Joan Irvine Smith and members of her foundation, James Irvine Swinden, and Jean Stern, for their complete commitment to the Joseph Kleitsch Project: a major retrospective with an accompanying book, *Joseph Kleitsch: A Kaleidoscope of Color*. Their unstinting support and encouragement was of significant assistance in the completion of the project.

Writing about Kleitsch's life was particularly difficult. The lack of personal archives resulted in the need to devote almost fifteen years of research to providing an account of his career. The assistance of many generous and devoted individuals has contributed to the realization of this project. I first thank my friend and colleague Janet Murphy, who willingly responded to my many research requests. Working together, we attempted to resolve unanswered questions about the artist's life. Janet shared with me the difficult task of reading microfilm and newspapers, and she demonstrated her skills on the Internet as well. Most important, she compiled a comprehensive bibliography for the book.

Another individual who generously volunteered his time to this project, specifically on chapter five, was Eric Jessen, chief of the Orange County Harbors, Beaches, and Parks Department, who identified the settings of certain Kleitsch paintings in the Laguna area. Eric Jessen and photographer Christopher Bliss trekked the streets of Laguna with me to discover the artist's vantage point for these paintings. My gratitude and fond friendship goes to both of them for their expert assistance.

To Janet Blake, curator of collections at the Laguna Art Museum, I express my appreciation for her willingness to share with me the museum's large archive of material and photographs related to the California plein-air painters and the Laguna Beach Art Association. I am also indebted to the museum's director, Bolton Colburn, who graciously approved the use of Kleitsch material from the publication *California Light*.

Joseph Kleitsch, *Diver's Cove, Laguna*, 1920. Oil on canvas, 26 x 34". Private Collection, courtesy of Redfern Gallery.

I would be remiss if I did not acknowledge the many dealers and collectors who also provided transparencies of their Kleitsch paintings: George Stern of George Stern Fine Arts; Ray Redfern of Redfern Gallery; Whitney Ganz and Patrick Kraft of William A. Karges Fine Art; DeWitt McCall of DeRu's Fine Arts; Paula and Terry Trotter of Trotter Galleries; the late Mark Hoffman and Colleen Hoffman of Maxwell Galleries; Thomas Gianetto, Donald Merrill, and Daniel

Nicodemo of Edenhurst Gallery; and Al Stendahl and Ronald W. Dammann of Stendahl Galleries. And kudos to the collectors who kindly allowed us to reproduce their fine works. They are acknowledged individually in the captions.

Two dealers in particular, David O'Hoy and Michael Kelley, also spent time on Kleitsch research and are passionately devoted to the artist. My thanks for their generosity in sharing their material with me and their assistance in locating paintings.

Joseph Kleitsch, *California*. Oil on canvas, 30 x 40".
Courtesy of Westphal Publishing.

Many individuals have generously supported this project, not only in California but throughout the United States and in Europe. A special expression of gratitude is extended to them for their invaluable assistance: Maksay Ádám, photographer, Romania; Captain Alejandro Alemán, Regional Military Museum, Seville, Spain; Russell Allen, attorney-at-law; Romaine Ahlstrom, Jill Cogen, Chris Adee, and Bert Rinderle, Huntington Library, San Marino, Calif.; Joseph Ambrose, Jr., and Michael D. Feddersen; William Atkins, graphic designer; Heather Becker, Conservation Center, Chicago; David Belardes; Fr. Robert V. Biroschak, J.C.L., J.D., Metropolitan Tribunal of the Archdiocese of Los Angeles; Barbara Blankman, First American Corporation, Santa Ana, Calif.; S. J. Boldrick, Miami-Dade Public Library System, Miami, Fla.; Katherine Bourguignon, Musée d'Art Américain, Giverny, France; Leslie Greene Bowman, Winterthur Museum; Cheryl Canfield, Hutchinson, Kan.; Eliane Carouge, Archives de l'Eure, Evreux, France; Brian Coburn, Atascadero-Martin Polin Library, Atascadero, Calif.; Georgianna Contigulia and Rebecca Lintz, Colorado Historical Society, Denver; Bobi Garland, Director of Research, Western Costume Company; William H. Gerdts, Professor Emeritus, Graduate School at the City University of New York; Diana Haskell, Lloyd Lewis Curator of Midwest Manuscripts, Newberry Library, Chicago; Scott M. Haskins, Fine Art Conservation Laboratories; Frank Hensley, historian, Palette and Chisel Club, Chicago; Alan Frazer and Jourdan Houston, Durango, Colo.; Mrs. Lubomir Hykel; Jane Janz; Harvey Jones, Art Department, Oakland Museum of California; Robert Jones, Laguna Beach, Calif.; Ágnes Király-Végi, Hungarian Consulate, Los Angeles; Susan Kistler, costume researcher; Marjorie Kleitsch; David O. Kleitsch and Family and the late Robert J. Kleitsch and Family; Phil Kovinick and Marian Yoshiki-Kovinick, Archives of American Art, Smithsonian Institution, San Marino, Calif.; Rev. William F. Krekelberg, Mission San Juan Capistrano Archives; Anne Labourdette, Musée Municipal A.G. Poulain, Vernon, France; Catherine Leonard, Christie's, Beverly Hills, Calif.; Scot Levitt, Bonhams & Butterfields, Los Angeles; Pam Ludwig, Grace Gallery, Laguna Beach, Calif.; Marlene McCord, executive assistant/attaché, Embassy of the United States of America, Rome; Mary McIsaac; Leslie Martin, Chicago Historical Society; Jim McCarty, Laguna Beach Public Library, Laguna Beach, Calif.; Edward Maeder, chair, Curatorial Department, Historic Deerfield, Inc., Deerfield, Mass.; Leroy H.

Miranda, Jr., director, Cupa Cultural Center, Pala, Calif.; Evelyn Moodey; J. Kenneth Moore, Metropolitan Museum of Art, New York; Fr. Dennis W. Morrow, SS Peter & Paul's Church, Grand Rapids, Mich.; Nancy Moure; Jonathan Nardone; Prof. James Oles, Wellesley College; Henri de Pierrefeu, Paris; John Powell and Katherine Gass, Photographic Department, Newberry Library, Chicago; Kathryn Rakich, assistant to the Consul General, U.S. Consulate, Florence, Italy; Marianne Richter, Union League Club of Chicago; Ruth Roberts, Indianapolis Museum of Art; Delmy Serrano, The New-York Historical Society; Jim Sleeper, author-historian, Orange County, Calif.; Deborah Barlow Smedstad and Angelo Gabriel, Los Angeles County Museum of Art, Research Library; Nora Smith, conservator; Al Stendahl, Ron and April Dammann, Stendahl Galleries; James Straub; Linda Taubenreuther; Athos Thiery; Jeffrey Trenton; Judith Throm, Archives of American Art, Smithsonian Institution, Washington, D.C.; Ed Van Ginkel and Nick Von Gymnich, Los Angeles Board of Education; Katherine Vollen, National Archives and Records Administration, Washington, D.C.; Sarah Vure, Orange County Museum of Art, Newport Beach, Calif.; Ruth Westphal; Sandy Wheeler, Mission San Juan Capistrano; Barbara Wilson; Professor Robert J. Wimberg; and Hon. Caprice Young, former president, Los Angeles Board of Education.

I owe my friend, art editor Jeanne D'Andrea, a debt of gratitude for her superb editorial assistance in reviewing the manuscript and clarifying and synthesizing the material.

And lastly, my continued love and devotion to my wonderful husband, Norman, who again supported me through all of the vicissitudes of this major project. I express my deepest gratitude to him for his constant support and his generous and kind ways.

Patricia Trenton
Principal Author and Curator

Joseph Kleitsch, *Model's Throne*. Oil on canvas, 40 x 30". Private Collection.

Introduction

Until the appearance of the present volume, a full-length study of the life and art of Joseph Kleitsch (1882–1931), the reputation of this outstanding painter was known only to a small coterie of admirers, collectors, and dealers who have concentrated on the art he produced in Southern California in the early years of the twentieth century. Even within such limitations, Kleitsch has been defined as one of the significant figures in the plein-air/Impressionist movement centered in Laguna Beach, the state's premier artists' colony of the period.

The fact that Kleitsch was Hungarian and had traveled throughout the world and the United States before arriving in Southern California to live there the last ten years of his life was not an uncommon characteristic among his California contemporaries. Indeed, along with Kleitsch, there were a significant number of foreign-born artists in that community. These included Austrian-born Franz A. Bischoff (1864–1929); Swedish-born Carl Oscar Borg (1879–1947); Maurice Braun (1877–1941), who, like Kleitsch, was born in Hungary; Conrad Buff (1886–1975) from Switzerland; Sam Hyde Harris (1889–1977) and William Lees Judson (1842–1928), who were born in England; Norwegian-born Paul Lauritz (1889–1975); and Jean Mannheim (1861–1945), William Ritschel (1864–1949), William Wendt (1865–1946), and Karl Yens (1868–1945), who were German-born. Indeed, other than Guy Rose (1867–1925), who was born in San Gabriel, and Percy Gray (1869–1952) and Armin Hansen (1886–1957), who were born in San Francisco, all other significant artists of this period in California came from other states; but once settled in California, they remained there the rest of their lives.

That Kleitsch should be recognized as a major figure in what has become a much-appreciated and sought-after school of regional Impressionism is not unjust. Certainly, his best-known paintings today are those he created in the 1920s when he was active in Southern California, and his identification with the Impressionist movement is also appropriate, given both his mastery of a broad spectrum of vivid chromatics, and his attraction to out-of-doors painting, much of it centered not only on the scenery surrounding Laguna Beach but also on exploring the town itself. Indeed, Kleitsch's "townscapes" of Laguna Beach are unique, as almost all of his Southern California colleagues devoted themselves rather to the Pacific coastline, the rolling hills beyond the town, or further east into the Santa Ana and San Bernardino mountains, and even up into the Sierra Nevada. In his outdoor paintings, too, Kleitsch shared in the fascination of the

Joseph Kleitsch, *First Street* (detail), 1924. Oil on canvas, 16 x 20". Private Collection, courtesy of The Irvine Museum.

distinctive heritage of early California as represented in the ruins of the San Juan Capistrano Mission, the beauty of which was so enhanced by the mission gardens, all bathed with the glorious sunlight and multitude of varied colors that provided an ideal subject for Impressionist painters.

Kleitsch emerged as a fully professional painter not in California, but in Cincinnati and Denver, also spending time in Mexico City from 1907 to 1909, and making return visits in 1911 and 1912. Mexico in the first decade of the twentieth century could be dangerous, but in fact, Kleitsch was not the only artist working there, and it would be intriguing to know if he crossed paths with such painters as New York artist William Lippincott (1849–1920), San Francisco Bay Area painter Xavier Martinez (1869–1943), Taos artist William Dunton (1878–1936), or the most noted Texan painter of the period, Julian Onderdonk (1882–1922), all of whom are known or believed to have been in Mexico at the same time as Kleitsch. Particularly intriguing is the possible relationship with African-American painter William A. Harper (1873–1910), who lived in Chicago, and died in Mexico City in 1910.

More importantly, Kleitsch became not only a mature but also a significant painter while living the entire decade of the 1910s in Chicago, the city from which so many of the so-called California Impressionists such as Wendt, Edgar Payne (1883–1947), and Alson Clark (1876–1949) also hailed. These artists continued to exhibit their works in Chicago, at times enjoying one-artist shows, and they found patronage in the Midwest as well as in California. Kleitsch's exhibition record in Chicago from 1914 to the end of the decade is impressive, both at the Art Institute of Chicago and the Palette and Chisel Club, probably the most active of the many artists' organizations in the city, though he was primarily identified in that city as an especially able portraitist. Even so, a division between the Chicago portrait painter of the 1910s and the California Impressionist of the 1920s is an oversimplification, as his *Problematicus*—exhibited at the Art Institute of Chicago in 1918—suggests, since it leads easily into his magnificent figural interiors painted in California a few years later. But even many of Kleitsch's likenesses go far beyond the standard practice of contemporary portraiture, being more concerned with psychological probing than with the vivid brushwork and rhythmic compositions of his Chicago colleagues such as Louis Betts (1873–1961) and Wellington Reynolds (1869–1949), whose reflection of the strategies of John Singer Sargent (1856–1925)

Joseph Kleitsch, *Evening Shadows*. Oil on canvas, 33 x 42". Payton Family Collection, courtesy of Redfern Gallery.

and William Merritt Chase (1849–1916) were not embraced by Kleitsch. And even during the 1920s, the basis for Kleitsch's income, if not the inspiration for his finest canvases, still lay in the realm of portraiture, a situation all too familiar with American artists of the past, such as Samuel F. B. Morse (1791–1872), and with such contemporaries as Joseph De Camp (1858–1923), Edmund Tarbell (1862–1938), and Frank Benson (1862–1951), the leading Boston Impressionists of the period.

Yet, with few exceptions, Kleitsch's Chicago years provide little hint of the coloristic explosion that would characterize his art during the 1920s, suggesting that the appearance of European Modernism in the extension of the famously controversial Armory Show, which originated in New York and then opened at the Art Institute of Chicago on March 24, 1913, found little reception with Kleitsch, or indeed with the vast majority of Chicago painters. Yet, once in California, active in the Laguna Beach art colony as well as in Los Angeles, Kleitsch went beyond the

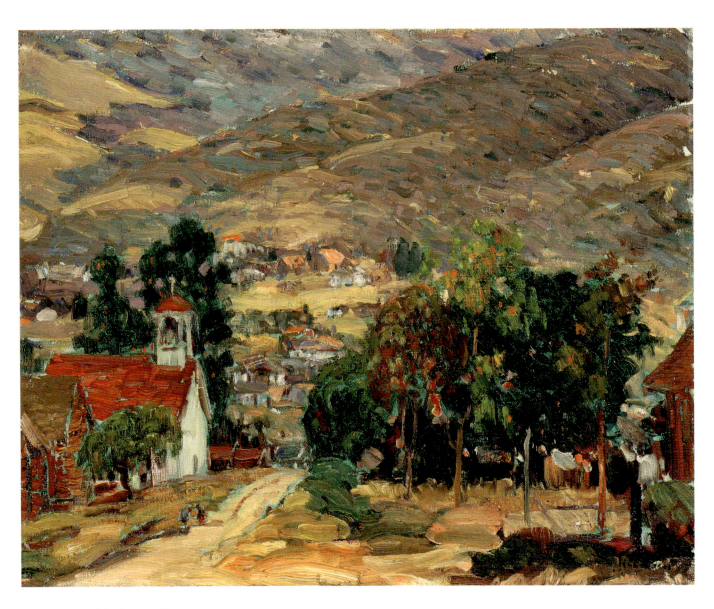

Joseph Kleitsch, *Foothill Village*, 1925. Oil on canvas, 16 x 20". S. & R. Arthur Collection.

primary emphasis on light, color, and atmosphere that characterizes Impressionist painting. Rather, he manipulated these natural elements with an Expressionist and very individual focus to create a body of work uniquely his own. Very few of Kleitsch's paintings, even his more straightforward landscapes painted in and around Laguna Beach, are distinguished by his particularly vigorous paint handling and his dramatic, even occasionally capricious, coloristic and tonal contrasts. It may be a measure of Kleitsch's individuality that in 1923 he was a founder and vice president of the Painters and Sculptors Club of Los Angeles, a group that was neither affiliated with the primarily Impressionist-oriented California Art Club nor with the more Modernist though often short-lived organizations that developed under the aegis of Stanton Macdonald-Wright (1890–1973) during the 1920s. Rather, the artists exhibiting with the club, in addition to Kleitsch, ranged from a few Impressionist painters such as Lauritz and John Frost (1890–1937), to more introspective painters like Haldane Douglas (1893–1980) and German-born Expressionist portraitist Max Wieczorek (1863–1955). And it may be a reflection of Kleitsch's European background that a number of the club's exhibitors hailed from Germany, Austria, and Eastern Europe, including Theodore Lukits (1897–1922), who came from the same region of Hungary (now Romania) near Temesvár.

Kleitsch's extended travel in Europe from January 1926 until November 1927 may have exposed him to a wealth of artistic endeavors by both old and new masters, but the experience does not seem to have impacted his art in any concrete way; indeed, some of his figural work of the later 1920s appears to retreat from the expressive handling of the earlier years of the decade. Despite the financial crash in October 1929 and the critical effect it had on his fortunes, Kleitsch would seem to have regained his momentum toward increasing Expressionism in his late Laguna beach scenes, done prior to his fatal heart attack in November 1931.

This definitive study of the artist by Dr. Patricia Trenton exposes the limitations of regional categorization. If Kleitsch's best-known works were painted while he was a resident of California, this covered little more than the final ten-year span of his activity, and even then he took time out to tour Europe in 1926 and 1927. For all the beauty and creativity of the paintings Kleitsch produced during this period, to categorize him as a "California Impressionist" is inappropriate on several counts. On the one hand, he adopted some, but only some, of the strategies of Impressionism late in his career; on the other, he had actually begun his artistic production as early as the turn of the century in his native Hungary, shortly before immigrating to the United States.

If, by the 1920s, Impressionism had long had its heyday in Europe and even the Eastern United States, it represented modern art on the West Coast, and the paintings by Kleitsch and his colleagues of "old California" in what was then still a Modernist aesthetic, these mission pictures mirrored the somewhat earlier art of the most celebrated of American Impressionists, Childe Hassam (1859–1935), who explored the traditional architecture of New England in colonial towns such as Newport, Gloucester, and Provincetown, utilizing the vivid coloristic strategies of Impressionism. Likewise, in Kleitsch's late Laguna beach scenes, the artist favored a vivid Expressionism far more dynamic than the delicate pastels of his colleague William Griffith (1866–1940), or even the playful coloration of Edward Potthast (1857–1927), the principal Eastern Impressionist of beach settings.

Even in much of his landscape and townscape paintings, Kleitsch's colorism took on stronger, and often more arbitrary dynamics than those of many of his colleagues, such as William Wendt, Frank Cuprien (1871–1946), and Anna Hills (1882–1930), and this is even truer of his indoor scenes, both still lifes and figure paintings. In fact, the sumptuously unctuous pigment that Kleitsch often favored is distinct from that of his California colleagues, and suggests rather affinities with the technique of early French nineteenth-century Modernists such as Manet and Courbet, though contemporary critics also likened his painterly methods to the work of the Dutch Old Master Frans Hals.

It would seem that Kleitsch's figurative interiors are his most distinct contribution to the repertory of the California Impressionists—though again, Impressionism can be interpreted here only loosely. Paintings of lovely, contemplative women in interiors were far more a staple of Impressionist painters of the American Northeast, especially the artists of the Boston School, led by Tarbell, but the elegant asceticism of their paintings are a world apart from the rich diversity of forms and strong contrasts of Kleitsch's interiors. Even more distinct is the sense of subdued tension that characterizes the women in Kleitsch's pictures, as opposed to the lassitude of their Eastern counterparts.

Much like the works of his colleague Karl Yens, who also exhibited with the Painters and Sculptors Club, Kleitsch's art defies easy and conventional classification. Trenton clearly notes the difficulty in "labeling, classifying or pigeon-holing" by opening this volume with a quote by Los Angeles critic Sonia Wolfson, who noted that Kleitsch's work "gives infinite joy." And so will this publication.

William H. Gerdts
Professor Emeritus of Art History
Graduate School of the City University of New York

Joseph Kleitsch, *The Oriental Shop* (or *The Jade Shop*) (detail), 1925. Oil on canvas, 32 x 26". Private Collection, courtesy of The Irvine Museum.

Joseph Kleitsch, *Vernonnet, France*. Oil on canvas, 18 x 21".
Private Collection.

Gardens of the Tuileries, the Louvre. Oil on canvas, 15 x 18 ¼".
Private Collection, courtesy of George Stern Fine Arts.

Joseph Kleitsch, *Still Life with Oranges*. Oil on canvas, 20 x 24". Private Collection, courtesy of George Stern.

Joseph Kleitsch, *Apples and Strawberries*. Oil on canvas, 16 x 24". Collection of Mr. and Mrs. Arthur Burdorf.

Joseph Kleitsch, *Mission Scribe*, c. 1925. Oil on canvas, 11 ½ x 16". Private Collection.

Joseph Kleitsch, *Ruins, San Juan Capistrano Mission*.
Oil on canvas. Collection of Lenoir Josey.

Joseph Kleitsch, *Woman at the Well*. Oil on canvas, 15 x 11". Private Collection, courtesy of William A. Karges Fine Art.

Joseph Kleitsch, *Geraniums*, 1930. Oil on canvas, 30 x 24". Private Collection.

CHAPTER I

Kleitsch's World: The Emerging Artist, 1882–1902

European-born Joseph Kleitsch (1882–1931) was a consummate artistic explorer. Constantly in search of new means of expression, his restless talent and perennial dissatisfaction were fed by an adventurous, bombastic, and charismatic personality. Kleitsch's roots and family environment undoubtedly contributed to the complex individual he became. His distant ancestors from Alsace-Lorraine migrated to Hungary during the reign of Charles III (1711–40), the Hapsburg king who offered largesse to German settlers.[2] An era of reconstruction from 1711 to 1848 led to the resettlement of Hungary by its native peoples and an opportunity for German migrants to repair the "destroyed Bulwark of Christendom" that Hungary had become. Over time the Germanizing of Hungary brought about a nationalistic reaction that blossomed into the Magyar cultural renaissance and economic and political reform.

Kleitsch was born on June 6, 1882, in Német Szent Mihály, or Sânmihaiu German, a village in the Bánát region of Hungary (present-day southwestern Romania),[3] about twenty kilometers from Temesvár (Timișoara), a large cosmopolitan city on the Bega River in Transylvania (PLATES 2–3; see also p. 257).[4] Accounts of Kleitsch's life from Theresa Kleitsch Haynel, a half-sister of the artist (PLATE 1),

above
PLATE 1. Kleitsch's half-sister Theresa (Resi) Kleitsch Haynel and Kleitsch's cousins Marie and Caroline Kleitsch, Cincinnati, 1919. Photograph courtesy of David O. Kleitsch and Family.

right
PLATE 2. Maksay Ádám, "The main entrance of the Roman Catholic church in Német Szent Mihály," 2002. Photograph.
PLATE 3. Maksay Ádám, "The main altar in the Roman Catholic church, Német Szent Mihály," 2002. Photograph.

opposite
Joseph Kleitsch, *Portrait of Edee-Lou Frazee* (detail), c. 1920. Oil on canvas, 40 x 36". Collection of The Irvine Museum.

give us insight into his early years.[5] Kleitsch's mother died when he was three and a half, and his father remarried about a year later. His stepmother recognized his artistic talent and fostered his interest in painting by supplying him with materials at an early age.

Kleitsch also displayed a strong musical bent that may have been stimulated early as well, perhaps when he was an altar boy assisting at high mass in the Roman Catholic church of St. Josephine on Scudier Plaza in Temesvár (PLATES 4 and 5).[6] The celebrating priest at these magnificent services was assisted by two deacons in richly embroidered dalmatics, acolytes carrying huge candles, and often a dozen altar boys moving through the sanctuary (PLATE 6). The vibrant, jewel-like color that appears much later in Kleitsch's paintings may have been imprinted on his memory during these sumptuous services in which the flickering light of the acolytes' candles was reflected in the richly embroidered liturgical

above
PLATE 4. Maksay Ádám, "The Roman Catholic Cathedral of St. Josephine on Scudier Plaza in Temesvár" (present-day Timişoara, Romania), 2002. Photograph. The church was built between 1736 and 1773 after drawings by Emanuel Fischer von Erlach and is in an Austrian baroque style.
PLATE 5. Maksay Ádám, "The interior of St. Josephine Cathedral," 2002. Photograph.
The main altar was designed by Josef Ressler, and the painting of St. George was done by Austrian artist Michael Unterberger.

right
PLATE 6. Maksay Ádám, "The main square, Temesvár (Timişoara); to the viewer's left, the National Theater and Opera House," 2002. Photograph.

garments. Music played a strong role, as a mixed choir accompanied by a small church orchestra sang the masses of Mozart, Beethoven, and Schubert.[7] In counterpoint to this classical influence, the ethnic mixture of Transylvania's small villages exposed Kleitsch to traditional Hungarian folk music, characterized by melodies that were often wildly exuberant, sometimes to the point of frenzied abandonment, like the artist's later vigorous, gestural brushstrokes.

At the age of thirteen or fourteen, Joseph apprenticed to a sign painter and mural decorator named Lanjarovics, who released Kleitsch from his contract within eighteen months because he had taught the boy all that he knew. No longer an apprentice, Kleitsch began to work as a freelance artist, applying his natural talents to portraiture. So successful was he at oil portraits that he soon opened an atelier and engaged an agent. His earnings allowed him to travel, and he made a trip to Munich to study.[8] Upon his return home he continued to prosper and engaged an additional agent. Kleitsch came to be known as "the little Munkácsy," a reference to Mihály Munkácsy (1844–1900), then Hungary's most celebrated artist.

Kleitsch's only extant portraits from this early period are charcoal drawings of his cousins Karoline and Johann Kleitsch (PLATES 7 and 8), executed in Temesvár in 1899 and 1901. Straightforward, bust-length portraits against neutral backgrounds, they seem to have been based on photographs.[9] Kleitsch, like many photographers of the time, employed a compositional formula; yet he was able to interpret the salient traits of his models at this early stage in his career. This would later set him apart from many of his colleagues, who usually chose not to portray the unflattering characteristics of their sitters. Idealization of the sitter was particularly prevalent among European portrait painters. During the early years of his career, Kleitsch continued to employ the formula he used here in portraying his cousins.

PLATES 7 and 8. Joseph Kleitsch, *Karoline and Johann Kleitsch* (*Two early portraits of relatives in Temesvár* [*Timișoara*]), 1899 and 1901. Charcoal drawing. Photograph courtesy of Lubomir C. Hykel.

Before coming to America in 1902, Kleitsch probably traveled again to Munich, where he would have seen many paintings by European masters. Several critics have noted his ardent admiration for Titian and the Dutch painters of the seventeenth century. These multiple influences led to a certain eclecticism that was evident throughout his career.[10]

On the advice of his family, Kleitsch called on the local bishop for support in expanding his career. According to Theresa, the church recognized Kleitsch's talent, but certain religious pictures they had ordered had not materialized.[11] Angered by the bishop's negative response, Kleitsch threatened to leave for America. When, somewhat later, the church offered to support his career, he refused its help. Soon after, in April 1902, Kleitsch left Hungary without a passport and crossed the border into Germany, a move that may have been prompted in part by the likelihood of military conscription.

From Hamburg, Kleitsch immigrated to the United States on the SS *Columbia,* arriving at the Port of New York on May 3, 1902, his cited destination "Cincinnati, Ohio" (see p. 258).[12]

CHAPTER II

The Survival Years: The Formative Period, 1902–1912

CINCINNATI—OVER-THE-RHINE (1902–1903)

From 1900 to 1914, Central and Eastern Europeans immigrated to the United States in vast numbers; "emigration to escape military conscription, as was true of Kleitsch, was common and time-honored."[13] Kleitsch's 1902 journey ended in Cincinnati's Over-the-Rhine district (PLATE 10), which had a concentration of Germans;[14] there he moved in with his nephew Jacob Pfeiffer at 1335–1339 Main Street.[15] Designed in the Italian Renaissance Revival Style, which was popular in the 1870s, this four-story building with limestone façade and decorative sheet-metal cornice still stands (PLATE 9). Pfeiffer's apartment was in the center above the street-level shops. At the turn of the twentieth century, the district's Main Street in Over-the-Rhine bustled with activity: three department stores and several other businesses attracted large numbers of customers. In 1902 about 80,000 people, most of them Germans, lived in this neighborhood. At that time Pfeiffer worked as a machinist, probably at a local machine tool company, or perhaps at one of the many breweries in town.

Over-the-Rhine offered numerous attractions and amenities for people of German descent, and it undoubtedly helped Kleitsch assimilate to a foreign land. Close by was St. Mary's Catholic Church, near 13th and Main streets, the church Pfeiffer and Kleitsch may have attended. Directly across the street from the apartment was Muehler's art supplies, and two blocks away the Sarah Banks art

PLATE 9. Robert J. Wimberg, "Kleitsch's residence: 1335-1337-1339 Main Street, Over-the-Rhine, Cincinnati," 2003. Photograph.
PLATE 10. Robert J. Wimberg, "Overview of Over-the-Rhine, Cincinnati," 2003. Photograph.

school, at 1219 Clay Street. Cincinnati was already a vital art center with an active art academy and several celebrated native-born artists, among them Frank Duveneck and Henry Farny.[16] Surely Kleitsch would have been comfortable in this climate. Although his name does not appear in the Cincinnati city directories from 1902 to 1904, we can assume that he engaged in some kind of professional art activity. The many German garden breweries in Over-the-Rhine were festively decorated with both easel and mural art, and he may have found work as an assistant to a mural decorator.

We can only speculate on how Kleitsch and his first wife, Emma Multner, met. It may have occurred at the May Festival at the Music Hall, or at a concert in one of the many Vine Street theaters. They may have met at a German festival at Turner Hall on Walnut Street in Over-the-Rhine. Or perhaps Emma taught English to immigrants, and Kleitsch was one of her students.

In 1902, Emma lived in Cincinnati's West End at 412 Clark Street (PLATE 11). She appears in the 1900–1903 city directories as a physician, and before that time as a teacher. She does not appear, however, in the Ohio directory of physicians and dentists for 1903. The history of the Eclectic Medical College published in 1902 did not list her as a graduate, although that school admitted women beginning in the 1870s. Gender bias made it a difficult time for women to practice medicine or work in hospitals. Possibly Emma was unlicensed and worked as a homeopathist.

Emma was born in Zanesville, Ohio, in 1857, which made her twenty-five years Kleitsch's senior.[17] Cincinnati's West End was a prosperous neighborhood, and her brother William was a successful grocer. (The author had thought that the marriage between Emma and Joseph might have been arranged to secure his passage to America, but on the ship's manifest, Kleitsch noted that he had paid for his own passage.) Emma was single, of German-Protestant descent, well educated, and of comfortable means. She was not, however, particularly attractive, with a rather matronly figure. Kleitsch's muscular build, wavy brown hair, good looks, and thick German accent must have been quite appealing to a spinster more than twice his age.

In 1903 Jacob Pfeiffer moved from Main Street to 1703 Frintz Street in Over-the-Rhine, smaller quarters that may not have accommodated Kleitsch. It seems that at this time, Kleitsch's talents had not yet been recognized in America—there were still no portrait commissions—and he may have decided to move in with Emma. Times were lean, and the successful portraiture career in Hungary described by his stepsister Theresa had not been replicated in Cincinnati. The new living arrangement was convenient for both Emma and Joseph: she had an attractive, gregarious, younger man in her life, and he gained the security that allowed him to pursue his career.

PLATE 11. Robert J. Wimberg, "Emma Multner's residence: 412 Clark Street, in the West End," 2003. Photograph.

PLATE 12. Joseph Kleitsch, *Still Life with Raspberries*, 1903. Oil on canvas, 14 x 18". Private Collection, courtesy of Redfern Gallery.

The only extant example of Kleitsch's art from the Cincinnati period is a simple still life, dated 1903, of a box of raspberries spilled onto an undefined surface in a theatrical setting that suggests a landscape (PLATE 12). Artificial in its conception, with the berries enveloped in a bright white light, the work's inspiration and source are clearly late-Romantic European art. This is the first evidence of Kleitsch's engagement with still life, a genre he was to develop over time into a more complex form. Traditionally, a mastery of still-life skills was required before an artist was ready to work in more challenging, elevated genres. Many painters began their careers with still life, because the subject matter was often readily available, inexpensive—and invariably immobile.[18] But for Kleitsch, still life became a creative wellspring and a source of income during his formative years.

Denver—"The Mile-High City" (1904–1907)

Both Kleitsch's and Emma's names disappear from the Cincinnati city directories in 1904. That year, they left by train for Denver, Colorado, where three of Kleitsch's cousins had moved for their health (Colorado was known as the Saratoga of the West). In Denver the couple arranged their marriage ceremony, officiated by Minister S. C. Orme and held October 5, 1904 (see p. 258).[19] Because they went to Denver to marry, we can assume that Emma was concerned about embarrassing her family: she was a woman of almost fifty from a well-respected Cincinnati family marrying a penniless foreigner half her age. From 1905 through 1907 Kleitsch is listed as a resident-artist in the Denver city directories.[20] He had expanded his repertory to include landscape and genre painting. According to a cousin, about 1904–5, Kleitsch painted a group of landscapes as advertising illustrations for the Union Pacific Railway. Two landscapes with wooded copse and trees in an apparently northern climate seem to have been painted out-of-doors.[21] Rather stiffly executed in the Barbizon mode, they nonetheless show some experimentation in breadth of composition and expanded color range. Neither, however, foreshadows Kleitsch's vibrant landscapes of Laguna Beach painted in the 1920s.

Sometime during his stay in Denver, Kleitsch painted a winter scene along the Platte River, with the snow-capped Rocky Mountains in the distance and bare-limbed cottonwoods along the river (PLATE 13). Although the scene is painted in a restrained color range and thinly applied pigments—without the rich color and impasto of his later work—the picture communicates the artist's poetic sensitivity to nature. He conveys here the bleakness and solitude of a cold wintry day.

PLATE 13. Joseph Kleitsch, *Platte River in Winter, Denver*, c. 1905–7. Oil on canvas, 16 x 20". Private Collection, courtesy of Bonham & Butterfields.

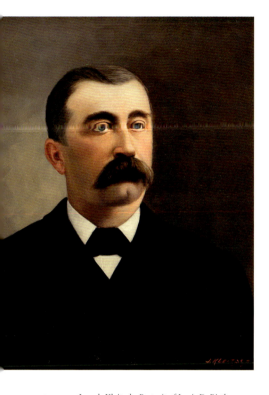

PLATE 14. Joseph Kleitsch, *Portrait of Louis D. Riethmann*, 1906. Oil on canvas, 24 x 20". Courtesy Colorado Historical Society, Decorative and Fine Arts Department.

In the late nineteenth century, many artists were lured to Colorado by its magnificent, primeval scenery; others moved there because of its climate. The colony of resident-artists that emerged had to struggle constantly against local indifference toward the arts. As the area rapidly grew wealthier, the influx of cultured families from Eastern cities encouraged the arts and brought new standards of taste to Denver. When Kleitsch and his wife arrived, the Artists' Club of Denver was a well-established society that was interacting effectively with the community in arranging exhibitions and sales.[22] There were also isolated pockets of Denver artists who were unaffiliated with established organizations, and who practiced and taught art in the city; several of these artists later migrated to California, including still-life painter William McCloskey (1859–1941), plein-air landscapist Hanson Puthuff (1875–1972), and German immigrant portraitist Jean Mannheim (1861–1945). Although Puthuff's and Mannheim's stays in Denver overlap with Kleitsch's, there is no evidence that they knew each other or were associated with the Artists' Club.[23]

Insight into Kleitsch's art activity in Denver can only be obtained from his extant paintings, since Denver publications do not mention his name.[24] We can assume that he continued to seek portrait commissions and that he developed a clientele for his small still lifes. In 1906 Kleitsch did a bust portrait of Louis D. Riethmann, a Swiss-German who was an early Colorado pioneer and prominent businessman (PLATE 14).[25] Riethmann owned a large grocery business, and undoubtedly the contact for this commission had come through Emma's brother William in Cincinnati, another prominent grocer. For a time, the artist continued to use the formula he had adopted in portraying his Hungarian cousins, but the model here is fleshier, rounder, and less mannequin-like. The competently handled flesh tones contrast with the muted tones of the man's apparel and the neutral background. Kleitsch's biographical sketch deposited at the Art Institute of Chicago indicates that he painted the portrait of another successful Colorado businessman, George J. Kindel, who later became a U.S. Representative from Colorado (1913–15).[26] Unfortunately, despite considerable effort, this painting has not been located.

In fall 1906, the German-Swiss artist Conrad Buff (1886–1975) suddenly appeared at Kleitsch's downtown studio-residence. Buff had left Cheyenne,

SURVIVAL YEARS

Wyoming, intending to relocate in Denver and pursue his artistic career. Buff recounted later in an interview with art historian Betty Hoag that "finally in an art store I saw some pictures exhibited by a name that I thought was German so I thought I'd look up the fellow. [I got] his address and he lived in a skyscraper, fifteen stories [high]. So I thought I'd go . . . see him. . . . I never heard of elevators so I walked up the fifteen stories. When I came into the room there were two fellows talking together. . . . I introduced myself and I said, 'My, how can you walk up here and down every day!' and they laughed and said, 'Didn't you hear of an elevator?' 'No, I didn't.' Well anyway the fellow was very nice and he offered me the use of his studio and he said I could paint little pictures and he thought I could sell them for about fifty cents or a dollar apiece. . . . [He introduced me to the man in the art store], so I tried that for a while but they didn't sell. [The artist's name was] "Kleich—Joseph Kleich [*sic*]. . . . He appeared in Los Angeles later on. . . . He was a nice fellow, he was a Slovanian [*sic*]."[27]

The advice to Buff was not idle, for Kleitsch himself continued to successfully produce and sell small paintings. These were primarily still lifes of comestibles on a ledge (PLATE 15).[28] Simple in format, they are illustrative of his

PLATE 15. Joseph Kleitsch, Untitled Still Life (*Cheese, Onions, Bread, and Tankard*), c. 1905–7. Oil on canvas, 16 x 24". Collection of Linda and Jim Freund, courtesy of Maxwell Galleries.

PLATE 16. Joseph Kleitsch, *Still Life with Apples and Oranges,* c. 1905–7. Oil on canvas, 16 x 24". Collection of Mr. and Mrs. Arthur Burdorf, courtesy of Redfern Gallery.

PLATE 17. Joseph Kleitsch, *Still Life with Fruit,* c. 1905–7. Oil on canvas, 16 x 24". Collection of Mr. and Mrs. Arthur Burdorf, courtesy of Redfern Gallery.

early work and recall Raphaelle Peale's "dining-room" or "kitchen pictures" of the early 1800s. In almost all of Peale's still lifes, objects are placed parallel to the picture plane on a simple, unadorned board or ledge.[29] Kleitsch adopted this formula for most of his early still lifes.

One still life (PLATE 16) depicts a cluster of apples and oranges, one of the oranges partially peeled, arranged on a rough-hewn wood ledge against a dark, neutral background. The artist deliberately draws the viewer's eye to the central focus of this piece: the highlighted, partially peeled orange.[30] Another of the group of four untitled ledge pictures (PLATE 17) executed during the same period

SURVIVAL YEARS 55

is a more complex composition with a variety of fruit and an upturned box of strawberries cascading onto an undefined ledge. The vivid colors of the brightly illuminated fruit against the dark ledge and background convey a sense of volume and create a trompe-l'oeil effect. The smooth finish and invisible brushwork add to the illusion. One can only speculate on whether Kleitsch's choice of blemished and spoiled fruit is intended as a metaphor for the transience of life or is merely a depiction of available props.

The Denver Art Company near Kleitsch's residence was another likely outlet for the sale of his work. The store sold both frames and pictures, including portraits, and it is listed in the classified section of the 1906 city directory. Given the number of still lifes Kleitsch turned out during this period, it can be assumed that he still depended on the sale of small pictures for some of his income, since portrait commissions were difficult to secure. In addition, Emma continued to support her young husband, however impractical his objectives may have seemed.

HUTCHINSON, KANSAS—A BRIEF ENCOUNTER (1907)

On the train trip to Denver in 1904, Kleitsch had encountered William C. Baker, an Easterner employed by the Union Pacific Railway. Like Kleitsch, Baker was penniless, and although he had business training, he aspired to be an artist. Both men were outgoing, and the two became immediate friends. In 1907, Baker persuaded Kleitsch and his wife to leave Denver and join him in Hutchinson, Kansas, where Baker intended to reenter the Hausman School of Penmanship at Salt City Business College to complete a penmanship course. He would arrange for Kleitsch to be appointed instructor in art.[31] L. H. Hausman even wrote a "testimonial" to Kleitsch's extraordinary work and talent, helping him obtain a commissioned portrait of an artist/musician friend Henry Milton Rudesill. Through Hausman, Baker secured rented rooms for all three, and Kleitsch received positive local press for both his painting and his teaching.[32]

MEXICO CITY—PRE-REVOLUTION (1907–1909)

Kleitsch's move to Hutchinson evidently failed to bring the success Baker had promised, and in late 1907, under Baker's instigation and direction, the two men and Emma headed for Mexico City. Kleitsch's visits to Mexico City in 1907–9 and again in 1911–12 involved crossing an uncontrolled border, and his departure in March 1912 was under extremely dangerous conditions.

In Mexico, Baker photographed Emma and Kleitsch in their modest, simply furnished lodgings (PLATE 18). Based on a response from Hausman in 1909 to a letter of Baker's from Mexico, it was clearly a difficult time. (A large hole in the sole of Kleitsch's shoe, visible in the photograph, may indicate their poor financial condition, even though the cost of living was less in Mexico.) Emma's money, it seems, was being depleted rapidly. Hausman responded: "You certainly have not found the distant pasture as green as it looked from a distance and have

PLATE 18. William C. Baker, "Joseph and Emma Kleitsch in Mexico," 1907. Photograph. Laguna Art Museum Archives, Laguna Beach, California. Gift of Jonathan Nardone.

only proven again that 'all is not gold that glitters.' I am very sorry that you have all been having such a trying time and truly hope you will be able to shake Hard Luck for good now. . . . Two years full of experience at least, I surmise."33

Despite their hard luck, Kleitsch was actively expanding his repertory. From this Mexican trip, five oil paintings and several drawings have surfaced, executed in an academic-realist style. Three are portraits, including two of his friend Baker, one of them signed and dated "Mexico, 1908," the other dated "1909"; a still life in the Peale family tradition; and a religious scene, probably based on an European engraving.34 There is an animated, freely sketched drawing of Baker playing a recorder with his parrot in a cage nearby ("never without his parrot," according to Baker's nephew Jonathan Nardone), signed and dated "Mexico, 1907" (PLATE 19). This is further tangible evidence of Kleitsch's drawing ability. A torso-length portrait of Baker painted in 1908 is handled in a similar manner to that of the artist's earlier portraits, but the sitter's personality is treated in a livelier fashion. A

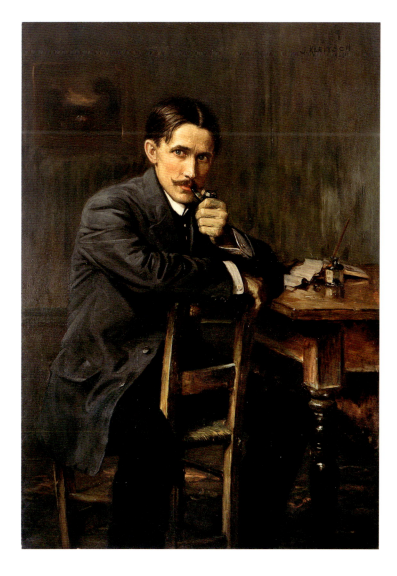

PLATE 19. Joseph Kleitsch, *Portrait of William C. Baker with His Parrot,* 1907. Pencil drawing, 11 x 8". Laguna Art Museum Archives, Laguna Beach, California. Gift of Jonathan Nardone.
PLATE 20. Joseph Kleitsch, *Portrait of William Baker,* 1909. Oil on canvas, 54 ½ x 38 ½". Private Collection.

opposite
PLATE 21. Joseph Kleitsch, *Self-Portrait*, 1909. Oil on canvas, 54 x 38". Collection of Joseph Ambrose, Jr., and Michael D. Feddersen.

above
PLATE 22. Joseph Kleitsch, *The Artist (Self-Portrait)* (detail), 1909. Oil on canvas, 30 x 25". Laguna Art Museum Collection, Museum purchase with funds provided in part from Janet Barker Spurgeon and John Roger Barker, courtesy of William A. Karges Fine Art.

PLATE 23. William C. Baker, "Joseph Kleitsch in Mexico"(?), c. 1909. Photograph. Courtesy of Kelley Gallery.

1909 portrait of Baker, however, captured at his desk in repose, with his penmanship tools spread out before him, is a grander and more accomplished picture (PLATE 20). Painted in an academic-realist style like Kleitsch's other works of this period, it is a more relaxed representation in a neutral palette with a smooth finish. The background is elaborated with strokes of muted color and a small picture on the wall, a treatment that appears again in Kleitsch's later portraits.

Although it, too, is an academic painting, Kleitsch's 1909 self-portrait seated at his easel recalls the influence of the Munich School in its brushwork and dark coloration (PLATE 21; see also PLATE 22). The painting is less tentative in execution than his earlier portraiture, indicative of his ability to move forward (though no record exists of any professional art training in Mexico).[35] In this picture, he captures his youthful appearance and his somewhat hesitant self-assurance. Appearance is obviously important to him in projecting the image of a successful professional. His apparel is fastidious: the neatly knotted tie; the artist's smock, worn over his business suit; the well-trimmed moustache; and the hair somewhat carelessly tousled but within acceptable bounds. In a photograph taken of Kleitsch by Baker that same year, the artist is dressed in a similar fashion (PLATE 23). Both of these images indicate Kleitsch's awareness of changing fashions. In keeping with the new mode of the first decade of the twentieth century, he wears a carefully tailored business suit and a white, wing-collared shirt with a dark patterned tie.[36] In this self-portrait, Kleitsch attempts to project a more mature image of himself through the intensity of his furrowed brow and his piercing eye contact with the viewer.

Self-portraiture is often considered a conduit to an artist's inner personality. It certainly requires skills beyond those needed for painting a still life. Perhaps Kleitsch's 1909 self-portrait shows "a deep, youthful self-involvement, bordering on narcissistic self-absorption," as one writer speculated about a Cézanne self-portrait that he felt had made that artist look upon himself to find "the emerging creative force." Kleitsch's youthful self-portrait, like those of Rembrandt and others, led to the admission of vulnerability seen in Kleitsch's later confrontations with his persona.[37] The several self-portraits he executed over his career as a challenge to both formal concerns and psychological interpretations mark definite transitions in his life and career.

Apples on a ledge figure in another Kleitsch still life from Mexico, this time less prominently. Cast in shadow but highlighted with daubs of yellow paint, they recede somewhat into the dark background, while the illuminated hairy coconut and profusion of scattered nuts are the focus of this composition (PLATE 24). (Later, in Paris, he would learn from fellow artists that Cézanne had warned against using highlights.)[38] Kleitsch uses the same rough-hewn wood ledge as a support for his objects but adds a decorative background treatment.

Times were clearly difficult, as Baker confirmed in a letter to Hausman. In late 1909 the three pulled up stakes for "greener pastures." Whether Baker went back to Denver or resumed his penmanship course in Hutchinson is unknown; he and Kleitsch, however, kept in contact over the years until Baker settled in South America in 1924. Kleitsch and Emma moved to Chicago, where he is listed as a "resident-artist" in the census of 1910.[39] Although the motive for this move is not documented, we can assume that the city's importance as an active art center and its large ethnic population offered an attractive environment, with several of Kleitsch's relatives who had settled in Chicago providing a supportive family base for the couple. A photograph in the Kleitsch family album shows him among friends, or family, at a Columbia Club Yachting Party in Fox Lake, Illinois, in 1910 (PLATE 25).[40]

Before Kleitsch's second visit to Mexico City in 1911, he painted *Behind the Fence* (PLATE 26), a scene of two street urchins hiding in an alley to steal a smoke. This scene recalls the many paintings of children and urchins by the American genre painter John George Brown (1831–1913).[41] The painting can be dated to 1910–11 because of similar clothing seen in numerous photographs of underprivileged children, particularly of young boys who worked in the mills and factories for little compensation. These "denizens of the alleys" typically wore

PLATE 24. Joseph Kleitsch, Untitled Still Life with Nuts, Coconut, and Apples, c. 1907–9. Oil on canvas, 16 x 24". Collection of Mr. and Mrs. Arthur Burdorf, courtesy of Redfern Gallery.

PLATE 25. "Joseph Kleitsch and Friends/Family at a Columbia Club Yachting Party at Fox Lake, Illinois," 1910. Postcard photograph. Courtesy of David O. Kleitsch and Family.

PLATE 26. Joseph Kleitsch, *Behind the Fence*, c. 1910–11. Oil on canvas, 38 x 24". Private Collection, courtesy of Redfern Gallery.

PLATE 27. "William Kleitsch, Sr. and Others in Cincinnati," n.d. Photograph. Courtesy of Marjorie Kleitsch.

PLATE 28. "Joseph Vollmer, Joseph Kleitsch, William Kleitsch, and Philip Vollmer, Cincinnati," 1910. Photograph. Courtesy of Hadley Marie Nagel.

short pants or knickers, long stockings, boots, and straw hats or caps.[42]

Shortly after Kleitsch painted *Behind the Fence,* the couple left for Cincinnati where, probably because of her health, Emma remained with her family during the artist's second trip to Mexico City. (A branch of Kleitsch's family had also settled in Cincinnati [PLATES 27, 28, and 29].)[43] There is tangential evidence that during his brief residence in Chicago, Kleitsch met Charles Schwab, the steel magnate from Pittsburgh, and that he returned to Mexico under Schwab's patronage.[44]

Mexico City—The Progressive Era under President Madero (1911–1912)

Kleitsch arrived in Mexico City in early 1911, after the official opening of the Asociación Cristiana de Jóvenes (YMCA), an impressive steel and concrete building offering room and board, billiard tables, a gym, bowling lanes, and reading rooms as well as classes in English, Spanish, and business. Inexpensive and open to all foreigners, the YMCA became Kleitsch's Mexico City residence.[45] George I. Babcock, formerly of St. Louis, Missouri, who had organized the nonprofit corporation, became Kleitsch's close friend and his contact with the colony of American

opposite

PLATE 29. Joseph Kleitsch, *William Kleitsch,* Cincinnati or Chicago, c. 1910–15. Oil on canvas, 40 x 30". Collection of Joseph Ambrose, Jr., and Michael D. Feddersen.

and foreign businessmen (PLATE 30).[46] The regime of President Porfirio Díaz (1876–1911) had had a long, reciprocal relationship with many foreigners that was especially beneficial to American investors, who boosted Mexico's economy and to a degree influenced its politicization. The American colony, according to Professor William Schell, author of *Integral Outsiders*, "was a latter-day 'trade diaspora' of expatriate cross-cultural brokers (integral outsiders) whose give-and-take relationship with their Mexican hosts was at once intimate and distant and whose relationship with Díaz was integral to a system of 'tributary capitalism' that provided the necessary resources for Díaz to stabilize *camarilla* politics through semi-constitutional *rotativismo* (rotation of elites in office) with himself at the center."[47]

This was the outwardly stable political environment that Kleitsch had experienced as an outsider on his first visit to Mexico. At that time, the Escuela Nacional de Bellas Artes (the Academy of San Carlos) was a conservative art gallery and school. By 1911–12 "there were fresh winds blowing in the Academy" with the introduction of European modern art.[48] Kleitsch's work, however, was not affected by these inroads of modernism; he continued to employ an academic-realist approach to his subjects. Nor did his work reflect the political unrest caused by the armed struggle between diverse factions of the Mexican population, which

PLATE 30. "Joseph Kleitsch in Mexico City," c. 1911–12. Postcard photograph. Laguna Art Museum Archives, Laguna Beach, California. Gift of Jonathan Nardone.

PLATE 31. Joseph Kleitsch, *Portrait of a Gypsy*, 1911. Oil on canvas, 46 x 34". Estate of Pearl Martin.

would eventually force Díaz to resign. But the stirrings of the Mexican Revolution, beginning in 1910, and the volatile nature of Mexican politics made Kleitsch's second stay in Mexico not only unsettling but dangerous.

Despite the political chaos, living was inexpensive, and Kleitsch continued to work. In 1911 he painted a young gypsy woman (PLATE 31) who reminded him of a childhood gypsy friend from his drawing class in Hungary.[49] Painted in dark, neutral colors, the almost full-length figure is in a stiff and conventional pose. A more interesting aspect of this picture is the veiled background with its sketchy, colored images of a bed and a chair, suggesting perhaps an intimate relationship between Kleitsch and the woman. Later in his career, rumors hinted at affairs with women, and certain family members referred to him as a "rogue."[50]

In 1911, during the turbulent times just before the Mexican Revolution, Kleitsch produced a meticulously rendered trompe-l'oeil still life (PLATE 33). Untitled [and now known as *The Interrupted Hand*], it may reflect the instability of life in Mexico City, symbolized by the empty six-shooter on the table. A pair of aces with a king high might have been the winning hand, since the money is still on the table. The half-filled carafe of wine and the smoking cigar suggest that this card game may have been suddenly interrupted and the winner forced to leave his gains behind. The artist has carefully arranged all of these elements to arouse a sense of intrigue, mystery, and adventure. That Kleitsch was there and a player in the game seems clear, because "J Kleitsch" is printed on the side of the matchbox. Fernando Nebot, a former owner of the painting, offered another interpretation: a violent end to the game that resulted in a suicide, since a bullet is missing from the gun's cylinder. During the 1920s, in California, the artist told a story about a poker game in which he had lost his money and returned to Tijuana in an attempt to recoup his losses; undoubtedly he substituted Tijuana for Mexico City.[51] Interestingly, this painting was given to Nebot's grandfather as payment for legal services performed for a client, probably a Wade, in Asturias, Spain. It may be one of the paintings Kleitsch's collectors—the Wade family—took to their new home in Asturias when they fled from Mexico in 1913.

PLATE 32. William Michael Harnett, *Still Life* (Copper tankard, box, apples, wine bottles, ginger pot, cigar box, and peeled orange), 1884. Oil on panel, 9 x 13".
Collection of the Flint Institute of Arts.
Gift of Mr. and Mrs. William L. Richards through the Viola E. Bray Charitable Trust.

PLATE 33. Joseph Kleitsch, Untitled Still Life (*The Interrupted Hand*), 1911. Oil on canvas, 24 x 31 ½".
Museum of Western Art, courtesy of Christie's.

Like the celebrated American trompe-l'oeil painter William Harnett (1848–1892) (PLATE 32), Kleitsch explores the tangibility and physicality of real objects in this complex illusionistic composition. From his early simplified arrangements of fruit on ledges, Kleitsch continued to develop the virtuoso technique seen in this composition, which leads later to his self-referential, baroque still lifes.

Political unrest in Mexico continued as the struggle between the forces of Francisco Madero and the government of Porfirio Díaz intensified. "Despite his family's well-being under President Porfirio Díaz, Madero deplored the callous treatment the majority received during the *porfiriato*. . . . In 1909, in the wake of Díaz's broken promise not to run again for the presidency, Madero formed the National Antireelectionist Party. . . . He was nominated in April 1910 by his party to run for the presidency. Díaz, in reaction, ordered Madero's arrest and the suppression of the party."[52] Escaping from prison, Madero fled to San Antonio, Texas, established a revolutionary headquarters, then reentered Mexico from El Paso on February 14, 1911. On May 25 Díaz resigned the presidency. Madero took office on November 6, 1911.

In 1912, Kleitsch attained prominence in Mexico as a result of his commissioned portraits of President Madero and his wife. This commission, and a gold medal, awarded by the Mexico Art Associates, led to more portrait commissions from other prominent Mexicans.[53] Amid these successes, Kleitsch's letter to his friend William Baker indicates serious concern about the unsettled political situation: "I am still alive with the shooting we have here; . . . now it's all well, but I don't know how long it will last."[54]

Kleitsch returned to the United States from Veracruz on March 22, 1912, aboard the steamer SS *Monterey* (see p. 258).[55] Staying long enough in New York to meet Baker, he then headed to Philadelphia to greet his sisters Agnes and Theresa, who had recently immigrated to America.[56] From there Kleitsch went to Cincinnati to get Emma, and the couple returned to Chicago. In the aftermath of Madero's murder on February 22, 1913, several collectors of Kleitsch's work were among the Mexicans who fled to Spain. When Kleitsch traveled to Spain in 1926, he visited these patrons, including a member of the Wade family who owned fifteen of his paintings.[57]

PLATE 34. Joseph Kleitsch, *The Angora Cats*, c. 1912. Oil on canvas, 19 ¼ x 25 ½". Collection of Mr. and Mrs. Arthur Burdorf, courtesy of Christie's.

CHAPTER III

Chicago in the 1910s: From Transition to Maturity, 1912–1920

A renaissance in the arts was well underway in Chicago when Kleitsch and his wife returned there in 1912. Yet many still perceived Chicago as a commercial city that exploited uneducated immigrants and neglected the poor. Upton Sinclair's *The Jungle* (1906) was among the number of contemporary books that called attention to urban immigrants, particularly from rural areas, who were ill-equipped to survive in the city because of a "stubborn individualism." Although culture in Chicago was still in its infancy, the Art Institute had already been in existence for forty years when *The Jungle* appeared. By 1900, Chicago was the most important art center between New York and San Francisco. By 1913, its annual exhibitions of work by living American artists, held since 1896, had begun to include artists from Chicago and the vicinity, although foreign names were the biggest attraction. "Traditional works . . . formed an important part of the public's art education. . . . [These works] were 'tastemakers' because of the inexperience of their viewers, the social prestige of their owners, the apparently monolithic taste of art officials, dealers, and critics. A traditional flavor was thereby imparted to the city's art scene which was almost totally undisturbed until the 1920's."[58]

To attract the very best in American art, Friends of American Art was formed in 1910. Initiated by Chicago artist Ralph Clarkson (1861–1942), who was most energetic in its development, the group's efforts enabled the Art Institute to spend $30,000 annually for the purchase of American art. In his 1912 review of the museum's prestigious Annual Exhibition of American Art, James William Pattison commented on the selection process for the annuals.[59] American artists in the United States and in Paris—artists of "superior abilities"—were invited by the Art Institute to exhibit in these shows, and a jury of painters and sculptors from the Chicago area and other parts of the country made selections from other works submitted. For Pattison, the jury system and the awarding of prizes focused attention on the "neglected knowledge of art."

The popularity of portraiture in Chicago must have influenced Kleitsch's decision to concentrate on this genre. He was undoubtedly aware of Chicago artist Louis Betts (1873–1961), who, after returning from Europe, quickly gained recognition as a portraitist (PLATE 35).[60] As Kleitsch considered the direction of his own career, he enrolled as a "special student" in the Saturday School of the Art Institute of Chicago, attending classes there from May 4 through June 16, 1912.

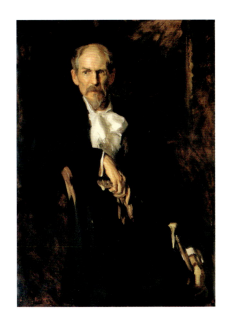

PLATE 35. Louis Betts, *Portrait of James William Pattison*, 1906. Oil on canvas, 48 x 34". Collection of the Union League Club of Chicago.

Because of his advanced qualifications he was not required to follow the prescribed program for full-time students.[61] Professional artists during this period attended figure painting and portraiture classes at the school in order to work from live models, and often, as special pupils, they devoted time to copying paintings in the museum galleries. Biographical data provided by Kleitsch for the Art Institute's registration form states that he was a "Professor" [his term] of art in the Chicago high schools. Chicago's Board of Education has lost its early employment records, so it is unclear how long Kleitsch taught in the public schools.[62] From the class registration form, on which Kleitsch gives his studio address as "834 Willow Street, Chicago," we can assume he was actively engaged in painting in 1912, but as yet no dated works from that year have come to light. His *Angora Cats* (PLATE 34) may date to this year, however, because of the use of brown tones and the conventional representation characteristic of his work from this time period.

Kleitsch's outgoing personality rapidly expanded his circle of artist friends. In 1913, he and Emma were among a group of artists photographed at a birthday party for Elsie Palmer Payne (1884–1971), wife of the landscape and mural painter Edgar Payne (1883–1947). "A costume ball" was held in the Paynes' Tree House Studio (PLATE 36). Edgar Payne had established a significant reputation with his many exhibitions of California landscapes and received numerous awards (PLATE 37). Payne would later influence Kleitsch's decision to move to Southern California and settle in Laguna Beach. There is little information on Kleitsch's artistic career in 1913, but several known events changed the course of his life and career. Emma's sudden death, from complications of nephritis, in Chicago on August 10, 1913, and her interment in Cincinnati in her family's plot undoubtedly affected him that year.[63]

PLATE 36. "Elsie Palmer Payne's birthday party, 'Masquerade Ball' or 'Costume Party,' Tree Studio Building, Chicago," c. 1913. Photograph.
Private Collection. Courtesy of DeRu's Fine Arts.
PLATE 37. Edgar Alwin Payne, *The Restless Sea*, 1917. Oil on canvas, 43 x 51". Indianapolis Museum of Art. Gift of Mrs. James Sweetser.

That fall, Kleitsch met Edna Gregaitis, an art teacher in the Chicago public schools. It was a significant transition, from a wife twenty-five years his senior to an attractive younger woman eight years his junior (PLATE 38). Edna, who was of Lithuanian descent, is reputed to have been born in Grand Rapids, Michigan, on January 16, 1890. Her birth date and birthplace, however, are not documented by a Michigan State birth certificate; the issue is confused further because her mother, according to the 1910 U.S. Census, did not come to America until 1892, two years after Edna's supposed birth date. A 1914 issue of the Palette and Chisel Club's monthly newsletter, *The Cow Bell*, alludes to Kleitsch's strong romantic interest in a certain young lady, undoubtedly Edna.

Kleitsch was approved for membership in the club, which had been organized in 1895 and incorporated in 1897, on December 4, 1913.[64] According to its 1896 constitution, the group's objective was to promote and educate its members in the art of drawing, painting, and modeling. To achieve this, the club planned to furnish at minimum cost suitable quarters and models for its members; arrange exhibitions of members' art; and advance their work during the summer months.[65] At first the club leased space in the Athenaeum Building at 59 East Van Buren Street, where its members met weekly, worked from live models, and then dined and drank into the night (PLATE 39). Nonetheless, the club had the serious goal of developing Chicago's art climate. On January 6, 1906, an article in the Chicago *Examiner* called the Palette and Chisel Club "the oldest and strongest practical art organization in the West."[66] Its active membership included painters, sculptors, graphic artists, decorators, and designers.

Club events had a profound effect on Kleitsch's career, and most certainly lifted his spirits. Always outgoing, he became heavily involved in the club's many

PLATE 38. "Edna (Gregaitis) Kleitsch in confirmation dress," c. 1904–6. Photograph. Courtesy of Kelley Gallery.
PLATE 39. Interior View, Athenaeum Building, 1914. Photograph. Courtesy of the Newberry Library. (See p. 259 for exterior view.)

clockwise from bottom right
PLATE 40. Palette and Chisel Club "End of 1914" in the Club's Logbook, vol. 2, 1914. Collection of the Newberry Library, Chicago.
PLATE 41. Vodvil [*sic*] Show (cover), in the Palette and Chisel Club Logbook, vol. 2, 1914. Collection of the Newberry Library, Chicago.
PLATE 42. Joseph Kleitsch and other band members, December 1914 in the Palette and Chisel Club Logbook, vol. 2. Photograph (detail). Collection of the Newberry Library, Chicago.
PLATE 43. "Cabaret on the Border." Joseph Kleitsch and other band members, December 1914 in the Palette and Chisel Club Logbook, vol. 2. Collection of the Newberry Library, Chicago.

activities, broadening both his artistic and social agendas. He participated in the club's numerous and varied exhibitions, including an annual juried show, smokers, "hi-jinks" (musical and theatrical shows), lectures, outings, and other activities. The club believed that "social activities of art organizations were key to bringing together members with shared ideals and common needs." Periodically, the club "scheduled receptions, concerts, . . . theme balls, ladies' nights, and 'high jinks' or burlesque entertainment written and staged by members."[67] In 1913 the club initiated a program of "awarding a prize to the best work in the annual fine art exhibition; Victor Higgins was the first to receive a gold medal."[68] That same year, the club began to publish *The Cow Bell*, naming it after the bell used to call meetings to order. The newsletter reported on members' activities as well as on the broader Chicago art scene.

On July 22, 1914, Kleitsch married Edna Gregaitis in a civil ceremony in Chicago, performed by a judge of the Cook County Municipal Court (see p. 259). Surprisingly, even though both had embraced Catholicism, the couple chose a civil ceremony instead of a religious one in the Catholic church. A son, Eugene, was born to the artist and his wife in Chicago on May 21, 1915.[69]

Kleitsch appears in the Chicago city directory from 1912 through 1917; in 1918 and 1919 no city directories were published. He was not in the 1918 and 1919 telephone directories, indicating that he had no phone;[70] his residency, however, is validated by the exhibitions in which he participated. Kleitsch's career can be traced from 1914 through 1919 in the Palette and Chisel Club logbooks at the Newberry Library; in exhibition records at the Art Institute of Chicago; in Chicago city directories; in a profile of Kleitsch and his work in the *Fine Arts Journal* (Chicago) of 1919; and in various exhibition reviews.

The logbook for 1914 indicates that he exhibited in the club's nineteenth annual exhibition (PLATE 40), and that he lent his talents enthusiastically to the club's "High-Jinks" each year as a musician and an actor. *The Cow Bell* (December 1914) offers insight into Kleitsch as the "Flamboyant Hungarian":

> "Vodvil [*sic*] Show" [PLATE 41]: The Kleitsch-Taylor-Carlsen trio proved a scream, the harmony was delicious in the extreme and reminded us of a "death rattle" we heard a guy do once who had gotten all mussed up in a railroad wreck.
>
> "Cabaret on the Border" [PLATE 43]: The club band covered itself with glory, and deserves a bundle of credit for a night's labor. With only one rehearsal before the show this flock of talented disturbers crawled out into the big pen and dragged forth from their various instruments a bunch of harmony that was immense. The band was under the leadership of Kleitsch, and is now being secretly observed by the state sanity commission [PLATE 42].

PLATE 44. Gallery view from the Twenty-Seventh American Paintings and Sculpture Exhibition (Room 25-N), Nov. 3d–Dec. 6th, 1914. Institutional Archives of the Art Institute of Chicago. Photograph courtesy of the Art Institute of Chicago.

The club held several "fantastical" parties each year, and Kleitsch seemed to enter fully into the spirit of these occasions, undoubtedly using the Palette and Chisel Club as a springboard into Chicago's art and social mainstreams. Under the club's auspices he met local and visiting artists as well as Chicagoans who supported the arts. Despite these associations, Kleitsch remained fiercely independent, charting his own direction without a dealer. When he painted at his studio in the Athenaeum Building, his primary models were relatives, friends, club members, and their families.

From 1914 through 1919, Kleitsch exhibited regularly in the annuals of both the Art Institute and the Palette and Chisel Club. In February and March 1914, he showed a painting titled *Isa* (no. 172) in the Art Institute's Artists of Chicago and Vicinity Eighteenth Annual Exhibition (the identity of the sitter has not been determined). With more than half of the 150 painters entering portraits or figure compositions, art critic Lena M. McCauley singled out Kleitsch's work as "meritorious" and a "direct portrait" of his sitter.[71]

In the Twenty-Seventh Annual Exhibition at the Art Institute of Chicago, November 3 to December 6, 1914, Kleitsch showed *My Sister* (no. 178), a portrait of his younger sister Theresa (Resi) at age twenty-one. Painted in Chicago in 1914, she is portrayed in a frontal, half-length pose, wearing a simple housecoat. While the painting is currently unavailable for viewing,[72] the owner's description makes it possible to locate the portrait in a photograph of the Art Institute's gallery room 25-N (PLATE 44). McCauley, writing in the *Chicago Evening Post* on November 5, 1914, remarked that *My Sister* had "particular merit." Of the 800 entries submitted to the jury, 345 canvases were by 275 American artists whose subjects were of "home material not foreign." It was a feather in Kleitsch's cap to exhibit among such prestigious artists as Childe Hassam (1859–1935), Robert Henri (1865–1929), Frederick Frieseke (1874–1939), and other eminent American painters from the East.

In 1915, Kleitsch and Edgar Payne were cited among the Palette and Chisel Club's exhibitors as "the strong painters of several seasons." That same year Kleitsch was awarded the A. H. Ullrich art medal for two portraits in the Palette and Chisel annual, an award "for the most creditable work by a member and not a prize on an individual picture."[73] One of the portraits was of Miss Helen Brown, the sister of the Palette and Chisel Club's president, and the other of the club's ex-president John B. Woodruff.[74]

As Kleitsch's paintings gained acceptance, his confidence grew, the scope of his work broadened, and its quality improved. In his *Self-Portrait* of 1915 (PLATE 45), exhibited in the Art Institute's Nineteenth Annual Exhibition, Artists of Chicago and Vicinity (no. 159), his demeanor suggests a career that is beginning to flourish. With the new responsibilities of a recent marriage and an expected child, his appearance reflects a man of maturity and station. The fedora set at a jaunty angle, the colorful, futurist-patterned cravat, and the red pin (Légion d'Honneur?) on his coat lapel all suggest his recent recognition.[75] The large overcoat with wide lapels, business suit, vest, and gloves complete this image of the artist as a mainline success with an expanded career and lifestyle. The eyes are interesting because they reflect a self-confidence not seen in his self-portrait of 1909. For fashion-conscious expatriate American artist James Abbott McNeill Whistler (1834–1903), "dress [also] played an essential role in his portraits . . . as an indicator of the character and status of the sitter."[76] This self-affirming portrait marks another transition in Kleitsch's life and career.

PLATE 45. Joseph Kleitsch, *Self-Portrait*, 1915. Oil on canvas, 40 x 30". Collection of James Taylor and Gary Conway.

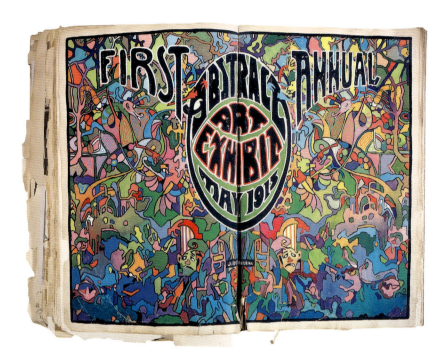

PLATE 46. Palette and Chisel Club, First Annual Abstract Art Exhibition (cover), May 1915, Logbook, vol. 2. Collection of the Newberry Library, Chicago.

The remarkable range and scope of Kleitsch's talent is reflected in an unidentified newspaper article of May 1915. "Cubism Has Advanced Beyond Cubes": "*Chemistry* by...Kleitsch, is a wild conception of atoms, molecules and gases gyrating in prismatic form. It is scientific to the last degree in the realm of abstraction." Unfortunately, this painting was accidentally destroyed several years ago.77

The Palette and Chisel's First Annual Abstract Art Exhibition opened the evening of May 17, 1915 (PLATE 46), "with a reception and dance, interspaced with some special features. Walter Ufer gave an abstract recitation....Joe Kleitsch read a choice poetical gem, replete with hitherto undreamed mortuary horrors. Four professional dancers were well received, in dances arranged for this occasion.... Enjoyed most of all, perhaps, were three compositions of Mr. Isadore [*sic*] Berger (see PLATE 56), inspired by certain paintings in the exhibit." The musical composition inspired by Kleitsch's *Chemistry*, according to *The Cow Bell's* writer, "proved full of color and movement."78

The Cow Bell also reported that the opening day of the abstract exhibition "drew a larger attendance than many entire exhibits of the past, and the show broke all records for attendance." Publicity from art critics undoubtedly helped to promote the show. In the *Chicago Evening Post* on May 20, Lena McCauley reported that the forty-two canvases by the Abstractionists at the Palette and Chisel Club were "delightfully colored cryptographs. Certain frames hold pictured brainstorms.... It is natural to classify the works with pipe dreams and the visions of lotus eaters." Tongue in cheek, she offers a favorable remark about Chicago's

"Abstractionists": "Remembering the display of Cézanne, Van Gogh and Gauguin, the comparison is in favor of the Palette and Chisel Club. The former painters were French madmen, the latter are clever and wholesome-minded Chicagoans. The western painters have avoided the trivial, the obvious and the vulgar. There is nothing to offend the academic or the impressionists. . . . The Palette and Chisel men will be better painters after the frolic. Immortal art has never been unintelligible, nor does it need an interpreter."

This was one of the first nonobjective exhibitions in the city since the Armory Show in 1913, which had made Chicagoans more aware of European avant-garde art.[79] Catalyst Samuel Kennedy, who had returned from Paris in 1914, and was credited by art reviewers as one of the club's leaders, roused enough interest among the membership to organize the exhibition. Victor Higgins (1884–1949), another initiator and participant, referred to the abstract pictures as "color symphonies" corresponding to Berger's musical interpretations (PLATE 47). Most of the exhibitors of abstractions, however, were otherwise representational painters who were not steeped in the theories or principles of modernism. This show was the club's first and final fling with nonobjective art.

PLATE 47. Victor Higgins, *Circumference,* 1914–19. Oil on canvas, 51 x 57". The Snite Museum of Art, University of Notre Dame. Gift of Mr. and Mrs. John T. Higgins.

PLATE 48. Joseph Kleitsch, *Studio Interior*, 1915. Oil on canvas, 30 x 40". Collection of Lenoir Josey, courtesy of George Stern Fine Arts.

When Kleitsch leased a studio in the Athenaeum Building in about 1915, the variety of his paintings became fully evident. Within a new space that offered a means of controlling light and exposure to an ever-increasing circle of artists, Kleitsch began to experiment with interior genre scenes—an extension of his developing creative powers. The studio and its furnishings became the setting for many of his fine interior scenes with figures. One of them, *Studio Interior*, painted in 1915 (PLATE 48), caught the attention of a reviewer when it was exhibited in the Palette and Chisel Annual Exhibition of April 1918:

> No one, we venture to say, has ever offered a nude and steam radiators in the same picture each as just an object in the scheme, the one not played up as a central figure, the other not appearing as an obtrusive novelty. Artists like this picture immensely because it shows the happy faculty of an artist in finding beauty in the commonest things. They delight in the fine bits of color afforded by the old rag carpet, cheap draperies and shabby studio properties,—color which is just as clear and just as interesting as that of silks and velvets. The nude model seen through the dressing room door in the far corner is only an incident of the scene. A touch of winter outside the window adds to the effectiveness though it does not seem consciously introduced.[80]

Although the painting is tonal, with close values, we see that Kleitsch's generally dark colors are becoming brighter. The picture offers a window into the artist's working space; the casual assemblage of drapery and clothing; and, perhaps as an afterthought, a voyeuristic glimpse of an out-of-scale nude dressing inside an open armoire. Light streaming through the window of the room at the rear illuminates the studio and creates a dramatic contrast to the subtler play of light and shadow.

A more elaborately furnished club room in the Athenaeum is the setting for Kleitsch's 1915 figural interior scene (PLATE 50). The sitter may be Miss Irene Petrtyl, the niece of August Petrtyl, president of the club in 1906 (PLATE 49), or a relative of Edna's from Lithuania, then part of Russia.[81] Indeed, she seems almost

PLATE 49 Joseph Kleitsch, *Portrait of August Petrtyl*, c. 1915. Pencil drawing. Collection of the Palette and Chisel Club, Chicago. Photograph courtesy of Frank Hensley.
PLATE 50. Joseph Kleitsch, Untitled Portrait in Athenaeum Club Room, c. 1915. Oil on canvas, 33 x 25". Private Collection.

Russian in appearance. What looks like a fur hat is actually a voluminous hairdo, held with a hairband and layers of silk milliners' net over a buckram base. Parted in the center, the hair is combed rather close to the head, dips down over the ears and is then caught up in a bun at the back. Both the costume and hairstyle reaffirm a 1915 date for the picture. "During the period following World War I," says costume historian Edward Maeder, "women did not have exposed foreheads!" Also substantiating the date for the painting is the very full skirt with its wide flounce and natural waistline. (After 1917, women wore barrel skirts.) "An overskirt . . . flares to just below the knees, covering a longer skirt, which is quite full, probably gored and may even have a deep flounce along the lower edge."[82] The sitter's fine jewelry indicates that she is dressed for a formal occasion. The room's traditional furnishings and accessories complement the elegant formality of the rich silk crêpe-de-chine dress. Tribal rugs from the Caucasus and a Navajo blanket thrown over the piano add further exoticism to the scene.

Kleitsch's tonalist harbor view *Chicago River* of 1915 has surfaced recently (PLATE 51). It reveals the extension of the artist's repertoire to the field of landscape painting and demonstrates his ability to effectively render the atmospheric effects of a foggy, wintry day.[83]

As an active participant in club activities, Kleitsch attended a life class held among the trees at the club's summer camp in Fox Lake, Illinois (PLATE 52). Caricaturing himself for the September issue of *The Cow Bell,* he sits on a rock, drawing a nude model who lets droplets of water fall over him (see p. 259). (Members were hard put to write a pertinent caption for the drawing.)

The Cow Bell's editor, Harry L. Engle, waxes eloquent over the beauty of the club's new camp on Mayapple Hill in the Fox Lake area:

> High above the surrounding country, in a fine grove of oak, hickory and ash, with lazy stretching slopes of waving grass, splotched with mayapple, primrose and day lily, and overlooking lower levels of shaded or sunny meadows, these in turn picked out with browsing cattle and white sketching umbrellos; then back of all the distant purple-drenched hills and lakes, that ring the camp like a cyclorama, the sturdy little clubhouse with the attendant commissary department and poker place; the outdoor dining-room trimmed with oak and ash; the 70 by 3 foot well of sparkling water—some camp, etc.[84]

opposite
PLATE 51. Joseph Kleitsch, *Chicago River [Dockside in Harbor],* 1915. Oil on canvas, 16 x 20". Private Collection, courtesy of Kelley Gallery.

above
PLATE 52. Palette and Chisel Club, Summer Camp, "Fox Lake, Oct. 1914." Photograph. Collection of the Newberry Library, Chicago.

right
PLATE 53. Palette and Chisel Club, "Twentieth Anniversary Jubilee," November 1, 1915. Collection of the Newberry Library, Chicago.

On Monday evening, November 1, 1915, Kleitsch attended the Twentieth Anniversary Jubilee of the club (PLATE 53) at the Art Institute, where newcomers celebrated the older members with "wreaths of bay and parsley and succotash hung about their hoary brows." Newspaper critics complimented the club on its advancement from a "semi-amateur group of men who painted for pleasure" to an efficient, vital, influential organization.[85]

In a *Cow Bell* feature titled "A Little Ditty on Worms," Kleitsch poked fun at himself on the rejection of one of his manuscripts, revealing his rather quirky sense of humor:

> It is serious to be funny, but a damn sight more funny to be in earnest serious. That's me. When it comes to criticizing my humor I get wild; I get furious. Because I was so serious, Dick could not see it that way. By gooly he didn't have to. All he had to do was laugh. He didn't want to, nor did Timmins want to. They're all alike, cuplink! If it wasn't for my kid, I'd be in a hell of a mixture, but as it is, he gets into it, and then speaks to me so sweetly and I am immediately consolidated. J.K.[86]

The manuscript must have been hilarious, with all the misspellings and grammatical errors Kleitsch's later letters display.

Many outside influences began to affect the direction of Kleitsch's work. With the city's rapid growth and the increasing involvement of Chicagoans in the contemporary art scene as well as in collecting, local galleries began to show impressionist and post-impressionist paintings, along with a stable of Old Masters and occasional examples of European abstract art. The Palette and Chisel Club provided a forum for discussion and debate with the outspoken progressive members on modernism. Although Kleitsch was always a vigorous participant, he was not easily understood when he spoke excitedly. These discussions gave him a new awareness of contemporary art and began to free him from the more derivative nineteenth-century forms and techniques.

Kleitsch continued to paint half- and full-length portraits of himself and his wife in different attitudes and dress. In a striking portrait of Edna from 1916 (PLATE 54), he begins to experiment with an impressionistic technique, a blond palette, and the placement of his sitter near a window. This allows the light to illuminate both the figure and the room, bringing out the sheen of Edna's satin dress and the warm glow of her face and hands. Through the window, a view of trees with bare branches indicates a wintry Chicago day outside. And Kleitsch lovingly crafts his wife's portrait to subtly reveal her true beauty and exquisite, soft features: the sweet mouth, dark eyes, and high cheekbones of her round face. *My Wife*—or *Mrs. K.*, as the portrait is sometimes called—was exhibited in the Twenty-First Annual Exhibition of the Palette and Chisel Club at the Art Institute in April and May 1916. Later that year, Kleitsch portrayed Edna with their son, Eugene, in a backyard setting, and in the same blond palette—not in an impressionistic style, but a more realistic natural environment. Unfortunately, this painting has been abraded and has lost a considerable amount of paint.[87]

PLATE 54. Joseph Kleitsch, *Portrait of Mrs. K.*, 1916. Oil on canvas, 45 x 35". Collection of Jim and Kathy Busby, courtesy of William A. Karges Fine Art.

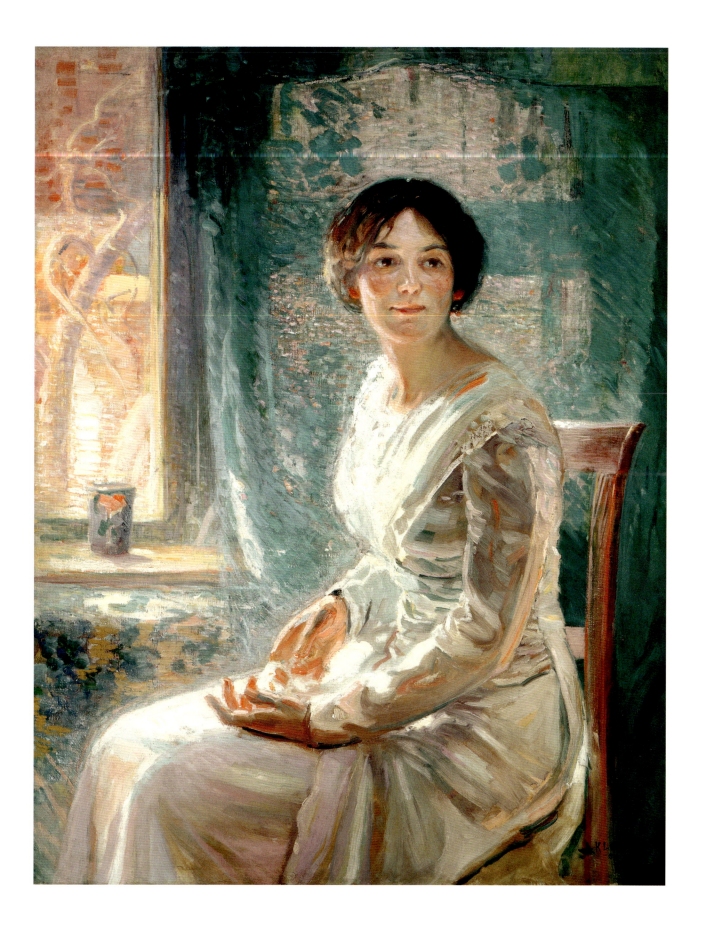

That same year, Kleitsch turned to the standard nineteenth-century practice of representing male subjects in *The Attic Philosopher* (PLATE 55), showing the sitter's face and hands amid the darkness of a black jacket.[88] In addition to commissioned portraits, like the well-received *Charles F. W. Nichols*,[89] he also painted friends, like the model for this work. A reviewer described the picture in glowing terms: "We have a masterpiece in portraiture. The whole character of the blond dilettante, a young Swedish friend of the artist in Chicago, is here—the dreamer, the musician, the philosopher, the sensualist, and the idealist. Kleitsch saw so much that his friend was reluctant to continue the poses, hence the picture was three months in the painting."[90] Kleitsch captured the Nordic appearance of his friend in a subtle characterization. The full lips and liquid blue eyes emphasize the sensuality of this young man, whose bohemian lifestyle was probably that of his artist friends. Kleitsch's success in capturing the personality of the model is complete with the strand of hair curled over the forehead, the cigar, and the jaunty neckpiece. Vigorous, sweeping brushstrokes replicate the sitter's animated personality and suggest the work of Wayman Adams (1883–1959), a popular portraitist of the day whose "gifted, brilliant, and colorful characterizations" were also achieved with the daring sweep of his brush (PLATE 57).[91]

PLATE 55. Joseph Kleitsch, *The Attic Philosopher*, 1916. Oil on canvas, 36 x 28". Collection of Mr. and Mrs. Thomas B. Stiles II.

PLATE 56. Joseph Kleitsch, *Portrait of Isador Berger [Rhapsody]*, 1917. Oil on canvas, 40 x 30". Collection of Dr. and Mrs. Edward H. Boseker, courtesy of George Stern Fine Arts.

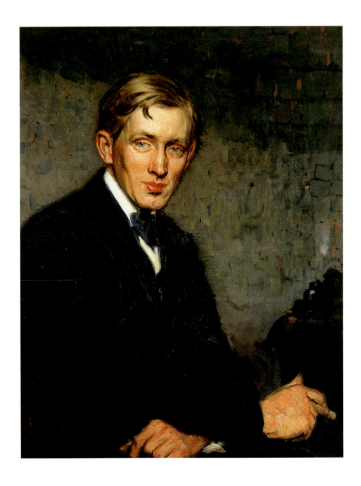

PLATE 57. Wayman Adams, *Portrait of William Preston Harrison,* 1924. Oil on canvas, 52 x 40". Los Angeles County Museum of Art. Mr. and Mrs. William Preston Harrison Collection. Photograph © 2003 Museum Associates/LACMA, courtesy of Laguna Art Museum, Laguna Beach, California.

In 1917 Kleitsch portrayed another close friend, a Chicago violinist, in *Isador Berger* (PLATE 56). Berger (1890–1964) had composed the musical score for Kleitsch's nonobjective painting *Chemistry,* shown in the Palette and Chisel's First Annual Abstract Art Exhibition (see p. 76). Berger and Kleitsch met in Chicago, where Berger was a soloist and concertmaster of the Chicago Philharmonic Orchestra as well as a violinist in the Chicago Civic Opera and Chicago NBC orchestras.[92] The musician had received his doctorate from the Royal Conservatory in Brussels, where he had performed as first violinist in King Albert's Royal Court Orchestra.

Kleitsch's keen appreciation for music led him to support the orchestra, and he was befriended by several of its members. (He could very well have pursued a career in music, with his skills at playing the violin, flute, and accordion.) When he received the portrait commission from his friend, Kleitsch must have thought carefully about how to portray the musician. The completed painting captures Berger's virtuosity and suggests the beauty of the sound of a Stradivarius in the hands of an accomplished performer.[93]

When Kleitsch exhibited Berger's portrait in the Annual Exhibition of the Palette and Chisel Club in April 1918, Evelyn Marie Stuart commented: "Where have we seen more spirit or absorption in the theme than in Kleitsch's master interpretation of a well-known musician wrapped in his virtuosity? Is not this the very essence and spirit of the man it portrays and does it not suggest life, action, rhythm and all that one associates with a musician? The head is beautifully placed, the face spiritually presented, the hands are full of nervous activity and seem actually in motion."[94] Kleitsch has managed to capture the experience of a beautiful violin sonata and the intensity of its performer by sharply illuminating his face, hands, and flashing bow. In *Rhapsody*—Kleitsch's alternate title—the violinist is superbly posed and lost to the outer world in an ecstasy of musical interpretation (PLATE 58).[95]

PLATE 58. "Isador Berger," Chautauqua traveling circuit brochure, c. 1920s. Photograph. Records of the Redpath Chautauqua Bureau, Special Collections Department, University of Iowa, Iowa City, Iowa.

PLATE 59. Joseph Kleitsch, *Self-Portrait*, 1917. Watercolor. Collection of Marjorie Kleitsch.
PLATE 60. Joseph Kleitsch, *In My Studio*, 1917. Oil on canvas, 30 x 25 ½". Collection of California Institute of Technology, Pasadena, California, courtesy of Laguna Art Museum Archives, Laguna Beach, California. Stendahl Art Galleries Collection.

After America entered World War I in April 1917, Kleitsch painted another self-portrait, this time beautifully modeled in watercolor (PLATE 59).[96] His technical brilliance is shown in his ability to handle the lighter medium. At thirty-five, the painter portrays himself as a mature Chicago citizen. Success and recognition by peers and collectors are reflected in his mode of dress—solid, proper, unostentatious, yet with a certain artist's flair in the way he wears his hat.

Although local newspapers printed numerous images of the ravages of war in Europe, most Chicago artists seemed to pursue subjects that had no reference to the conflict. However, Kleitsch's reaction to America's intervention in the European war may be evidenced in this serious, even sober, self-portrait. In 1919, critic William Pattison recalled a story that Kleitsch had invented of having a French name and a boyhood in Alsace, where a German priest who baptized him changed his Gallic name to a Teutonic one. During and after World War I, a strong bias against people with Teutonic names developed, which led many citizens of German ancestry to change their names, or to justify them as Kleitsch's invention did. Since the author's research sheds doubt on the facts of this story, an explanation is needed.[97] The author believes Kleitsch's fiction was a result of the public antagonism toward Germans and the unpopularity of the war.

As Kleitsch perfected his skills as a portraitist in Chicago, he continued to illuminate his interiors with backlighting, as he had done earlier in *Studio Interior* and *Mrs. K* (see PLATES 48 and 54). His exposure to Vermeer and the "little Dutch masters" is evident in his work during these transitional years. The interior series is certainly autobiographical, produced under familiar, controlled conditions: the artist's studio, his paintings, his wife, and his moods. Like Vermeer, Kleitsch places his figures before a window, allowing the light to partially illuminate the figure and the objects in the room. And, like the Dutch master, Kleitsch "recognized the important psychological functions of light and how its intensity and distribution affect the mood of a figure or setting."[98] He also understood the importance of color, texture, and decorative patterning in evoking a mood through setting and character. Soft light and somewhat subdued tonal qualities characterize the work of this period and reflect the gray wintry months in Chicago.

In 1917 Kleitsch showed three oils at the Art Institute in the Twenty-First Annual Exhibition of Artists of Chicago and Vicinity: *In My Studio, Natsi,* and *Von M*. The setting in each of these paintings is the artist's Athenaeum studio. Kleitsch's continuing awareness of the subtle play of light and shadow in an interior space manifests itself in paintings like *In My Studio* (1917, PLATE 60), *Problematicus* (1918, PLATE 61), and *Miss Ketchum* (c. 1918, PLATE 62), part of a series of interior scenes painted in his studio.[99] The first picture is a double portrait:

PLATE 61. Joseph Kleitsch, *Problematicus,* 1918. Oil on canvas, 60 x 55". Collection of Robert and Susan Ehrlich.

the artist and his wife, Edna, thoughtfully study the picture, perhaps of themselves, on the easel.[100] Newspaper accounts commented that the painting had "little color," that it was primarily "an arrangement of gray and yellow" of subdued tonal qualities and "mellow luminosity."[101] Elizabeth Bingham, in *Saturday Night*

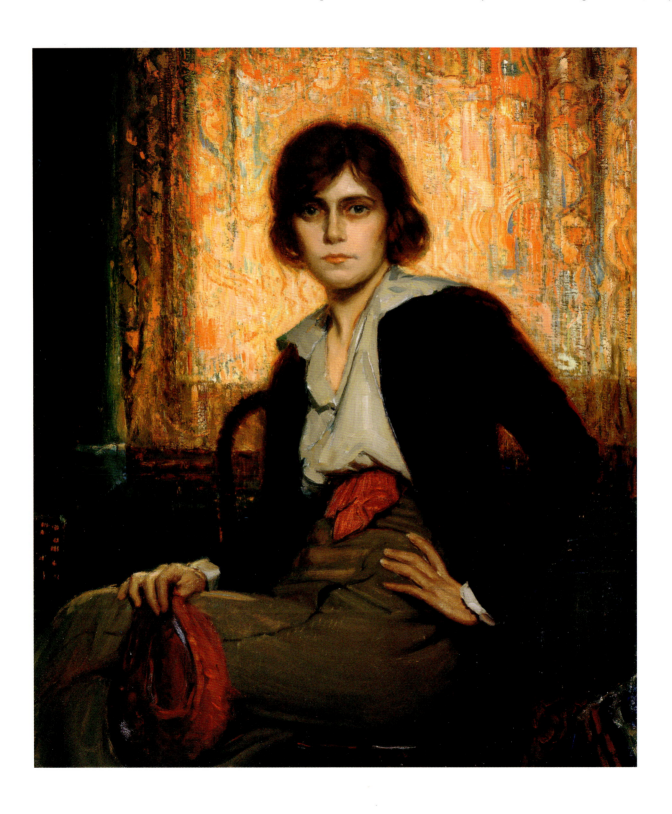

PLATE 62. Joseph Kleitsch, *Miss Ketchum*, c. 1918. Oil on canvas, 42 x 36". Edenhurst Gallery.

on June 9, 1923, called *In My Studio* one of Kleitsch's "masterpieces," adding that "the dominant interest lies in the sense of intimacy within the darkened room, but the passage above the two heads, the window shade, the light both within and without, is really the chief point of contact."

The second picture, *Problematicus*, a figure in an interior of "mellow luminosity," hung in the Art Institute's Twenty Second Annual Exhibition by Artists of Chicago and Vicinity in 1918. In it, the artist's wife is lost in contemplation of a picture on the easel, most likely of herself. The painting creates the same mood as *In My Studio*, with backlighting that flows through the amber-colored window shade to cast highlights on her hair and body. The close tonal arrangements of golds and gray-blues give it an elusive, poetic quality. Perhaps influenced by Matisse, the artist adds colorful decorative patterning in the rug and vest. Later, in his California pictures, a profusion of colorful decoration would become Kleitsch's hallmark. Although *Problematicus* is primarily a tonal painting, some impressionistic brushwork is evident in the gray-blue wall and in the buildings seen through the window. There is a certain stylistic irresolution as well in the inconsistent use of planar and rounded forms and in the perspective. In addition, Kleitsch's gestural brushwork is used arbitrarily in the figure, not necessarily to model forms or to create highlights. When *Problematicus* was exhibited at the Art Institute, reviewer Lena McCauley singled it out as one of "the figure paintings to be remembered."[102]

The third picture, *Miss Ketchum*, from about 1918, is a portrait of a young, attractive, independent woman, a successful New York designer who visited the Kleitsches in Chicago. Her direct personality is conveyed through her striking pose and her deep-set, gray-blue eyes.[103] The mood of the painting emerges in the determined face, particularly the eyes, the expressive hands, the shapely figure, and indeed in the costume. "Hats will be worn" was the order of the day in 1918, but in *Miss Ketchum* it is not worn, it is held. The small red tam in her right hand indicates a certain break with the establishment; she is not wearing her hat, but still maintains decorum, convincing the viewer that the hat is available in the event it is needed. Her attire suggests proper dress for a spirited walk through the woods for exercise. As a liberated woman, she is not wearing a corset, but she looks comfortably chic nonetheless. The stylish placement of the red sash, with its soft bow just in front of her right hip, was apparently arranged by the artist. Her less-than-perfect hairstyle indicates that fashion is not everything to her, in character with her independent personality.[104] Miss Ketchum's attitude is clearly that of a modern woman.

Kleitsch's portrayal of individual expression as well as his freedom of thought and action are especially discernible in his uncommissioned portraits, such as *The Attic Philosopher* and *Miss Ketchum*. These more spontaneous portraits seem to be of people he knew, whose mannerisms and personalities were familiar to him.

Confident of his skills as a portrait and figurative painter, Kleitsch began to experiment with small landscape studies made on his summer haunts with Palette and Chisel Club colleagues. A reviewer of the show at the Bryden Art Galleries, writing in the *Chicago Evening Post* on January 29, 1918, pointed out "a wonderful example," *The Dunes,* that should attract [the attention of] the Prairie Club members, and others who have tramped the sands on the east shore of Lake Michigan." This review is the first mention of Kleitsch expanding his repertory to include landscapes, and is perhaps a hint of his successful future in this genre in California. Kleitsch continued to paint landscapes, and in the summer of 1919, produced *A View Across the Lake, Saugatuck, Michigan* (PLATE 63).

By 1919, Kleitsch's status as an outstanding portraitist had been affirmed by his peers and critics. His art was widely seen in local exhibitions, and he had received several awards and significant recognition. In the June 1919 *Fine Arts Journal*, William Pattison wrote a laudatory article comparing Kleitsch's talents to

PLATE 63. Joseph Kleitsch, *A View Across the Lake, Saugatuck, Michigan,* 1919. Oil on canvas, 30 x 40". Collection of the Lorna and Milton Berle Trust.

those of such notable artists as the Spaniard Joaquín Sorolla (1863–1923) as well as Rembrandt and other painters of the Dutch School.[105] Singling out Sorolla as one of "the best portrait painters. . .ever mindful of the rich beauty of the softened light of a fine interior," Pattison added that "one who can master this lighting has gone far in portraiture and for this reason the work of Joseph Kleitsch may be said to be representative of the best element of the younger portrait painters of today. This artist is indeed essentially a portrait painter." Pattison continued, "Kleitsch is a substantial painter, engrossed in the character of his subject as expressed in his person and gifted with an innate faculty for good *arrangements of mellow light and rich shade*."[106]

In the same article, Pattison highlighted two recent paintings by Kleitsch: one the *Sicilian Girl* (PLATE 64) and the other a full-length portrait, *The Artist's Wife* (PLATE 65). He specifically noted the "lovely head of the little Sicilian girl," remarking that Kleitsch had "brought out all the innate refinement of the girl's

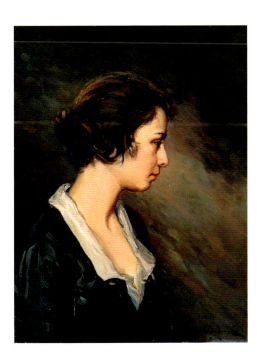

PLATE 64. Joseph Kleitsch, *Sicilian Girl,* c. 1919.
Oil on canvas, 24 x 18". Collection of Mrs. Chris Sweely.
PLATE 65. Joseph Kleitsch, *The Artist's Wife,* 1919.
Oil on canvas, 62 ¼ x 52", courtesy of Edenhurst Gallery.

CHICAGO IN THE 1910S

nature" manifested by the "arrangement of her simple attire with all the taste and charm of a great lady." Pattison noted too that "it is something for an artist to see, recognize and paint whatever of elegance his subjects may possess. It shows him as appreciative of the more gracious aspects of life even while not out of sympathy with the charm of simplicity." The charm and decorative quality of the portrait had for Pattison "the mark of a fine Romney." The writer also praised the superbly painted flesh tones: "Mr. Kleitsch paints an olive complexion deliciously. Few artists of our time have so completely realized on canvas the subtle beauty of a transparent dark skin with the warm olive tint glowing softly in its high lights." Pattison attributes this special skill to the artist's long stay in Mexico, "where an olive complexion is seen in its fullest perfection among the old Spanish aristocracy."[107] For whatever reason, Pattison missed recognizing the beauty of the sitter's sensuality with the subtle exposure of her breasts.

Pattison was particularly impressed with the monumental and elegant portrait of Kleitsch's wife. Indeed, this stunning portrait is one of the artist's most masterful works. Pattison admired her pretty, "smooth round cheeks" with a tinge of "rose," and "the pearly and opalescent tones of the white satin gown," which made "a fine foil for the vivacious face with its frame of dusky hair." Her curvaceous, shapely figure is revealed by the soft, flowing satin fabric of her dress, its butterfly sleeves of silk net edged with embroidered metallic thread, sequins, and/or crystal beads, inspired by the popular Ballet Russe.[108] Edward Maeder elaborates on her costume:

> It seems that the figure is wearing a corset. The straight line of her back and the way she is seated on the settee look formal, even though the artist's casual placement of her right hand on the hip and her left hand carelessly draped over her left knee give the opposite impression.... There is an indication that the "v" of the neck has been strengthened by the "insertion" of a pink silk satin ribbon. This would, again, have been typical [of the period] and would emphasize the femininity of the sitter and show off her pale skin. The transition of style change is illustrated by the use of flimsy, nearly see-through textiles such

PLATE 66. Joseph Kleitsch, *Miss Gregg*, c. 1919. Oil on canvas, 48 x 30". Collection of Michael Kizhner Fine Art.

as the light satin and the silk net that were a prelude to the outrageously "indecorous" styles of the 1920s, when "naughty" flappers let nearly everything show.

Maeder believes that Edna is wearing both lipstick and rouge, which were acceptable at the time. To the author, Edna's formal costume suggests that she was a fashionable modern woman.

As teenagers, Edna and her sister Martha were known as the belles of Grand Rapids, Michigan, according to Edna's godchild Marianne Barto.[109] Martha Gregaitis also sat for Kleitsch after her move from Grand Rapids to Chicago, where she became a teacher in the public schools. In Grand Rapids, Martha had lived in a convent for thirteen years as a member of a religious order. Once established in Chicago, she made an effort to change her life, choosing Marcia as her given name and Gregg as her surname. After Kleitsch's death, Marcia and her husband, businessman A. Paul Jones, generously supported Edna, who had been left in serious financial straits.

Her portrait is appropriately titled *Miss Gregg* (PLATE 66). Marcia and Edna resembled each other: both were tall, statuesque, and beautiful. In the portrait, Marcia wears a richly embroidered lavender silk blouse and a gold-colored shawl casually draped over her shoulders and arms, complementing the warmer flesh tones of her gently smiling face framed by her dark hair. Like Edna, Marcia was conscious of the latest fashions.

Like the American expatriate artist John Singer Sargent (1856–1925), who occasionally portrayed close male friends in a relaxed mood, "casually seated with a cigar in . . . hand," Kleitsch often adopted a similar approach to his portraits of male friends.[110] In Kleitsch's day, smoking had become an accepted convention in male portraiture, and he employs it in both *The Attic Philosopher* (see PLATE 55) and *August Petrtyl* (see PLATE 49). By contrast, Kleitsch's commissioned portraits, like the one of the businessman Charles F. W. Nichols, are rather stiff and formal, in keeping with the sitter's demeanor and position in society. The first version of Nichols' portrait, shown at the Art Institute's Twenty-Third Annual Exhibition by Artists of Chicago and Vicinity in 1919, received favorable criticism in the local newspapers. The second version (see p. 218) received still higher praise from

William Pattison. It "eclipsed" the first one, he wrote, because it was "an even more serious work of art." And for its "dignity and beauty" it was "unsurpassed in the difficult field of modern male portraiture."[111]

One of the high points of Kleitsch's career in Chicago was the acceptance of his *Self-Portrait* of 1919 (PLATE 67) in the Art Institute's Thirty-Second Annual Exhibition of American Oil Paintings and Sculpture, held in December 1919. This was a clear indication that painters from the East Coast no longer enjoyed exclusivity in the event. Several years earlier, a trustee of the Art Institute had questioned the practices for judging art in the museum's annuals: "Why are the artists of our own city not accorded a similar treatment" to that of the Eastern cadre of artists? "Personally, I believe in throwing all exhibitions open to competition."[112] This led to the adoption of a new procedure that immediately exposed local art to a competitive selection process. The open competition was positive for everyone, Easterners and Westerners, and especially for Kleitsch.

In 1919 Kleitsch applied for naturalization but did not activate his request until 1924, when he planned to go to Europe to further his career. He probably had intended to make the trip on the earlier date.[113] What deterred him from this trip is unknown, although rumors in local newspapers suggested that he and Edna had disagreed about his plans to go abroad. Instead, the rumors had it, they settled their differences and went to California. Kleitsch's *Self-Portrait* of 1919 reflects the serious side of his nature and his resolution to further advance his career. The intensity of his eyes suggests a passionate desire to compete and to maintain his successful status. This almost frontal self-portrait seems specifically autobiographical, hinting too at a certain vulnerability, and it marks a significant transition in his life.[114]

PLATE 67. Joseph Kleitsch, *Self-Portrait*, 1919. Oil on canvas, 30 x 24". Collection of Mary E. Olden, courtesy of A. J. Kollar Fine Paintings.

With Kleitsch's career as a portraitist well assured, his decision to leave for California comes as a surprise. The Kleitsches' move, on about January 3, 1920, is documented by information in his petition for naturalization, dated January 30, 1924.[115] *Los Angeles Times* critic Antony Anderson asked why the artist pulled up stakes and moved only to "bury himself in a village on the continent's terminal point?"[116] Several factors probably influenced Kleitsch's decision. His friend and successful colleague Edgar Payne had established studios in both Chicago and Laguna Beach, and Laguna was rapidly becoming an attractive haven for artists. In Laguna, there would be no more harsh winters with long periods of indoor confinement, allowing Kleitsch the opportunity to pursue his recent interest in landscape painting. The author believes that Kleitsch—the businessman-artist—also recognized the opportunities offered by the rapid growth and expansion of Southern California. His special talent and achievements as a portrait painter would be immediately acknowledged because of his successes in Chicago and Mexico. Moreover, there were few portraitists of Kleitsch's stature and reputation in Southern California. Indeed, he had already been commissioned to paint a portrait of Simon William Straus, a prominent financier who became instrumental in financing the Ambassador Hotel in Los Angeles (PLATE 68).[117]

PLATE 68. "Simon William Straus," n.d. Photograph. Chicago Historical Society, ICHi-36274.

CHAPTER IV

Southern California: Coming of Age, 1920–1931

"In the Southern California of the 1920s, the whole saga of frontier growth and westward expansion, the story book version of the American Dream, was given its penultimate staging in a semi-tropical setting at the western edge of the continent."[118] During this decade, the shifts in economic development, from agriculture to industrialization and urbanization, "came in such rapid succession that the region's growth seemed staged or contrived, like an outdoor pageant or a motion picture being shot on location."[119] As the railroad system extended over the region, it fueled successive land booms, creating a dynamic population that included patrons of the arts. The history of Southern California is a chronicle of the area's growth and the entrepreneurial empire builders who forced that growth through booster tactics and self-promotion. This great Los Angeles boom of the 1920s was just beginning to gain momentum when Kleitsch arrived in Southern California. While artists of the time were attracted to the area for its dynamic growth as well as its extraordinary climate and geography, it was the unique quality of Southern California's light that brought them together. Kleitsch's strong response to the region's color and light led him first to be enchanted and then finally compromised by the locale.

Initially, he had intended on only a three-month sojourn to explore some of the state's scenic highlights, traveling to locations such as Laguna Beach, Carmel-by-the-Sea, San Juan Capistrano, San Diego, and San Francisco, with its famed Chinatown. Then, after a trip to Taos and Santa Fe, New Mexico, he planned to return to Chicago.[120] His visit was undoubtedly inspired by the work of fellow Chicago artists who had painted the region's endlessly intriguing motifs: hills and meadows, deserts and mountains, rivers and ocean.

Instead of returning to Chicago, however, Kleitsch and his family moved into "the small Edwards's cottage, on the front, above the [Old Laguna] Hotel" (see PLATE 200).[121] In Laguna, the artist responded to the rhythms of the sea as well as the mountains and the varied landscape of the coastal region. The stimulation and unfettered freedom of this new environment began to transform his paintings. The contrast between the thriving Chicago metropolis and the small village of Laguna had a positive effect on Kleitsch as an artist, and it was certainly a healthier environment for his wife and son.

PLATE 69. Harold Parker, "Covered Bridge with Wicker Chairs at the Huntington Hotel, Pasadena, California," c. 1914–20. Photograph. The Huntington Library, San Marino, California.

The Santa Ana Daily Evening Register of 1920 details Kleitsch's activities during the first half of that year in California. On February 4, it reported that Kleitsch, who came to California from Chicago to paint the portrait of Mr. Straus, the New York and Chicago banker, "has decided to rest in Laguna some time before commencing his picture." On March 4, the artist was at work on Straus's portrait in Pasadena, where the banker was spending his vacation at the fashionable Huntington Hotel. Straus ostensibly came to California for a rest, but in fact he had been charged with financing the California Hotel (conceived in 1919 and later called the Ambassador Hotel), scheduled to open in Los Angeles on January 1, 1921.[122] Kleitsch's portrait of him has yet to be located.

According to the *Register*, Kleitsch returned to Pasadena around March 20 to paint another commissioned portrait, but the article does not identify the sitter.[123] Two elegant female portraits have surfaced recently, both painted at Pasadena's Huntington Hotel. In both of them, a young woman is seated in a wicker chair on the hotel's terrace; in the background is a Monet-like impressionistic garden (PLATE 69). We know that Straus had commissioned Kleitsch to paint his oldest daughter, who had accompanied him to California, and one of these pictures portrays Mrs. Herbert Spencer Martin (née Madeline Straus), wearing the elegant apparel of a wealthy society matron of the era (PLATE 70). Her hat gives the portrait a formal air and helps project the image of a married woman of Mrs. Martin's social class: her walking stick is a reflection of the latest fashion.[124]

Kleitsch carefully describes his sitter's elegant fashion-plate look. Her soft, flowing skirt with its natural waistline falls slightly above the ankles. The brim of her hat—not quite a cloche—is tipped close to her eyes, and the carefully adjusted angle "just touching the sitter's left eyebrow is highly fashionable." The stiffened brim, squarish crown, and inverted feathers with quills jutting up at a jaunty angle were stylish contrivances of the early 1920s. Instead of the longer upswept hair of the 1910s, Madeline's is shorter and bobbed. By holding her gloves and exposing her hands to view, she makes a more open, "modern" gesture. "The dress . . . [may be] actually made of a knit fabric, the collar and cuffs of white, possibly linen," either detachable or attached to a blouse underneath. The silhouette of her dress can be dated to 1920, the year Kleitsch painted this portrait.[125]

PLATE 70. Joseph Kleitsch, *Portrait of Mrs. Herbert Spencer Martin* (née Madeline Straus), 1920. Oil on canvas, 42 x 34". Collection of James Taylor and Gary Conway.

The other portrait is of the artist Isaac J. Frazee's youngest daughter, Edee-Lou (PLATES 71 and 72).[126] In contrast to the elegance of Madeline Martin's attire, Edee-Lou's clothing is casual. Clearly a spirited young woman with an individual sense of style, she wears a flower in her hair and a red shawl over an orange dress. Kleitsch perceptively portrays her free, vivacious nature. A dappled light dances across the portrait. Both sitters are modeled in a realistic manner against an impressionistic background.

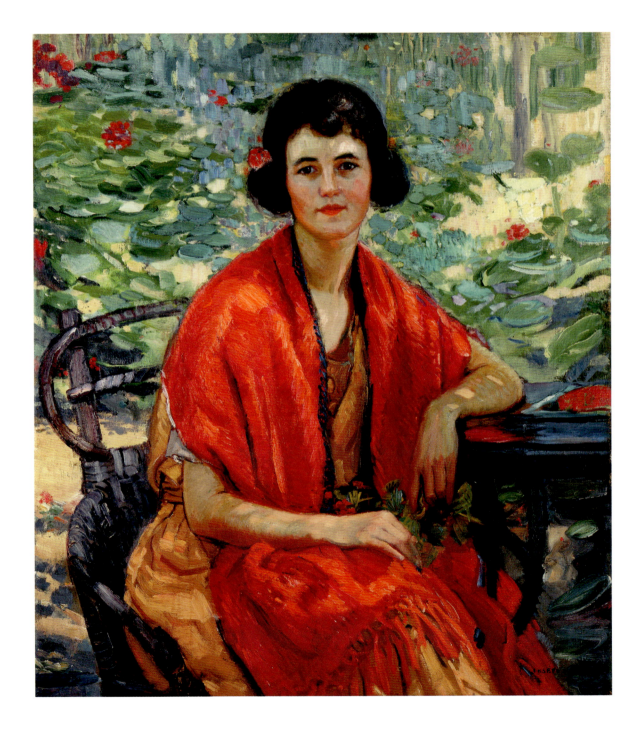

During the first half of 1920, Kleitsch painted portraits of several other local patrons in Pasadena, Laguna, and Santa Ana: Miss June Harding of Laguna; Mildred Whitsen and Elizabeth Scott of Santa Ana; and a larger-than-life-size portrait of Mrs. Paul E. Hurst (Hedda Nova, a Russian silent film actress). In the portrait of Mrs. Hurst, not yet located, she is dressed in white and seated at a table. Exhibited at a reception held at the Laguna Beach Art Association Gallery on May 27 honoring Joseph and Edna Kleitsch, the portrait received "much favorable comment," and was "painted [expressly] for an exhibition to be shown in large galleries." While the actress was on location in Laguna for *The Bird of Dawn*, a movie produced by the newly organized Laguna Del Rey Art Film Company,[127] the Hursts and Kleitsches became close friends, perhaps because of their shared European background. The Kleitsches and their son Eugene and local investors in the film company were hosted by the Hursts at a birthday dinner for Mrs. Hurst. At the time, Kleitsch must have painted two portraits of Hedda Nova, because another depicts her half-length wearing a bouffant, black evening gown that accentuates her arms and shoulders seductively with black net lace (PLATE 74).[128] Her short, full hair is in keeping with the sultry look of the 1920s that she epitomizes in a studio photograph (PLATE 73).

opposite
PLATE 71. "Edee-Lou and Isaac Jenkinson Frazee," c. 1920. Photograph courtesy of Craig Walker.
PLATE 72. Joseph Kleitsch, *Portrait of Edee-Lou Frazee*, c. 1920. Oil on canvas, 40 x 36". Collection of The Irvine Museum.

above
PLATE 73. "Hedda Nova as Silent Movie Actress," c. 1919. Photograph. Courtesy of the Academy of Motion Picture Arts and Sciences.

right
PLATE 74. Joseph Kleitsch, *Portrait of Hedda Nova (Mrs. Paul Hurst)*, c. 1920. Oil on canvas, 34 x 23". Photograph courtesy of Jack Jacobs, Oxford Galleries/Fine Arts & Imports.

PLATE 75. "Exterior View: Laguna Beach Art Association, First Art Gallery, Old Town Hall, Laguna Beach," c. 1918. Photograph. Laguna Art Museum Archives, Laguna Beach, California.

In June 1920 the Kleitsches left for New Orleans, where the artist planned to do a group of paintings of Creole life for a traveling exhibition in the fall. New Orleans' unique population, history, and cuisine proved to be bountiful stimulation. Returning to Laguna late in the year, they decided to settle there permanently.[129] Kleitsch immediately became involved with the Laguna Beach Art Association, initiated and founded in 1918 by his friend and colleague Edgar Payne. The association was a perfect vehicle for introducing Kleitsch and his art to the community (PLATES 75 and 76).[130] Edna probably informed the *Santa Ana Daily Evening Register* that her husband had painted several prominent personalities, such as President Madero and his wife, U.S. Representative George Kindel, and Joseph Smith, founder of the Church of Latter-Day Saints.[131] By year's end, Kleitsch was considered the dominant portraitist in the Laguna art community. Among his many commissioned portraits were those of Mr. and Mrs. E. E. Jahraus, Mr. Isaac Jenkinson Frazee (PLATE 77), Miss Borghild Leren, and Mrs. C. A. Brookes.[132] From then on, Kleitsch was very much in demand as a portraitist, attracting numerous commissions from prominent citizens in both Laguna and Los Angeles.

PLATE 76. "Interior View: Laguna Beach Art Association, First Art Gallery, Old Town Hall, Laguna Beach," c. 1920. Photograph. Laguna Art Museum Archives, Laguna Beach, California.

PLATE 77. Joseph Kleitsch, *Isaac Jenkinson Frazee*, 1921.
Oil on canvas, 30 x 24". Collection of Craig Walker.

Kleitsch continued to rely heavily on portrait commissions as a source of income. About 1920–21 the eminent Dr. Walter Jarvis Barlow (1868–1937), founder of the first respiratory hospital in Los Angeles, sat for his portrait.[133] The physician is shown with the instruments and books of his profession; the correct business suit he wears for the portrait suggests that it was commissioned by his board of directors (PLATE 78). Laguna artists also became subjects for Kleitsch's brush. In 1921 he painted and exhibited a portrait of his artist-friend Robert Fullonton (1876–1933).[134] Kleitsch chose to portray the seriousness and candor of Fullonton's personality (PLATE 79). His piercing blue eyes, seen through pince-nez glasses, and his patterned tie provide focal points of color against the flesh tones and the neutral, textured background. The composition is extraordinary in its portrayal of the sitter's relaxed yet alert demeanor.

The years from 1921 to 1925 were exceedingly productive for Kleitsch. He explored the Southern California landscape and motored to the Bay Area (PLATE 80). His restless nature, perceptive eye, and appetite for color were rewarded with countless subjects to paint and record. This is best illustrated by *Rocky Cliffs, Laguna* of 1920–21, which depicts Edna and young Eugene at play on the rocky beach, a work that demonstrates the artist's new facility with an impressionistic brush and blond palette, effectively capturing the brilliant, glaring California light on a sunny day (PLATE 81).

below
PLATE 78. Joseph Kleitsch, *Portrait of Dr. Walter Jarvis Barlow,* c. 1920. Oil on canvas, 36 x 32". Collection of Barlow Respiratory Hospital, courtesy of George Stern Fine Arts.
PLATE 79. Joseph Kleitsch, *Portrait of Artist Robert Fullonton,* 1921. Oil on canvas, 40 x 34". Laguna Art Museum Collection. Gift of Marjory Adams.

opposite
PLATE 80. Joseph Kleitsch, *Joice Street (Nob Hill), San Francisco,* August 1922. Oil on canvas mounted on board, 15 x 11 ½". Private Collection, courtesy of the Oakland Museum of California.

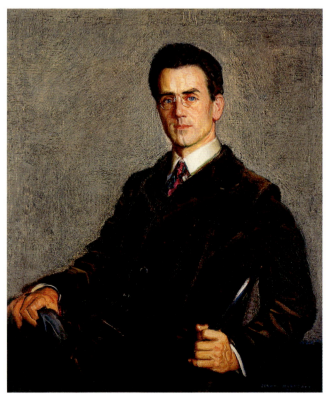

SOUTHERN CALIFORNIA 105

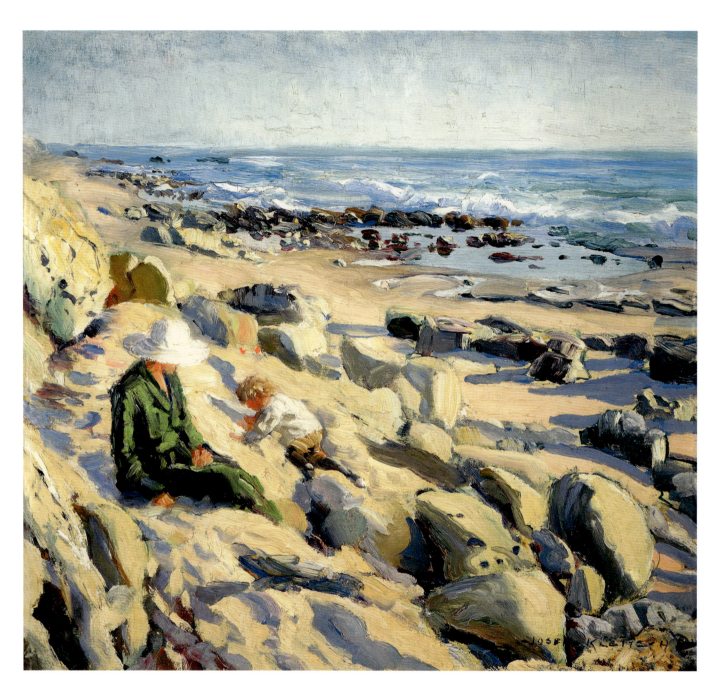

PLATE 81. Joseph Kleitsch, *Rocky Cliffs, Laguna (Edna and Eugene)*, c. 1920–21. Oil on canvas, 18 x 20". Private Collection.

Laguna Life on July 15, 1921, reported that "an exhibition of the paintings of Joseph Kleitsch containing all of his best pictures of Laguna Beach done here in the past two years" was held at the Fine Arts Building in Chicago. These paintings included a number of portraits of prominent New York and Chicago society women—*Mrs. Herbert Spencer Martin* (sometimes called "the woman in white") and *Hedda Nova* among them.[135] As Kleitsch's career continued to flourish, Edna assumed its management, which included the responsibility of organizing his exhibitions and handling the sales of his work. At this time she was also expecting their second child, who was born in Chicago on August 17, 1921. Unfortunately, Bernard Joseph Kleitsch lived only a short time, dying on October 2, 1921, in Grand Rapids, Michigan. He was buried in Sts. Peter and Paul Lithuanian Catholic Cemetery in the Gregaitis family plot.[136]

Although the loss of their second child was a serious emotional and spiritual setback for the Kleitsches, they quickly returned to California, where an ever-increasing, demanding schedule awaited them. In November the artist entered his portrait of Fullonton in the Southwest Museum's first annual exhibition of paintings by California artists. *Los Angeles Times* art critic Antony Anderson, who would play a decisive role in the appreciation and understanding of Kleitsch's work, commented on the portrait: "It is thoroughly characterized in posture and expression, is true in modeling, a trifle harsh, yet not unpleasant, in color, and in brief, is alive. It compels your admiration."[137] Encouraged by the receptivity to his work, the artist entered a portrait (unlocated) of his son, *Eugene,* in the Laguna Beach Art Association exhibition in December. Critics admired "the small boy of singular beauty standing at the seashore," but felt that he was overshadowed by the dominant, almost "crudely" colored landscape.[138] They recognized the affection Kleitsch felt for his son in the beautifully modeled portrait. The recent death of his infant son may explain the tenderness expressed in the painting.

There was occasionally time for leisure in California, and during the summer months Kleitsch performed as a flutist in Isaac Frazee's Indian Pageant Play of the Peace Pipe based on the story of Kitshi Manido, "The Great Spirit," and held under the auspices of the Laguna Beach Art Association.[139] The following year he was welcomed as a performer in Frank Adams' "Circus," playing Hungarian melodies on his accordion.

Kleitsch and his wife also entered into Laguna's social life by hosting dinners and informal card games in his studio. A man with many interests and talents, the artist delighted in card games and sports in addition to playing several instruments and involving himself in many community activities. With Kleitsch's full schedule, it was no surprise to see *Laguna Life* remark that he had gone to "Los Angeles for a few days of much needed rest."[140]

PLATE 82. "Front Entrance and East Porch, Ambassador Hotel, Los Angeles, California," c. 1920s. Postcards, courtesy of Carlyn Frank Benjamin.

PLATE 83. Christopher Bliss, "Lobby, Ambassador Hotel, Los Angeles, California," 2003. Photograph.
PLATE 84. "Earl Stendahl's Banquet for Artists at Stendahl Art Galleries, Ambassador Hotel, Los Angeles, California," c. 1928. Photograph. Courtesy of April Dammann, from the forthcoming book on Earl L. Stendahl.

In 1922 Kleitsch gave Kanst Gallery, one of the oldest art dealers in Los Angeles, two portraits to sell: *Robert Fullonton* and *Mrs. R. Clarkson Coleman*.[141] A critic singled out the second work as a "splendid character" study: "The artist in his hours of labor on this painting had analyzed the innermost thoughts of his subject in so far as they appear in the moulding of her features, the pose and carriage of her head, [and] had penetrated far below the surface into the essential soul."[142] Edna, acting as her husband's representative for a Pasadena exhibition, was successful in selling two of his recent landscapes.[143]

On March 16, 1922, Kleitsch signed an exclusive contract for Southern California with the well-known Stendahl Galleries. Earl Stendahl was well aware of Kleitsch's favorable critical reviews and the sizable patronage he already enjoyed. An association with Stendahl ensured timely scheduling of exhibitions and offered the artist ample media exposure. The contract gave Earl Stendahl 50 percent of gallery sales and Mrs. Kleitsch a 15 percent commission for outside sales.[144] Stendahl opened his gallery on January 1, 1921, in the new Ambassador Hotel, which had become the social center of Southern California (PLATES 82–84).

As early as *Problematicus* of 1918 (see PLATE 61), color and decorative pattern had begun to emerge as essential to Kleitsch's compositions. These elements are even more pronounced in the California pictures, in which he seems to fully embrace the spirit of Hungarian painting. Christian Brinton characterized Hungarian painting as follows in his critical review of the Panama-Pacific International Exposition of 1915 in San Francisco: "The art of Hungary is before all else a typically rhapsodic expression. You feel in it a marked degree of rhythm and a rich, vibrant harmony rarely if ever encountered elsewhere. . . . In each [painting] you meet the same deep-rooted race spirit, the same love of vivid chromatic effect, the same fervid lyric passion."[145] Four paintings by Kleitsch of California subjects—*The Oriental Shop, Creek—Laguna Canyon, Laguna Road,* and *Highlights*—illustrate the depth and sensitivity of his awakened understanding of color.

The Oriental Shop of 1922 (PLATE 86) dazzles the eye with a galaxy of color and a profusion of decorative objects. Employing the entire color spectrum, Kleitsch gives the painting the opulence of movie palaces of the 1910s and 1920s. Although a writer for the *Los Angeles Times* complained on April 20, 1924, that the picture lacked "coherence," he praised the artist for a "virtuosity that . . . [made one] gasp" and singled out the woman [Edna] on the viewer's left as "a little masterpiece of itself." Kleitsch's virtuosic brush moves freely in swirling arabesques, and the dark, vibrant colors, applied dark-on-dark in the same intensity with a wet technique, suggest the subtle shapes and forms of his objects. Against a white ground, the colors appear richer and more contrasted.[146]

Kleitsch sculpts the hands and faces of his subjects with a variety of colors to produce delicate or swarthy flesh tones that are glowing and opalescent, just as the rich colors of their hair reflect the light of lamps and mirrors, blending in a chromatic crescendo. The brushstrokes of the clothing create soft, natural folds and the bridging of many colors that look like scintillating flickers skipping off fabric, as light dances on water. The artist often employs a tilted perspective to draw the eye back to the impressionistic, light-filled windows revealing figures passing by, reminiscent of the Tiffany windows of the 1920s.

In *The Oriental Shop,* the model for the fair-complexioned redhead reclining in a wicker chair was Florence Marsh, wife of the manager of G. T. Marsh and Company, an Asian import shop in the Ambassador Hotel, where Kleitsch set this painting (PLATE 85). Marsh's father, G. T. Marsh, who founded the House of Marsh in San Francisco in 1876, was among the first to introduce Asian art to the West Coast.[147]

PLATE 85. Christopher Bliss, "Interior View: G. T. Marsh Shop, Ambassador Hotel Arcade, Los Angeles, California," 2003. Photograph.

PLATE 86. Joseph Kleitsch, *The Oriental Shop*, 1922. Oil on canvas, 32 x 40". Collection of Joseph Ambrose, Jr., and Michael D. Feddersen.

In a smaller, altered version, *The Oriental Shop* (or *The Jade Shop*) of 1925 (PLATE 88), Kleitsch included only a single figure, perhaps Edna, who is almost incidental to the multicolored decoration and patterning. Less distinctive and more abstract than the 1922 painting, it seems to reflect a change of mood by the artist. Kleitsch resolved the later composition by reducing the painting's width to eliminate the profusion and jumble of drapery on the left side of the original version (PLATE 87).

PLATE 87. Joseph Kleitsch, *The Oriental Shop*, 1925. Original painting before alteration. Photograph. Laguna Art Museum Archives, Laguna Beach, California. Stendahl Art Galleries Collection.

PLATE 88. Joseph Kleitsch, *The Oriental Shop* (or *The Jade Shop*), 1925.
Oil on canvas, 32 x 26". Private Collection, courtesy of The Irvine Museum.

PLATE 89. Christopher Bliss, "Interior View: Kleitsch's Studio, Ambassador Hotel Tower, Los Angeles, California," 2003. Photograph.

The reactions of the press to Kleitsch's exhibitions from 1922 through 1925 detail his career path of those years. In June 1922, his first one-man show of thirty-eight paintings was held at the Stendahl Galleries in the Ambassador Hotel, where Kleitsch later established his Los Angeles studio (PLATE 89). A review by Vandyke Brown in Laguna Beach's *Life and Art* on July 28, 1922, makes it clear that the artist had begun to receive highly favorable press reviews:

> Joseph Kleitsch that uncompromising belligerent with the broad brush. And most of the thirty-eight canvases are pictures of Laguna Beach, at that. The portraits and figures are very few, yet even these are almost all lovely ladies from Laguna. Our friend Joseph has not found it necessary to go far afield for subjects....Kleitsch is certainly a painter. Of an equal certainty he is an artist. What exuberant vitality and what gorgeous schemes of color we find in these canvases! And what poetry, too, in many of them. You never dreamt, till you looked at these pictures, that Laguna offers to the artist a diversity in composition and subject hard to beat anywhere else.

Kleitsch's brilliant, colorful, and varied interpretations of Laguna Beach attracted many critics, who remarked on his transition from portraitist to painter of landscapes. Kleitsch's "eagle eye," Vandyke Brown wrote, had captured Laguna Beach "inside and out—its hills, its rocks, its beating surf, its quaint streets, its lovely gardens, its handsome women." The infinite beauty of the gamut of colors Laguna offered, from "gray to gold, from gold to vermillion, from these to green and blue, and then back to gray again," was displayed in these thirty-eight works.[148]

Probably the most striking of the group was *The Village,* an arrangement of trees and houses spread across the sloping hillside, with the veiled and sunlit Mystic Hill in the background (PLATE 90).[149] In this picture, Kleitsch offers a glimpse of the small settlement that would provide endless images for his canvases in succeeding years. Among the paintings in the Stendahl exhibition were the atmospheric *Jeweled Coast,* the sunset along the shore in *Bird Rock,* the eucalyptus trees on misty hills in *Gray Symphony*, a girl (Edna) in red walking through a eucalyptus colonnade on a dusty road; *Diver's Cove*; *Golden Cliffs* (PLATE 91); and *Rocky Cliffs, Laguna* (see PLATE 81).[150]

PLATE 90. Joseph Kleitsch, *The Village (Laguna)*, 1922. Oil on canvas, 24 x 29".
Private Collection. Photograph courtesy of George Stern Fine Arts.

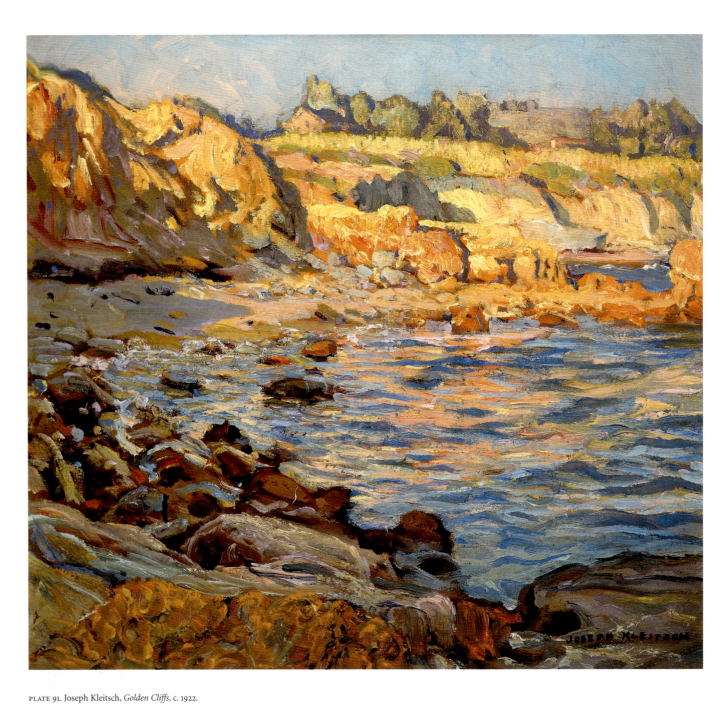

PLATE 91. Joseph Kleitsch, *Golden Cliffs*, c. 1922.
Oil on canvas, 19 x 21". Private Collection, courtesy of
Joseph Ambrose, Jr., and Michael D. Feddersen.

PLATE 92. Joseph Kleitsch, *The Flower Garden—Laguna*, 1922. Oil on canvas, 24 x 30". Private Collection, courtesy of George Stern Fine Arts.

Kleitsch also entered two paintings in the third exhibition of the Painters and Sculptors of Southern California at the Los Angeles Museum of History, Science and Art in Exposition Park, April 21 to May 28, 1922. A reviewer of *Portrait*, which depicted a young woman in a red shawl, called it a "vigorous piece of painting" that was "brilliantly alive in color" (see PLATE 72).[151] Although Antony Anderson found *The Flower Garden—Laguna* "vigorously realistic in treatment" and the distant hills beautifully rendered, he felt that the "riotous colors" could be more subdued (PLATE 92).[152]

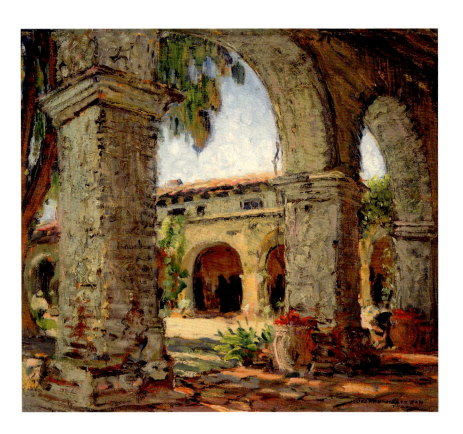

PLATE 93. Joseph Kleitsch, *Through the Arches, Mission San Juan Capistrano*, 1922. Oil on canvas, 18 x 20". Collection of Dr. Kevin Jeworski, courtesy of George Stern Fine Arts.

Earl Stendahl adhered to his contract with Kleitsch, maximizing his exposure to the media and organizing frequent exhibitions to promote sales. Stendahl's gallery seems to have exhibited a sizable inventory of Kleitsch's works at all times. This inventory contained a large number of landscapes, sometimes enlivened with figures, portraits, and a view of Mission San Juan Capistrano (PLATE 93).[153] Kleitsch was captivated by the picturesque architecture and setting of this mission and the yearly migration of the swallows. In the next several years he painted the mission and its environs often, recording it from various vantage points at different times of the day to capture the nuances of light. The paintings that resulted from these passionate labors came to be recognized as some of the most brilliant and spiritually moving of his career.

An accounting statement from Stendahl to Kleitsch, dated April 1, 1922, to January 1, 1923, covers the first year of their association, indicating sales of sixteen paintings totaling $1,860.00 and debits of $1,985.75. This included cash draws, framing, automobile exchange for $600.00, and miscellaneous expenses. The difference between credits and debits shows that Kleitsch owed Stendahl $125.75. The statement did not include any paintings that Kleitsch might have sold independently.[154]

Stendahl was pleased with both the sales of Kleitsch's work and the response from the press. On August 27, Stendahl, his wife and child, and Kleitsch were reportedly en route to San Francisco and would stop off at Carmel on their return. They had different agendas: Stendahl's was to check out the northern city's galleries and Kleitsch's was to search for new sketching grounds, including Carmel-by-the-Sea. The press expressed concern that the artist might succumb to this picturesque spot and give the "go-by" to Laguna Beach, where he was now well known. The Ambassador exhibition, the critic added, had been "a highly successful one—which may account for the 'grand tour' that artist and dealer are taking together. Nothing like money to cement friendships of this sort."[155] The only study to surface from this 1922 trip is a small view of Nob Hill in San Francisco (see PLATE 80).

October was an active month for Kleitsch and his family as they moved into the Turner House near Isch's grocery and general store.[156] He was also involved with the Laguna Beach Art Association exhibition, held in the organization's gallery.[157] Kleitsch chose to exhibit *Enchantment*, an animated painting full of vigorous brushwork and vibrant color. The composition focuses on Edna in a

PLATE 94. Joseph Kleitsch, *Enchantment*, 1922. Oil on canvas, 22 x 18 ¼". Private Collection, courtesy of The Irvine Museum.

PLATE 95. "The Old Post Office," n.d. Photograph. Courtesy of David O'Hoy.

red jacket and white dress, dabbling her feet in a pool of water and surrounded by looming, craggy rocks made up of daubs of color (PLATE 94). With this picture, Kleitsch demonstrated his talent for plein-air painting.

"Nick Isch's old store and post office where everyone sat and whittled on the railing while they were waiting" was another subject for Kleitsch in early fall 1922 (PLATE 96).[158] Looking across the porch of the old board-and-batten post office on Laguna Avenue at Coast Highway, the artist was able to convey a sense of Old Laguna—a small beach community with an art colony where residents still had "to wade through mud, to plow through dust, to import water, to cook with kerosene, to pant up steep hills" (PLATE 95). The cropped foreground and steep angle of the composition with surrounding houses, eucalyptus trees, and "a genuine un-subdivided" hill add dimension to the picture. The play of light and shadow leads the eye first through the deep shade of the Old Post Office porch and then back to the parched sunlit hills in the background. This was Old Laguna, rural in setting, with a strong feeling of tranquility.

In late April 1923, this treasured landmark was razed. Isch's general store and post office—Old Laguna's village meeting place—gave way to "50 modern cottages and apartments and an administration building." Kleitsch's impressive painting would preserve Old Laguna and its once-familiar landmark for future generations, despite the inroads of "progress." For Kleitsch the destruction of village landmarks became a clarion call to preserve on canvas as many of these historic sites as possible. Recognizing that Old Laguna would succumb to development, he became one of the early preservationists of his time (see chapter five).

PLATE 96. Joseph Kleitsch, *The Old Post Office* (*Laguna Beach*), 1922–23. Oil on canvas, 40 x 34". Laguna Art Museum Collection. Gift of the Estate of Joseph Kleitsch in memory of his wife Edna.

The author has previously referred to the artist as a multifaceted man. A facet not yet touched upon is Kleitsch the "pool shark." An issue of *Laguna Life* from December 8, 1922, contains a description of his gregariousness and versatility:

> Tonight at Ed Hofer's amusement parlor the aspirations of one faction for the title of local pool champion will go into the dust. The laurels, at present, rest with the artists, who are represented by Joe Kleitsch and Austin Cody. But, the runners-ups, and the contractors Frank Champion and Lester McKnight, are the challengers and the deciding game must be played tonight. In Mr. Kleitsch's own words, (but sadly lacking his pleasing enunciation): Speeches will be made at the banquet . . . to celebrate the artists' victory . . . . When the final game was played victory perched on the banner of the contractors . . . . [Kleitsch] still undaunted . . . challenged the winners for a return match . . . to [be] played after New Years.

A versatile sportsman as well, Kleitsch was elected vice president of the Laguna Beach Gun Club at a meeting the following year.

During the same season that Kleitsch was demonstrating his prowess at the pool table, an item in *Laguna Life* on December 8, 1922, reports that he was building a new house on the hill above First Street (present-day Glenneyre) with a sweeping view of the land and sea. In 1924, Kleitsch painted a view near this site (PLATE 97). Property records, however, indicate his March 1923 purchase of a lot for a house and future studio at Legion and Through streets as well as two lots in Arch Beach Heights that were not filed with the recorder until December 1928.[159] In a conversation, Kleitsch told a reporter that he had considered purchasing the lot for his future residence as early as December 1922.

PLATE 97. Joseph Kleitsch, *First Street (now Glenneyre) at Legion Street,* 1924. Oil on canvas, 16 x 20".
Private Collection, courtesy of The Irvine Museum.

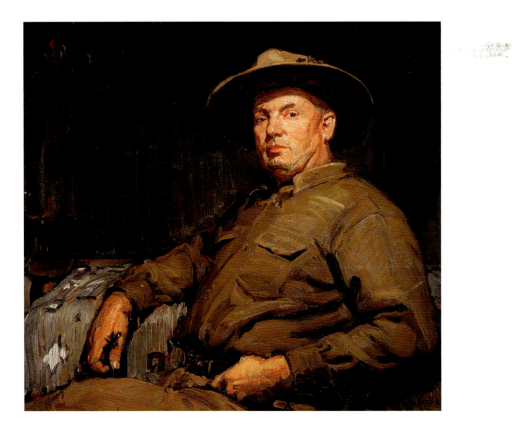

 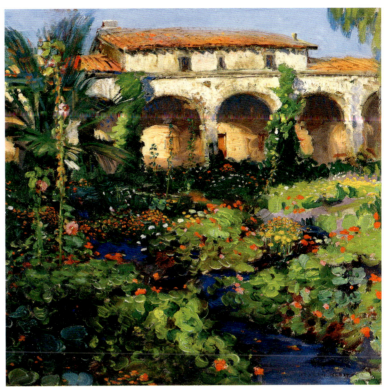

opposite
PLATE 98. Joseph Kleitsch, *Mission Canyon,* 1922. Oil on canvas, 29 x 33". Collection of Lenoir Josey. Photograph courtesy of William A. Karges Fine Art.
PLATE 99. Joseph Kleitsch, Unidentified Male Portrait, Pala Indian Reservation, Pala, California, 1922–23. Oil on canvas, 30 x 40". Collection of E. Gene Crain.

above
PLATE 100. Joseph Kleitsch, *A Favorite Spot (Fisherman's Cove, Laguna Beach),* 1923. Oil on canvas, 20 x 18". Private Collection.
PLATE 101. Joseph Kleitsch, *Capistrano Courtyard,* 1923. Oil on canvas, 20 x 18". Private Collection, courtesy of Redfern Gallery.

In mid-December 1922, Kleitsch began a painting tour, visiting San Juan Capistrano to paint more scenes of the mission, and San Luis Rey to depict nearby Mission San Antonio de Pala in northern San Diego County. He also set up his easel in the back canyon country to depict *Mission Canyon*, with its tangled branches of gnarled gray sycamores "lifting their burden of golden leaves above a river-bottom green with winter" (PLATE 98).[160] His *Pala Mission* lacks the brilliance and vigor of the paintings of Capistrano, a location he often returned to paint.[161]

Edna reportedly joined him over the holidays, and they spent a month at a ranch near "an Indian reservation."[162] The ranch was probably on the boundary of the Pala Indian reservation, where Kleitsch may have painted a virile, rugged, unidentified male portrait (PLATE 99). The individual's uniform would suggest his affiliation with the federal government in the administration of Indian affairs. The blanket his arm rests on appears to be Navajo, and he sports a feather in his hat.

Kleitsch had intended to be away for more than a month, but his many commitments for portrait commissions and the Stendahl Galleries exhibitions required him to change his plans. On March 9, 1923, because of his numerous commitments in Los Angeles,[163] the Kleitsches moved into a new residence there and began to divide their time between the city and Laguna. Kleitsch continued to paint in Laguna Beach (PLATE 100) and Capistrano (PLATE 101).[164]

PLATE 102. Joseph Kleitsch, *Red and Green* (*Mission San Juan Capistrano*), 1923. Oil on canvas, 36 x 40". The Irvine Museum.

On May 4 Kleitsch entered his *Self-Portrait* of 1915 (see PLATE 45) in the Fourth Exhibition of the Painters and Sculptors of Southern California. The June 3 headline of Antony Anderson's *Los Angeles Times* column "Of Art and Artists" read: "Joseph Kleitsch's Brilliant Exhibit." Critics were surprised by the magnitude of this show at the Stendahl Galleries, which included seventy-one paintings. Anderson was eloquent: "Kleitsch is an artist with a temperament and with not a little of the divine fire. I am not saying that ... Kleitsch is 'driven,' but I do believe that he often works inspirationally—or at all events at a white heat of creative esthetic energy—call the moment what you will—and that he occasionally gives us pictures that are truly masterly." Anderson singled out *In My Studio* (see PLATE 60), *Problematicus* (see PLATE 61), *Miss Ketchum* (see PLATE 62) and *The Attic Philosopher* (see PLATE 55): "These few are the masterly ones—I may even venture to term them masterpieces—that merge emotion and technique with absolute completeness, that show a perfect adjustment of means to ends, and that have the elusive, the poignantly thrilling and touching beauty that we find in all works of art of a high excellence—in music, poetry, sculpture, and painting."

Anderson concluded his column with a reference to several recent paintings of California subjects in which Kleitsch expressed a "different mood and manner," such as *The Breakers, The Oriental Shop, Capistrano, Baptismal Font,* and *Mrs. Herbert Spencer Martin*. With this diverse list of titles, one had "to admit Kleitsch's versatility," said Anderson. Clearly Stendahl's reason for including Chicago subjects—to impress Kleitsch's patrons with the breadth of the artist's talent—had proven valid.[165]

During this productive period, Kleitsch found time to start an artists' club. Earlier, he had confided to Earl Stendahl his idea of forming a new art club in Southern California for a select membership, primarily of former members of the Palette and Chisel Club and the Salmagundi Club, an organization that would rival the conservative Painters and Sculptors of Southern California.[166] In early July 1923, he and Fred Grayson Sayre (1879–1939) founded the Painters and Sculptors Club of Los Angeles. At the club's first meeting, held at Kleitsch's Ambassador Hotel studio on July 10 (see PLATE 89), John Cotton (1869–1931) was elected president; Joseph Kleitsch vice president, and F. Grayson Sayre secretary-treasurer.[167] On July 15, 1923, the *Los Angeles Times* stated that "the objective was to form a democratic working club for men only which shall provide a studio with [live] models where members may draw or paint in any medium they wish, without interference or instruction. . . . The atmosphere will be one of absolute freedom." The club was patterned after the Palette and Chisel Club of Chicago, in which both Kleitsch and Sayre had been active, and the Salmagundi Club of New York. Provision was made for associate as well as artist members, allowing businessmen to mingle with artists in theatricals, minstrel shows, and mixers, an arrangement that had been extremely successful in both cities.

Minutes of the regular business meetings indicate that Kleitsch was busy with club activities and that his studio remained its meeting place until October 9, when the club approved the rental of a studio in the Lyceum Building at 231 South Spring Street. The club also accepted a Mr. Frolich's generous offer of the use of the Norse Studio Club in Hollywood for social mixers on Friday nights "to boost associate memberships and fellowship." Members managed to raise $461 for the club through an auction of small works donated by the artists. The club's first annual exhibition was scheduled for February 25, 1924. Kleitsch and Sayre had been successful in attracting many of the leading artists of Los Angeles, Pasadena, and Laguna as members.[168]

In late July, Kleitsch began an extended sketching trip to San Juan Capistrano. His keen color sense responded to the rich beauty of the colorful gardens and the subtle loveliness of the mission walls and cloisters. *Red and Green*, a strikingly beautiful painting, exemplifies his response to this environment (PLATE 102). The same riotous, vibrant colors seen in Kleitsch's recent figurative paintings occur again in this landscape. In the mission's front garden, Edna, in her familiar red jacket, shades her eyes as a young Mexican girl kneels nearby among the flowering plants. The soft adobe color of the mission's south wing in the background contrasts with the figures, the colorful garden, and the large, leafy pepper tree. The bright summer sunlight makes the small kneeling figure almost invisible. Kleitsch evokes a sense of the deeper religious significance of the old mission's faded grandeur and tranquility.

Among the many mission studies that Kleitsch made on this trip was *Mission Flowers*, picturing the front garden and south wing (PLATE 103); *Mission Poinsettias*, depicting the south wing, looking east toward the ruins of the Old

PLATE 103. Joseph Kleitsch, *Mission Flowers*, 1923. Oil on canvas, 21 x 22". Collection of Dr. and Mrs. Edward H. Boseker, courtesy of Kelley Gallery.

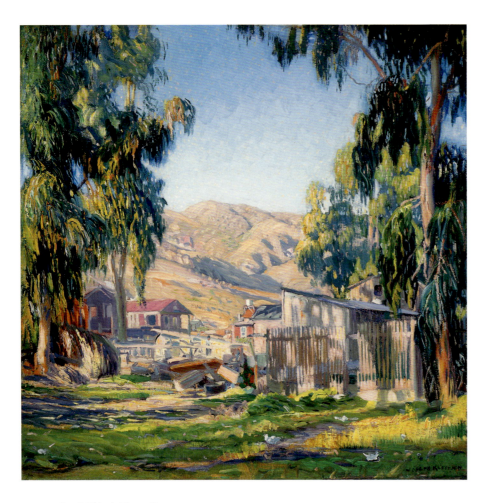

PLATE 104. Joseph Kleitsch, *Pioneer Homes*, 1922–23. Oil on canvas, 40 x 40". Collection of the Russak Family, courtesy of Redfern Gallery.

Stone Church; and *Geraniums*, vibrant with red flowers, indigo shadows, and a pale blue sky. All of these pictures were exhibited that October with other mission scenes at Leonard's Gallery in Hollywood.

On August 3, *Laguna Life* announced that "for the first time in many months Joseph Kleitsch is exploiting his own paintings in a one-man exhibit at the Cravath and Hall realty office," adding that "although the building was not conceived with an especial aim for artistic lighting it serves admirably for an exhibition room."[169] *Pioneer Homes* may be one of the scenes singled out for Kleitsch's vivid depiction of Laguna's streets and shoreline in his "inimitable" style (PLATE 104). Stylistically, the picture is similar to the *Old Post Office* in terms of the use of color, light, and shadow. The shed and nearby cottages are framed on either side by the ubiquitous eucalyptus trees, with a sunlit Mystic Hill in the background. The free-range chickens in the dappled light of the grassy foreground add further realism to an everyday scene in Old Laguna.

Still other scenes of streets, tangled eucalyptus trees, and tranquil Old Laguna sunsets (see p. 271) were included in the exhibit,[170] along with several portraits and Capistrano mission pictures. The *Laguna Life* reporter continued, with

PLATE 105. Joseph Kleitsch, *Our Garden*, 1923. Oil on canvas, 11 x 14". Collection of David and Linda O'Hoy.

a glowing appraisal of Kleitsch's technique: "For sometime Mr. Kleitsch has been gaining in popularity in artistic circles. Not that he is a 'best seller,' as best sellers go but because his art is compelling and arresting. His sense of drawing is exceptional and combined with the scrutinous view of the portrait painter, with the broad and exacting eye of the colorist, the result is a Kleitsch picture of incomparable loveliness or piquant 'difference.'" The reporter may have been thinking of *Creek—Laguna Canyon* of 1923 (see PLATE 191).

During the summer months of 1923, Kleitsch painted a small gem, *Our Garden* (PLATE 105), a view of the ocean and the surrounding landscape seen from his Laguna backyard. Splashes of dazzling color, fluid, virtuosic brushstrokes, and the rendering of late afternoon sunlight make nature come alive.[171] That fall, Kleitsch's *In My Studio* of 1917 (see PLATE 60), frequently praised and often shown, won the grand prize for a figurative painting in the Laguna Beach Art Association's Fourth Annual Exhibition. The special Jury of Awards, consisting of the dean of painters William Wendt (1865–1946), Carl Oscar Borg (1879–1947), and Alson Skinner Clark (1876–1949), bestowed this distinguished honor on Kleitsch on September 12, 1923.[172]

Before returning to Los Angeles in late October, Kleitsch was moved to paint several pictures in autumnal colors at twilight. In one of these, *Evening Light, Laguna,* "the twilight lies like a carpet on the country road that leads to the quiet humble, country church," whose small steeple lifts itself "prayerfully among the trees [PLATE 108].... A powdery, crystalline light touches the roofs and the tree tops with an unearthly glory in the darkness."[173] The church in Kleitsch's picture had a rich history. Originally built as a Mormon schoolhouse by the Latter Day Saints in 1888 at the intersection of El Toro and Laguna Canyon roads (PLATE 106),[174] it was later used by two different schools and then served as a Catholic church. Moved three times from its original site, it was located finally at the corner of Legion and Through streets in 1931, when Kleitsch, the preservationist, purchased the building for his studio (PLATE 107).[175]

Golden Haze speaks to the "poignant hour of the year when autumn comes down the hills of Laguna" (PLATE 109).[176] The little houses lining the village street are brushed by the soft, diffuse autumn haze of Indian summer. Kleitsch had painted the same site earlier in *The Village* (see PLATE 90), but at a different hour and season.

The large exhibition at Leonard's Gallery in Hollywood garnered rave reviews from the press. Antony Anderson remarked on how well the artist had adapted to the color and light of the West in his California subjects: "Kleitsch fell into the sunshine of California with a sort of happy abandonment, yielding his impressionable spirit to its seductive charm without a struggle.... Joseph Kleitsch is a true artist, ever on the alert for the new word in any manifestation of nature,

above
PLATE 106. "Mormon Schoolhouse, Toro Canyon," n.d. Photograph. Laguna Art Museum Archives, Laguna Beach, California.
PLATE 107. "Studio-Church and Edna Kleitsch, 'July 9, 1940.'" Photograph. Courtesy of Robert and Susan Ehrlich.

right
PLATE 108. Joseph Kleitsch, *Evening Light, Laguna,* 1923. Oil on canvas, 24 x 30". Collection of Robert and Susan Ehrlich.

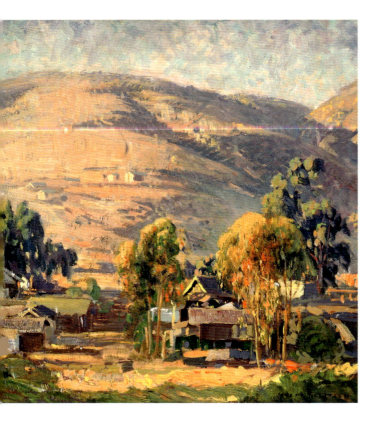

PLATE 109. Joseph Kleitsch, *Golden Haze*, 1923. Oil on canvas, 24 x 26". The Fieldstone Collection.

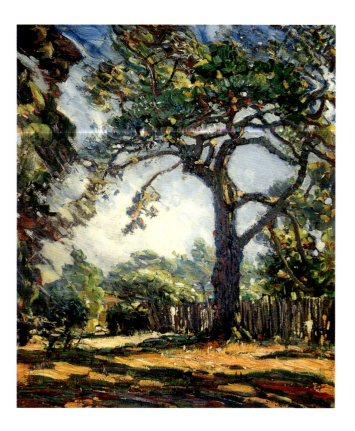

PLATE 110. Joseph Kleitsch, *Carmel Cypress*, 1923–24. Oil on canvas, 30 x 26". The Fleischer Collection.

and with an exquisite responsiveness to its meaning to him, the interpreter. California had no new language for him, only a few fascinating new words in the old. Yet, till he came here he had not been a landscape painter, but a very successful maker of portraits and figure pictures."[177]

Although Anderson was effusive in his praise, he maintained that Kleitsch's portraits and figure pictures "still remained his finer and stronger works." Somewhat later, the artist's brilliant, dynamic landscapes and marinescapes would prove the critic wrong.

On December 8 the *Carmel Pine Cone* reported that Kleitsch was painting in Carmel for the winter season.[178] The artist, however, was not enchanted with Northern California: the color and climate were "a trifle cold for his temperament." The few Carmel scenes he painted conveyed subtly and convincingly the difference between the northern and southern climates. *Carmel Cypress* is an unusual composition that conveys the windswept, often cold climate of this part of California (PLATE 110). *Fish Market—Monterey*, somewhat reminiscent of a European locale, is a vibrant, colorful picture of fishermen's boats banked along the shore next to the seaside buildings of Cannery Row (PLATE 111). In these pictures Kleitsch accurately records the cloudy, overcast weather with cool colors and

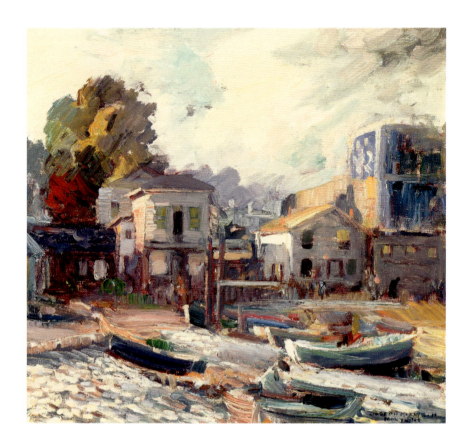

PLATE 111. Joseph Kleitsch, *Fish Market—Monterey*, 1923–24. Oil on canvas, 18 x 20". Collection of Paul and Kathleen Bagley.

dashing, diagonal brushstrokes. Both paintings were exhibited at the Biltmore Salon on March 2, 1924.[179]

While Kleitsch was working, Edna enjoyed wandering the high cliffs among the pines that engulf Carmel. She agreed with him, however, that Laguna's light and color offered a better environment for his painting. Although the artist worked on some important portrait commissions in Carmel as well as the landscapes, the highlight of their season occurred when Eugene, following in his father's footsteps, "carried off the honors in the Thanksgiving theatrical program." It was no surprise to find the gregarious Kleitsches well established in Carmel's art and social activities during their short stay.

The following year Kleitsch was involved in a number of exhibitions in Los Angeles and Laguna. In January, the Ebell Club of Los Angeles showed ten of his paintings, including his "masterpiece" *In My Studio*.[180] Kleitsch's popularity was evident when he attended the June banquet of the Painters and Sculptors Club at the Ambassador Hotel. That same month, the club scheduled its first annual exhibition at the Stendahl Galleries. Edna was also active that month, as a Laguna Beach delegate to the Catholic Women's Convention in Los Angeles.[181] Although the Kleitsches were not married in a Catholic ceremony, Edna seems to have returned to the church, probably for the sake of their child, and possibly at the urging of local priests.

PLATE 112. Joseph Kleitsch, attr. *Portrait of the Artist's Wife*, n.d. Oil on canvas, 32 x 26". Collection of John and Regina Rowe.

PLATE 113. Joseph Kleitsch, *Grace,* n.d. Oil on canvas, 32 x 28". The Buck Collection.

In an article in the July 1924 issue of *California Southland*, titled "The Laguna Art Colony," Kleitsch is described "as a sun-browned young man whose virility invades his canvases" and his wife as "a woman with a personality as vibrant as a Sorolla, and an excellent intermediary between the world and her restless painter-husband" (PLATE 112).[182] The writer noted that the "artistic influx to Laguna began with Gardner Symons . . . who was eminent among eastern painters. Today there is a 'colony' whose proportions are sufficiently extensive to give the Village its tone. Babbitry has done slight damage as yet—though something of a building boom has developed—the fishermen, town-folk and creative intruders dwelling piously in peace." Curiously, instead of illustrating a Laguna scene by Kleitsch, the editor chose to reproduce a poignant and sensitive portrait titled *Grace* (PLATE 113). Although she is not a fashion plate, the model projects a sense of style and sophistication through her hairdo, informal clothing, and casually held cigarette holder.

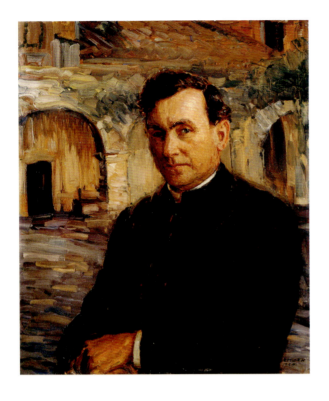

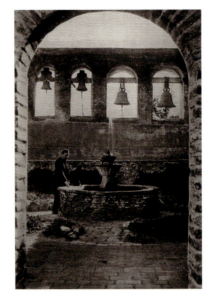

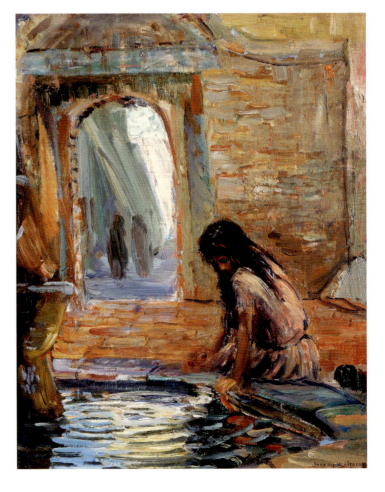

above
PLATE 114. Joseph Kleitsch, *Portrait of Father St. John O'Sullivan,* 1924. Oil on canvas, 30 x 25". Mission San Juan Capistrano.
PLATE 115. "Father O'Sullivan at the Sacred Garden Fountain, Mission San Juan Capistrano," c. 1920s, courtesy of Rev. William F. Krekelberg, Mission San Juan Capistrano archivist.

right
PLATE 116. Joseph Kleitsch, (*A Moment's Reflection, The Sacred Garden, Mission San Juan Capistrano*), c. 1924–25. Oil on canvas, 20 x 16". Private Collection, courtesy of Kelley Gallery.

PLATE 117. Joseph Kleitsch, *Going to Church* (*Sunday Morning*), *Capistrano*, 1924. Oil on canvas, 40 x 36". Edenhurst Gallery.

Kleitsch returned that summer to Capistrano and painted *Father St. John O'Sullivan* (PLATE 114), a portrait of the resident priest who was largely responsible for restoring Mission San Juan Capistrano after he arrived there in 1910. Through his vigorous efforts, Father O'Sullivan repaired Serra Chapel, built a new mission school, created the flower gardens, and installed several fountains (PLATES 115 and 116).[183] Kleitsch characterized the priest as "pensive and resolute," placing him in front of Serra Chapel and the rectory on the mission's east wing.[184] Father O'Sullivan strongly encouraged visiting writers and artists to carry his vision of the mission to the outside world with their writings and art.[185] Kleitsch seized that opportunity, returning repeatedly to the mission to record it with great affection.

At the Capistrano mission that same summer, Kleitsch captured worshippers about to attend Sunday Mass at the newly restored chapel in the original version of his *Going to Church* (alternately titled *Sunday Morning*). Kleitsch showcases two young Mexican girls in their Sunday best, accompanied by their parents.[186] Sometime later, in an attempt to improve the composition, the artist removed the onlooking parents in the top right quadrant, making the colorful costumed girls the focal point of the painting (PLATE 117).[187] Kleitsch's skillful use of vibrant colors and multi-textured surfaces enlivens the mood of the picture.

PLATE 118. Joseph Kleitsch, *Mission San Juan Capistrano*, 1924. Oil on canvas, 24 x 30". The Joan Irvine Smith Collection.

In his exceptional rendering of *Mission San Juan Capistrano* in 1924, Kleitsch turns his back on the mission and faces the town, adjacent to the Soldiers' Barracks. In this long view of the riotous and verdant colors of the front garden and its large pepper tree (PLATE 118), his impressionistic brush skillfully conveys the brilliant natural light and tranquility of the setting. From a similar vantage point but closer to the town, Kleitsch captures a view of the red brick Hotel Capistrano in San Juan Capistrano, surrounded by hollyhocks with the hills in the distance (see p. 259).[188]

One of Kleitsch's more unusual paintings of Capistrano is *Cloister, Mission San Juan Capistrano,* with its recession and symmetrical forms. The artist presents an arresting view down a corridor "framed by a series of arcs and perspective lines, creating [a third dimension] with an immense space that continually expands towards the viewer" (PLATE 119).[189]

PLATE 119. Joseph Kleitsch, *Cloister, Mission San Juan Capistrano*, c. 1924. Oil on canvas, 17 x 20". Private Collection, courtesy of The Irvine Museum.

opposite
PLATE 120. Joseph Kleitsch, *Bougainvillea, Mission San Juan Capistrano*, 1924. Oil on canvas, 30 x 24". Private Collection, courtesy of The Irvine Museum.

above
PLATE 121. Joseph Kleitsch, *Rancho near Capistrano*, 1924. Oil on canvas, 20 x 22". Private Collection, courtesy of George Stern Fine Arts.

As he was leaving the mission, Kleitsch's eye caught the deep red bougainvillea cascading over a rough adobe brick wall (PLATE 120). In a nearby area, he rendered the color and peacefulness of day's end in an impressionistic twilight landscape at a ranch near Capistrano (PLATE 121).

During August, the *Los Angeles Times* reported, Kleitsch was at work in his Ambassador Hotel studio on a portrait commission from Dr. Elias Fedorovitch Morgenstiern. Morgenstiern was a Russian philanthropist and an eminent psychographologist and psychoanalyst who planned to settle in Los Angeles.[190] In 1925,

PLATE 122. Joseph Kleitsch, *The Garden Fence*, 1923. Oil on canvas, 36 x 40". Collection of Mr. and Mrs. Thomas B. Stiles II.

PLATE 123. Joseph Kleitsch, *Tangled Branches, Laguna Canyon*, n.d. Oil on canvas, 23 x 17". Collection of W. Donald Head, Old Grandview Ranch, courtesy of George Stern Fine Arts.

Morgenstiern left Los Angeles for Chicago, where he lived until 1928, when he was sought by the police and arrested for committing grand larceny.[191] Kleitsch never received full payment for the portrait.

On September 16, Kleitsch entered eight paintings in the Golden Jubilee Exhibit of the Painters and Sculptors Club of Southern California at the Park House of Carmelita Gardens in Pasadena.[192] Most of these were earlier paintings, such as *Enchantment, Mission Canyon*, and *In My Studio*.

During 1924, Kleitsch painted a prodigious number of scenes of Old Laguna. In morning, noon, and evening light, he depicted its distinctive shoreline, its opalescent sea, its distant hills (PLATE 122), and the original structures that lined its dusty mud roads, in canvases like *Early Morning in Laguna* and *Laguna Road*.[193] He painted Laguna's ubiquitous eucalyptus trees in sun and shadow, blown by Pacific breezes, or with their golden leaves hanging in the heat of a summer noon (PLATE 123), conveying "the richness of massed leaves without losing the characteristic droop of the gum tree's vertical foliage."[194] Framed by eucalyptus trees, *Laguna Road* of 1924 (PLATE 124) gives an evocative sense of Old Laguna. Kleitsch's vigorous brush, loaded with myriad, rich colors and manipulating the ever-changing light, effectively captures the mood of the old village. (For a later version, see PLATE 198.)

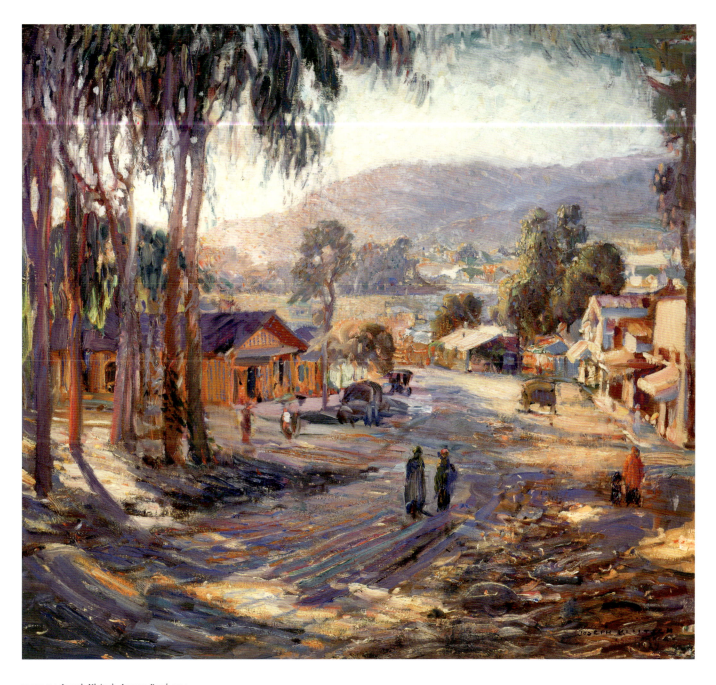

PLATE 124. Joseph Kleitsch, *Laguna Road*, 1924. Oil on canvas, 36 x 40". Collection of the City of Laguna Beach.

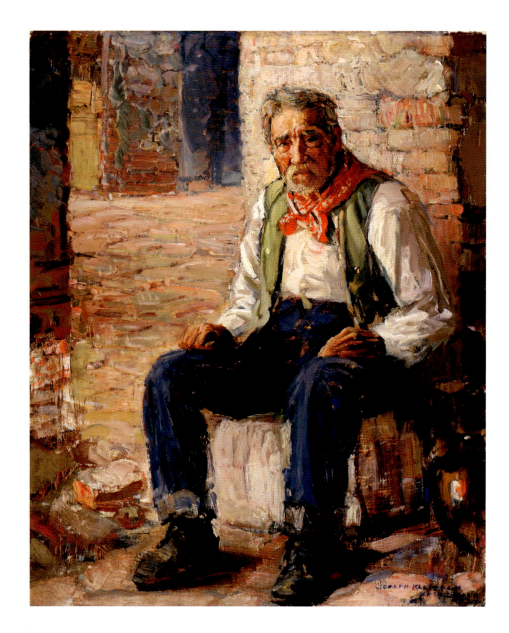

right
PLATE 125. Joseph Kleitsch, *El Peón* or *José Juan [Olivares]* or *Old Man Yorba, San Juan Capistrano*, 1923. Oil on canvas, 30 x 25". Collection of James W. and Sarah T. Miller.

below
PLATE 126. "José Juan Olivares, Augustin Manriquez, José de Garcia Cruz (Acu)," 1920s. Collection of Alfonso Yorba. Photograph. Courtesy of David Belardes.

In October, Kleitsch attended several special business meetings of the Painters and Sculptors Club to prepare for the November exhibition at the MacDowell Club and the subsequent bidding sale at the Art Center in December.[195] He submitted a number of works for both shows, and won a silver medal for his entry *José Juan [Olivares]* at the Art Center (PLATES 125 and 126). A critic commented on this "successful piece of characterization," but felt the foreground details showed a "lack of care."[196] The unidentified subject was probably a local laborer involved in the restoration of the Capistrano mission. Because of its intense characterization, the painting has been referred to by several names: *José Juan, El Peón,* and *Old Man Yorba*. The same subject, his identity no longer a mystery, was again a central figure treated with warmth and understanding in several compositions completed the following years.[197]

The year 1925 could be considered a banner one for the artist. Anticipating his departure for Europe in late October, Kleitsch dealt with a demanding schedule, and his production of paintings was sizable.[198] At the annual meeting of the Painters and Sculptors Club on January 6, 1925, he was reinstalled as vice president and appointed to serve on the model committee. Kleitsch and Leland Curtis (1897–1989) were directed to make the necessary arrangements for securing rooms in the Grosse Studio Building. Lack of consistent financial support meant frequent changes in the club's studio location. The entertainment committee planned special fundraising events like the Quartz Art Ball, with a fee of a dollar per couple. A Valentine's Day dance was planned for February 14, and another dance for March 14. These successful social mixers helped offset a large part of the club's debt.

In January, Stendahl opened a bidding sale and exhibition of the work of Los Angeles artists. According to a reporter, the idea for the sale was "unique in Los Angeles" but had already been a great success in Chicago and other cities. Art works were restricted to "small canvases none over 20 x 24 inches" selected for quality and merit. Kleitsch was among the participants in the month-long sale. The plan was described as follows: The sale was to begin on January 5, and "the catalog prices remain in force for one week. On January 12 the prices will be reduced 5 percent, and on every day following, excluding Sundays, there will be another 5 percent reduction on the catalog prices, 'til all the paintings are sold."[199] The results of the sale, in dollars or in paintings sold, were never disclosed.

On February 1, 1925, Antony Anderson exuberantly reviewed the exhibition of forty paintings by Kleitsch at the short-lived Stendahl-Hatfield Galleries: "Ah those still-lives! You will pounce upon four or five in the gallery that are simply overwhelming in their virtuosity. If Frans Hals were alive today—Kleitsch reminds us of the Jolly Dutchman more than once—he would toss up his cap and shout, 'I greet you brother, for you sure can tickle the canvas and make it laugh for joy.'"[200]

Anderson continued to rhapsodize over the artist's ability to transform the canvas: "Kleitsch does make the canvas laugh for joy, and simply and solely because he himself is so joyful and expert, so absolutely alive, when he paints. That cardinal red difficult? Not at all! A sweep or two of the brush and there you are. Those amber beads? There, and there, and there. Aren't they sparklers?" Anderson was struck by the painting known as *Oriental Still Life* and sometimes referred to as "Yellow and blue Cloissonee"[*sic*] (PLATE 127), in which the yellows and blues are vibrant accents against a rich red textile covering and a dark green background. The tilted perspective and amorphous shape of the red textile border on abstraction. Noted American art historian William Gerdts correctly observes that "the blue scarf, the dark blue bottle, the amber beads, the yellow cloisonné bowl, a cosmetic box or a cachepot perhaps for beads, in turn, suggest the toiletries and adornment of a woman's intimate world."[201]

Anderson next invites his readers to linger over *The Turquoise Buddha* ("the largest piece of carved turquoise in the world"), which he finds "more subtle and more exquisite in its gradations of tone and color than 'Yellow and Blue Cloissonee[*sic*].'" Exalting over the many textures the artist achieved in rendering

PLATE 127. Joseph Kleitsch, *Oriental Still Life*, 1925. Oil on canvas, 16 x 20". Collection of Lenoir Josey.

PLATE 128. Joseph Kleitsch, *Orientale*, 1925. Oil on canvas, 22 x 24". Private Collection, courtesy of John Moran Antiques & Fine Art Auctioneers.

"a cup lined with gold, a ruby-colored goblet, and shimmering [Asian] fabrics with threads of gold and silver running through them," he avers that the work is "an amazing tour de force in paint." This complex, baroque composition is a prelude to Kleitsch's outstanding still life *Highlights,* painted a few years later. However, Anderson missed in his review the recently discovered exuberant and colorful still life titled *Orientale* (PLATE 128), with its profusion of antique Asian objects placed on an exquisite fringed, embroidered Chinese dragon robe.[202] The setting is recognizable as G. T. Marsh and Company in the Ambassador Hotel.

In another article about the Stendahl-Hatfield exhibition, Anderson finds Kleitsch's portraits fine examples of composition and drawing as well as interpretation of character. The critic asks whether without Kleitsch's "synthetic tact" he could "have painted that virile portrait of *Major John C. Walker, Jr.*, those equally puissant portraits of *Edward B. Good* and *Dr. Elias Morgenstiern*," or the splendid figure he sometimes calls "Rhapsody" (see PLATE 56).[203] Regarding the portrait of the violinist Isador Berger, Anderson observed that the "very spirit of music seem[ed] to pervade the canvas." Edward B. Good (1861–1936), an industrialist from Lancaster, Ohio, was so pleased with his portrait that he became a strong supporter and patron of the artist (PLATE 129).[204] Records indicate that Good purchased his first Kleitsch painting, *Sicilian Girl*, in 1923 (see PLATE 64), and that eventually he owned ten of the artist's paintings. The industrialist also offered Kleitsch financial support on several occasions.[205]

In the same show, Kleitsch included several figurative paintings. One of them, *Curiosity* (PLATE 130), depicts two little girls from Capistrano intensely absorbed in the mysterious contents of the artist's palette and paint box. The youth and beauty of the children in the setting outside the mission is expressed with spontaneous, impressionistic brushstrokes in strong, harmonious colors. Whether the artist actually observed their action or posed the girls for his composition is a matter of conjecture. The dark-haired girl with her face turned toward the viewer appears in several other mission paintings by Kleitsch.[206] For *The Story Teller* (PLATE 131) Kleitsch posed the elderly José Juan, patriarch of

PLATE 129. Joseph Kleitsch, *Portrait of Edward B. Good*, 1925. Oil on canvas, 30 x 25". Collection of James W. and Sarah T. Miller.

PLATE 130. Joseph Kleitsch, *Curiosity* (*Mission San Juan Capistrano*), 1924. Oil on canvas, 25 x 30". Collection of Mr. and Mrs. Thomas B. Stiles II.

PLATE 131. Joseph Kleitsch, *The Story Teller* (*Eugene and El Peón [José Juan Olivares]*), 1925. 18 x 22". Private Collection.

PLATE 132. Joseph Kleitsch, *Mission San Juan Capistrano*, c. 1925. Oil on canvas, 16 x 20". Collection of James and Janet Murphy.

Capistrano, with the artist's son, Eugene, who is listening intently to the old man. In a decided change of pace and mood, Kleitsch painted a somber mission interior with a shrouded worshipper in an ethereal, monastic setting (PLATE 132).[207]

SOUTHERN CALIFORNIA 147

Kleitsch received special recognition at the 120th Annual Exhibition of the Pennsylvania Academy of the Fine Arts for *In My Studio* (see PLATE 60), exhibited from February 8 to March 29, 1925. The painting was also shown at the Art Institute of Chicago, the Des Moines Art Association, and possibly the Philadelphia Art Week Association.[208]

From March through June, Kleitsch was busy producing work for several exhibitions in Los Angeles and Laguna, traveling back and forth between the two communities. In June he exhibited *El Peón* and *Curiosity* (also called *The Paint Box*) in the Laguna Beach Art Association summer show and received favorable comments on them from the *Laguna Beach Life* reporter.[209]

During the 1920s and into 1931, Kleitsch continued to pursue portraiture as his principal source of income. The *Lifeguard* of 1922, a portrait of artist William Griffith's son Nelson, shows how much Southern California light had brightened his palette (PLATE 133). Many commissioned works, such as *Mrs. Benjamin Frank* of 1925 (PLATE 134),[210] *Ruth Renick* of 1928 (see PLATES 181 and 182), and *Ruth E. Bach* of 1930 (PLATE 135) reveal the influence of Hollywood on the artist's style. The attitudes of his models become highly mannered and the surrounding objects still lifes in themselves. In these portraits, there is less of the individual expression and interpretation that set Kleitsch apart from his colleagues earlier in his career. Portraits of elderly men, however, such as *El Peón, José Juan,*

PLATE 133. Joseph Kleitsch, *Portrait of Nelson Griffith (Lifeguard)*, 1922. Oil on canvas, 40 x 36". Laguna Art Museum Collection. Gift of Ida Griffith Hawley and Charles C. Hawley.

PLATE 134. Joseph Kleitsch, *Portrait of Mrs. Benjamin Frank,* 1925. Oil on canvas, 30 x 25", courtesy of Carlyn Frank Benjamin.

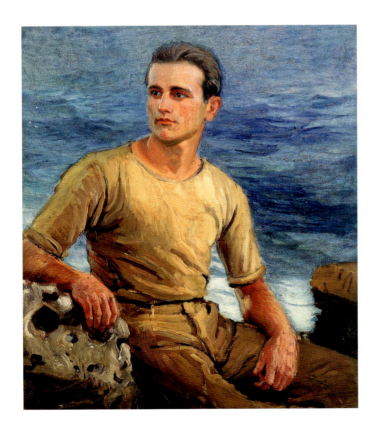
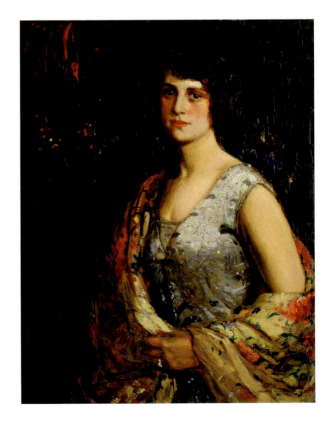

or *Old Man Yorba* of 1923, 1925, and 1929 respectively (see PLATES 125, 131, and 136), painted in Capistrano, or the *Spanish Officer,* painted in Seville, Spain, in 1926 (see PLATE 144), remain consistent in treatment.[211] Their most characteristic feature is a forceful, somewhat rough technique. The wrinkled, weather-beaten faces and large expressive hands recall the art of the Dutch master Josef Israels (1824–1911), whose work Kleitsch studied when it was exhibited at Moulton and Ricketts Galleries in Chicago in 1914.[212]

Between July and October, Kleitsch exhibited at the Artland Club, Carmelita Gardens, the Friday Morning Club, and Stendahl Galleries. By late summer 1925, he had been a resident of Southern California for five and a half years. Although he genuinely enjoyed living and working in Laguna and Los Angeles, the artist had grown restless and seriously contemplated a change. Kleitsch was now forty-three years old, and although he had gained recognition and acceptance from many of his peers, he still did not enjoy the national respect that many of his contemporaries, such as Maurice Braun (1877–1941), Alson Clark, Guy Rose, and William Wendt, had received. Still regarded as a Chicago and a California painter, Kleitsch had not been elected to the National Academy. He had not been out of the country for thirteen years, and he felt the need for travel and further European study. Undoubtedly he conferred with Stendahl, who was very much in favor of the trip.

PLATE 135. Joseph Kleitsch, *Portrait of Ruth E. Bach*, 1930. Oil on canvas, 38 x 26 ½". Collection of Marcel Vinh and Daniel Hansman.

PLATE 136. Joseph Kleitsch, *Old Man Yorba* (*José Juan Olivares*), 1929. Oil on canvas, 30 x 25". The Fieldstone Collection.

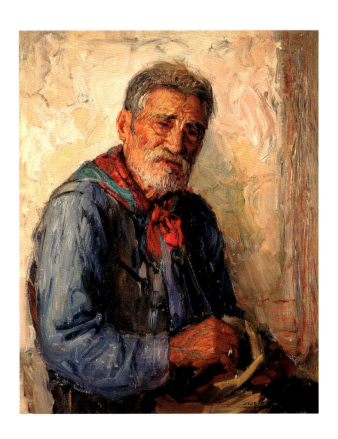

Kleitsch and his family began their trip in October 1925,[213] stopping first in Chicago, where he was feted by colleagues and given a fine reception by patrons, collectors, and old friends.[214] The Kleitsches then went to Grand Rapids, Michigan, where Edna had lived as a child.[215] There, they stayed at the Rowe Hotel, the social center of Grand Rapids, projecting an image of the artist's success to the local population. On November 11, Kleitsch wired Earl Stendahl from the Rowe Hotel asking him to wire back funds from exhibition sales. On November 20, Stendahl responded, asking Kleitsch to accept an offer of two hundred dollars for *The Story Teller,* fifty dollars less than his stipulated price.

During their stay in Grand Rapids, the artist painted a unique self-portrait in a landscape setting (PLATE 137). Here Kleitsch projects a very serious mood, unlike those of his previous self-portraits, which can be interpreted as the beginning of a change in his career path. With palette in hand, standing on a hilly terrain overlooking the river, the artist is the picture of maturity and self-confidence. His well-trimmed Vandyke beard enhances the image of a successful practitioner of the arts. Working outdoors, Kleitsch wears a shirt with a cutaway collar and a hand-painted tie tucked under a vest that is part of a three-piece suit. A felt hat completes the de rigueur ensemble for the well-known painter.[216]

The autumnal colors and cornstalks in the background verify the season of the painting. In the far distance across the river, smokestacks of furniture factories are visible (see p. 260), indicating that the portrait was painted in a rural setting near a large industrial city. Edna's parents, who were furniture factory workers, lived in a section of town where Lithuanian and Russian immigrants had settled.[217]

PLATE 137. Joseph Kleitsch, *Self-Portrait (Grand Rapids, Michigan),* 1925. Oil on canvas, 30 x 22". Orange County Museum of Art Collection. Gift of Mr. and Mrs. Roy Childs.

Influences from Abroad—Tour of Europe (1926–1927)

Kleitsch's passport, issued January 21, 1926,[218] tells us that the artist and his family traveled to New York City and stayed at the Herald Square Hotel. In New York, they decided that Edna would remain in the States with their son, whose schooling was of primary importance, although financial issues were probably another consideration.[219] Kleitsch sailed for Europe on the *President Roosevelt* on February 6, 1926. A letter from Edna to Stendahl on February 14 states that Kleitsch had arrived in Paris, where an important commission awaited him.

During his stay, just off the Champs-Elysées at Hotel California, 16 rue de Berri (PLATE 138), he painted a casual, almost full-length self-portrait using a mirror (PLATE 139).[220] Because the painting is a mirror image, the artist's right hand is in his pocket as he paints with his left. From his hotel window, Kleitsch looked out over the rooftops of Paris to paint the scene on the street below (PLATE 140).

above
PLATE 138. Henri de Pierrefeu, "Hotel California, Paris, France," 2003. Photograph.

right
PLATE 139. Joseph Kleitsch, *Self-Portrait, Paris, France,* 1926. Oil on canvas, 18 x 15". Collection of Brent Gross.

opposite
PLATE 140. Joseph Kleitsch, *Paris,* 1926. Oil on canvas, 36 x 36". W. Donald Head, Old Grandview Ranch.

SOUTHERN CALIFORNIA

right
PLATE 141. Joseph Kleitsch, *Oui (France)*, 1926. Oil on canvas, 21 x 18". Private Collection, courtesy of Kelley Gallery.

below
PLATE 142. Norman Trenton, "Gardens of the Alcázar, Seville, Spain," 2003. Photograph.

Like many visitors and expatriates, Kleitsch frequented the lively cafés and bistros of Montparnasse, where the gatherings of artists and intellectuals also attracted young Parisian women. Many of Kleitsch's informal character studies of women were probably motivated more by personal than professional concerns. In *Stendahl's Art Review,* Summer 1928, J. C. Bulliet comments on Kleitsch's appealing portrait of a *demoiselle*, "a Parisian of the people: The artist calls it 'Oui' because, as he whimsically declares, this girl, . . . [like] all other French girls, has a prettily pursed mouth that is shaped from saying oui so often and so smilingly. The flesh is pearly in color and texture, the pose and the scheme suggest a Titian—perhaps a Rembrandt" (PLATE 141).[221]

A short time later Kleitsch traveled to Madrid, where he spent many hours in the Prado Museum studying the Old Masters, especially Titian (c. 1488–1576) and Velázquez (1599–1660), both of whom he greatly admired.[222] The artist also visited several exhibitions and did a number of paintings of the city. His next stop was Asturias in northern Spain, where he had been commissioned to paint por-

traits of the Wades, an English family involved in silver mining there. Major patrons of Kleitsch in Mexico, the Wades had acquired some fifteen of his paintings during his second Mexican visit in 1911–12.

In the early spring of 1926, Kleitsch spent several months in Seville.[223] Gaining permission to paint in the gardens of the Alcázar (PLATE 142), he witnessed the gorgeous pageantry of the Nazarene processions throughout Holy Week. His love of the city is evident in the number of paintings he made there and in the many hours he spent studying the Spanish masters in the museums and galleries. Very much at ease in the Museo de Bellas Artes, he painted a graceful view of an inner court, with its fountain and verdant plants framing an arched doorway (PLATE 143; see also p. 260). At the Plaza de San Francisco, he was attracted by the beautiful Baroque architecture and flowers, and in a Sevillan courtyard he captured children at play. Even the local military is represented, in the person of an elderly infantry colonel dressed in full military regalia with the insignia of his rank (PLATE 144).[224] Kleitsch became captivated by Sevillan customs and traditions, as well as the city's splendid architecture and general ambience.

PLATE 143. Norman Trenton, "Inner Court, Museo de Bellas Artes, Seville, Spain," 2003. Photograph.
PLATE 144. Joseph Kleitsch, *Spanish Officer (Colonel in Infantry), Seville, Spain,* 1926. Oil on canvas, 34 x 27". Private Collection, courtesy of Maxwell Galleries.

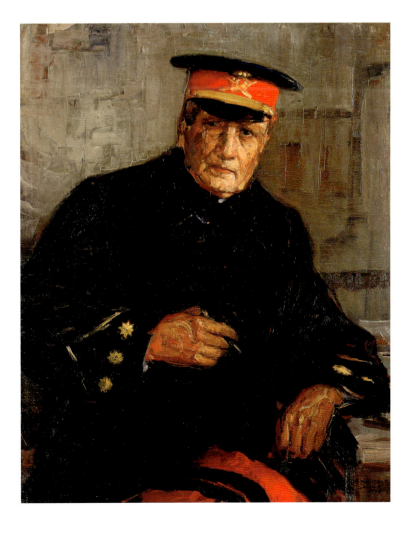

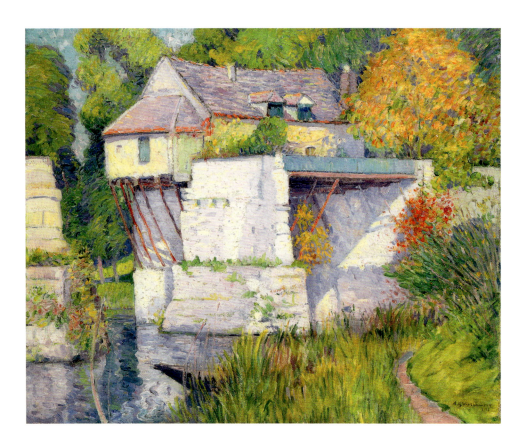

PLATE 145. Abel G. Warshawsky, *Le Vieux Moulin* (*The Old Mill*), *Vernon, France*, 1912. Oil on canvas, 25 ½ x 32". Private Collection, courtesy of Edenhurst Gallery.

When Kleitsch returned to Paris, he met American artist Abel George Warshawsky (1883–1962), an Impressionist painter from Cleveland, Ohio, who had resided in Paris. Warshawsky related his vivid impression of Vernon and Giverny, a region he had visited with artist Samuel Halpert (1884–1930) in 1910:

> While we were at Vernon, we visited several times the art colony at Giverney [*sic*], three kilometers away, tucked neatly between the rolling hills on the rambling little creek called the Epte River. . . . Compared with the spacious, unspoiled atmosphere of Vernon, Giverney seemed cramped and overcultivated. Vernon's lovely moss-covered bridge tiptoed to the island on graceful arches, its streets held remnants of Norman and Gothic architecture . . . a fine 14th Century cathedral, and extremely paintable gardens while its vistas were of pale chalk cliffs set among the green and blue hills. . . . At Vernon I felt for the first time since . . . [my] southern [Spanish] tour free of the weighty power of the great masters, conscious only of the influence of nature. . . . Every morning and afternoon we sketched away. Objects which had looked quite commonplace at one time of day, would suddenly become gloriously transfigured by a slanting sunlight [PLATE 145].[225]

Impressed by Warshawsky's enthusiasm for the Normandy village, Kleitsch joined him and his friends Leon and Natalie Gordon on a trip to Vernon and Giverny in June 1926. Although his host had not revisited the quiet Norman town in fifteen years, Warshawsky found "hardly anything had changed," only the old Hôtel Soleil d'Or, whose "façade had been repainted and its charming name replaced by the more up-to-date one, Normandie Plaisance" (see p. 260). The proprietor's amiable wife, Madame Espagnon, was still behind the counter, and "the kindly *Patron*, grown a little grayer, there to greet us with his former hospitality." Kleitsch was certainly aware of the couple's blonde daughter Simone, whose direct loveliness he effectively portrayed (PLATE 146). Warshawsky's and Kleitsch's rooms had views of the village with its towers and gardens, and both sketched from their windows as Warshawsky had done on his previous visit.

PLATE 146. Joseph Kleitsch, *Simone, Vernon, France*, 1926. Oil on canvas, 24 x 18". Private Collection.

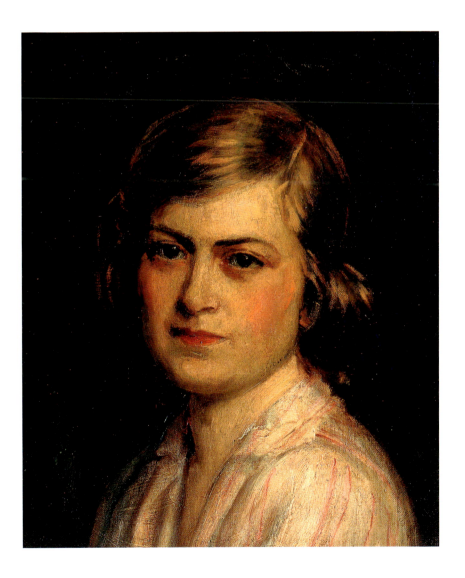

PLATE 147. Joseph Kleitsch, *Vernon to Vernonnet, Vernon, France*, 1926. Unaltered version. Photograph taken 1928. Laguna Art Museum Archives, Laguna Beach, California. Stendahl Art Galleries Collection.

Warshawsky lamented, however, that one could no longer paint by the roadside because of heavy motor traffic. But for the two men, "the riverbanks and hillsides still offered many quiet nooks where one could work undisturbed" without clouds of dust and sprays of gravel endangering their canvases. Giverny was now being overrun with a new group of Americans, more pleasure seekers than serious artists, making it less attractive for both painters.

Vernon, unlike Giverny, still retained much of its older atmosphere of simplicity and tranquility. Kleitsch was charmed by the French village, which reminded him of his native Hungary. For Warshawsky, "Joe was the most astonishing mixture of ingenuousness and cunning, that . . .[he] had ever met. His attempts at French were terrifying, yet in some mysterious fashion he managed to convey his every wish to the hotel personnel, though they spoke not a word of English." Warshawsky complimented Kleitsch on the "many fine canvases imbued with poetical feeling" that he painted at Vernon.

Stimulated by the French countryside, Kleitsch painted a number of striking works at Vernon. In several of these he depicted the Old Stone Bridge, with its graceful arches spanning the Seine from Vernon to Vernonnet (seen in a historic photograph, p. 260). A Stendahl Galleries photograph informs us that the composition of *Vernon to Vernonnet* was altered slightly from its original form (PLATE 147), in which a lone woman walks down the promenade toward the viewer. Most noticeable among the changes in the altered version (PLATE 148) are the difference in perspective, the cloud formations, and the addition of upright moorings to the punt. It can be argued that this is either another version of the old bridge or an alteration of the extant painting.[226]

PLATE 148. Joseph Kleitsch, *Vernon to Vernonnet, Vernon, France,* 1926. Oil on canvas, 34 x 34". Collection of Christopher Walker.

right
PLATE 149. Joseph Kleitsch, *Lunch Hour, Vernon, France*, 1926. Oil on canvas, 18 x 21". Collection of John and Regina Rowe.

below
PLATE 150. Joseph Kleitsch, *Bathers along the Seine, Vernon, France*, 1926. Oil on canvas, 28 x 34". Collection of Herbert and Earlene Seymour.

In Kleitsch's *Lunch Hour* (PLATE 149), the same stone bridge provides a backdrop for a French family's outing on the grassy banks of the Seine near Vernon. The eye is drawn to the two women strolling along the path near the family. A white cross beyond the bridge raises the question of Kleitsch's religiosity at this period in his life. (In his twenty-two months in Europe, there is no evidence that he painted any religious subjects—perhaps because religious pictures were no longer popular.) *Lunch Hour* is a spontaneous study in vibrant color, as is *Bathers along the Seine*, another view of everyday activity along the river (PLATE 150). The short, broken brushstrokes and the soft colors of his palette indicate that the artist was moving toward a more impressionistic painting style. The provocative bathers, nude and partially clothed, are summarily treated, as are the bathers in his later Laguna Beach scenes.[227]

Warshawsky's impressionistic work may have stimulated Kleitsch to move away from a more traditional treatment of his subjects (PLATE 151). Indeed,

PLATE 151. Abel G. Warshawsky, *Poplars near Vernon, Fall,* 1909. Oil on canvas, 31 x 24". Private Collection, courtesy of Howard Agriesti, Cleveland Museum of Art.

exposure to Europe had already led Kleitsch to experiment with technique, form, and subject matter in his attempt to reinterpret in his own idiom the work of the Old Masters, Impressionists, Post-Impressionists, and Paris School. This can be seen clearly in much of the work he produced in Europe. An outstanding example is the Vernon painting *Ancient and Modern Normandie* of 1926 (PLATE 152), described later by a critic as "shining like a jewel." Rays of sunlight illuminate the old Norman roofs and the Gothic collegiate church and towers of Notre Dame in the distance.[228] Dazzling, vivid reds, yellows, blues, greens, browns, and pinks— a gamut of colors—run wild in complete harmony. A gnarled tree and its branches frame the old quarters of Vernon. In what seems to be a backyard view, the houses are arranged to act as a screen that blocks out the village, and the view is enlivened by the small foreground figures. Although Kleitsch has used short, impressionistic brushstrokes, he, unlike most French Impressionist painters, never dissolves his forms. *Ancient and Modern Normandie* is as close as Kleitsch ever came to painting like Monet.

PLATE 152. Joseph Kleitsch, *Ancient and Modern Normandie, Vernon, France,* 1926. Oil on canvas, 36 x 40". Collection of Marcel Vinh and Daniel Hansman.

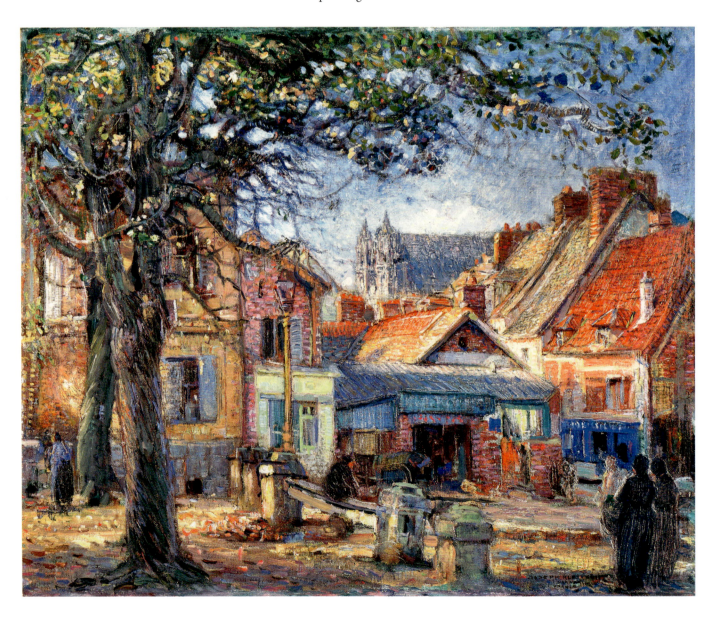

top left
PLATE 153 Joseph Kleitsch, *Pacific Ripples*, 1925. Oil on canvas, 24 x 30". Private Collection.

above left
PLATE 154. Joseph Kleitsch, *Just before the Showers (San Juan Capistrano)*, 1925. Oil on canvas, 16 x 20". Private Collection, courtesy of Redfern Gallery.

above right
PLATE 155. Joseph Kleitsch, *Looking thru Eucalypti (Autumn Idyll)*, *Laguna*, 1925. Oil on canvas, 20 x 18". Private Collection.

Enamored of Vernon and its environs, Kleitsch nonetheless had to return to Paris to await Earl Stendahl's arrival.[229] The dealer arrived in Europe in mid-July 1926 to tour with Kleitsch until mid-October (see p. 261). Stendahl immediately updated the artist on the successful sales from the major exhibition of forty-five paintings at his gallery.[230] Among these were several important pictures, including *Oriental Shop, In My Studio, Portrait of Mrs. Kleitsch, Just before the Showers, Laguna Cove, Pacific Ripples* (PLATE 153), and *Houses among the Eucalypti*. Stendahl also informed him of the widespread enthusiasm for his work. *Los Angeles Times* critic Antony Anderson, for example, had devoted a full paragraph to Kleitsch's views of Capistrano.[231] In a visit to the mission, Kleitsch had observed the gathering clouds, and *Just before the Showers* is a small, wonderfully free study of an atmospheric effect (PLATE 154). *Laguna Cove* of 1925 (see PLATE 203), also extravagantly praised by the critics, is a dynamic, colorful, sweeping panorama of Laguna's northern coastline. Most appealing to Anderson were Kleitsch's canvases depicting "the little houses and tangled eucalyptus trees in the village of Laguna." Anderson must certainly have had in mind the late afternoon scenes of *Houses Among the Eucalypti* of 1925 (see PLATE 202) and *Looking thru Eucalypti (Autumn Idyll)* (PLATE 155).[232]

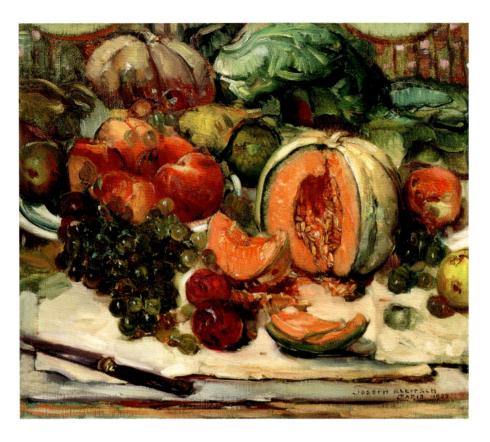

PLATE 156. Joseph Kleitsch, *Cantaloupe, Paris*, 1927. Oil on canvas, 15 x 18". Collection of Joseph Ambrose, Jr., and Michael D. Feddersen.

Stendahl and Kleitsch traveled together throughout Europe that summer and early fall, visiting Munich, Rome, Florence, Vienna, and Budapest, as well as cities in Romania and England. Surprisingly, Kleitsch "did not care for Rome—its grandeurs, ancient and modern, jumbled together, confused and disquieted him."[233] When they were not visiting exhibitions and galleries, or enjoying European cuisine and wines, Kleitsch painted incessantly in almost orgiastic outbursts of energy. This stimulating excursion gave both men time to visit and discuss at leisure Kleitsch's opportunities for the future.

After his return to America in late fall, Stendahl wrote Kleitsch, "I have written a letter to Mr. Good telling him what we talked about, asking him to see to it that your wife and boy were sent over so they could take care of you." Stendahl added: "All I can say Joe is to finish up enough stuff for a big exhibition. I don't care what you do or how much, just plant yourself and paint."[234] Nothing was to come of Stendahl's seeming generosity.

Kleitsch found Paris exhilarating, and he spent considerable time studying the paintings at the Louvre and frequenting galleries on the Left Bank. From comments by critic J. C. Bulliet, we learn that Kleitsch "liked the 'ideas' of the French in art, but he was equally taken with the 'finish' of the English. He considers some of the still-life painting of the modernists remarkable work, and he even did some himself with much satisfaction" (PLATES 156 and 157). Reveling in the

PLATE 157. Joseph Kleitsch, *Peonies, Paris*, 1927. Oil on canvas, 25 x 21". Collection of Mr. and Mrs. Thomas B. Stiles II.

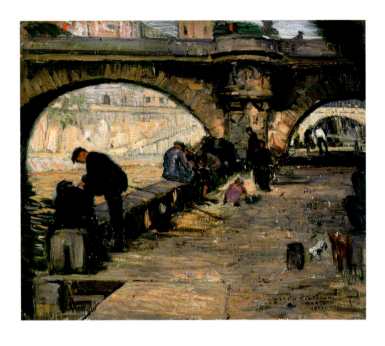

above
PLATE 158. Joseph Kleitsch, *Along the Seine, Paris*, 1927. Oil on canvas, 18 x 21 ¾". Private Collection, courtesy of William B. Dewey.

right
PLATE 159. Joseph Kleitsch, *Reposer, Pont Neuf, Paris*, 1927. Oil on canvas, 36 x 36". Reed and Chris Halladay Collection.

opposite
PLATE 160. Joseph Kleitsch, *Pont Neuf with Statue of Henry IV, Paris*, 1927. Oil on canvas, 15 x 18". Michael Kizhner Fine Art, courtesy of Christie's.
PLATE 161. Henri de Pierrefeu, "Pont Neuf, Paris," 2003. Photograph.

Parisian environment, Kleitsch painted extensively, attracted above all by the activity along the quays and below the bridges of the Seine in the heart of the Latin Quarter (PLATE 158),[235] bridges that have fascinated artists for generations. In *Reposer* (PLATE 159), Kleitsch brings the viewer to the underside of Paris. The painting expresses the abject despair of hopeless derelicts through its somber tones. Kleitsch heightens the effect by placing himself in the picture as an observer of the depressing scene under an arch of the Pont Neuf. This work is unique for Kleitsch in its evocation of deep human emotion.[236] Another painting of the Pont Neuf, identifiable by the statue of Henry IV, is a scene of active life along the Seine (PLATE 160; photo, PLATE 161).

PLATE 162. Joseph Kleitsch, *Luxembourg Gardens, Paris*, 1927. Oil on canvas, 15 x 18". Michael Kizhner Fine Art.

PLATE 163. Joseph Kleitsch, *Tuileries, Paris*, 1927. Oil on canvas, 15 ¼ x 18 ¼". Collection of Rod Harris, courtesy of George Stern Fine Arts.

PLATE 164. Joseph Kleitsch, *Jardin du Carrousel, Paris*, 1927. Oil on canvas, 18 x 21". Collection of Christopher Walker.

Among Kleitsch's inventory of smaller paintings, most of them outdoor studies, are the notably fresh views of the colorful gardens of Luxembourg (PLATE 162), the Tuileries (PLATE 163), and the Carrousel (PLATE 164). Several of these are quick, spontaneous studies in "cool tones with lively greens and white sunlight."[237] In addition, Kleitsch completed several richly painted figurative pictures. One of them, *Blue Thread* of 1927 (PLATE 165), is of a woman sewing,

PLATE 165. Joseph Kleitsch, *Blue Thread*, 1927. Oil on canvas, 40 x 30". Orange County Museum of Art Collection. Gift of Mr. and Mrs. Donald Winston.

PLATE 166. Joseph Kleitsch, *Madonna and the Apples, Paris*, 1927. Oil on canvas, 28 x 36". Collection of John and Regina Rowe.

PLATE 167. Joseph Kleitsch, *The Artist's Dresser, Paris*, 1927. Oil on canvas, 18 ¼ x 22". Courtesy of Edenhurst Gallery and Kelley Gallery.

PLATE 168. Joseph Kleitsch, *Interior with Woman Sewing, France*, 1926. Photograph taken 1928. Laguna Art Museum Archives, Laguna Beach, California. Stendahl Art Galleries Collection.

Another, *Madonna and the Apples* (PLATE 166), focuses equally on the woman and the still life and recalls Cézanne's studies of apples. "There is a story to this still life of rich red fruit with cake, glass, and tablecloth. In the Café de Dome one night the painters were arguing about their work. The still current phrase 'It is as hard to paint an apple as a Madonna' was heard in many forms. But, it developed, one must not paint anything any more with 'highlights.' One 'realizes' the planes, puts a thick outline round them, but under no circumstance puts on a high-light."[238]

A large glass pitcher seen in *Madonna and the Apples* reappears in the upper right corner of a small still life, *The Artist's Dresser*. Placed on the dresser is a mélange of objects, including Kleitsch's ubiquitous cigar (PLATE 167). The pitcher included in both paintings could suggest a possible liaison between Kleitsch and the attractive model.

Los Angeles critics were impressed with Kleitsch's vivid, realistic portrait of a French woman bending over her sewing basket. They commented on her "fine character, racial quality and the magnificent composition of full curving masses" and considered the canvas among the best of his European paintings.[239] Interior scenes of women sewing and embroidering had been painted by Velázquez, Chardin (1699–1779), Frederick C. Frieseke, Richard Miller (1875–1943), and other well-known painters.[240] Kleitsch also painted a woman sewing in a historic house in Vernon, focusing more on the interior than on the figure (PLATE 168).[241] Another portrait, half-length, of a woman sewing, is similar in composition to a painting attributed to Velázquez (PLATES 169 and 170).[242] Several of Kleitsch's interior scenes, including *Reflections* (see PLATE 177), seem to have been inspired by works of Manet (see PLATE 176), Monet, Matisse, and others.

Except for Simone, Kleitsch's French women remain anonymous, since his (or Stendahl's) titles specifically avoided naming them (PLATE 171). One wonders whether they were artist's models, café acquaintances, or companions for a lone artist. Understandably, when Kleitsch returned to Southern California in 1928, rumors abounded about possible liaisons during his twenty-two-month stay in Europe.[243]

Kleitsch's experience in Paris is best characterized by Abel Warshawsky, who described a new American population in Paris during the 1920s:

> It almost seemed as if Greenwich Village en masse had emigrated to the Quarter. What had formerly been real bohemianism now became a sham, a part of Montparnasse sideshow. The Dôme Café was crowded to the limit. . . . Across the street the once modest Rotonde had blossomed forth into a rival of the Dôme. . . . Entire wall space being devoted to a permanent exhibition of paintings and drawings of artist clients, while upstairs every evening a large dance orchestra played jazz to a jostling crowd of gyrating couples. The center of Paris night life had

PLATE 169. Diego Rodríguez de Silva y Velázquez, *The Needlewoman*, c. 1640–50. Oil on canvas, 29 ⅛ x 24 ⅝". Andrew W. Mellon Collection, Image © 2003 Board of Trustees, National Gallery of Art, Washington, D.C.

PLATE 170. Joseph Kleitsch, *Woman Sewing, Paris*, 1926. Oil on canvas, 21 x 17 ½". Trotter Galleries.

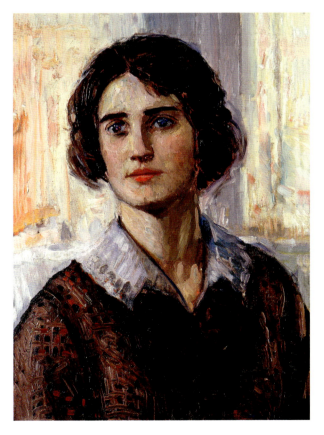

PLATE 171. Joseph Kleitsch, *M'lle 'E'*, 1926. Oil on canvas, 21 x 17". Private Collection, courtesy of Julie Hopkins.

PLATE 172. Joseph Kleitsch, *Paris Café*, 1927.
Oil on canvas, 15 x 18". Collection of James D. Zidell.

been transferred from Montmartre to Montparnasse. As a result, the Quarter was rapidly losing its former air of quiet and unpretentiousness. Cafes [PLATE 172], American bars, and "dancings" were springing up all along the Boulevard du Montparnasse. A new Babylon had been launched in Paris.[244]

Montparnasse's international character made it home to many foreign artists' associations, such as the American Art Association, the American Students and Artists Center, the Association des Artistes Scandinaves, and others. For Kleitsch, Paris of the 1920s was stimulating and provocative. On occasion he sought out colleagues, aspiring painters like Warshawsky, who were not primarily interested in the Parisian avant-garde.

But the frenetic pace of Paris finally proved to be too distracting, and Kleitsch, like Warshawsky, looked to the tranquility of a small, picturesque French village (PLATE 173).[245] Kleitsch's longest European stays had been in Seville and Vernon (PLATE 174),[246] because these places had the most aesthetic appeal for him. In late spring of 1927, he left Paris and returned to Vernon and Giverny.

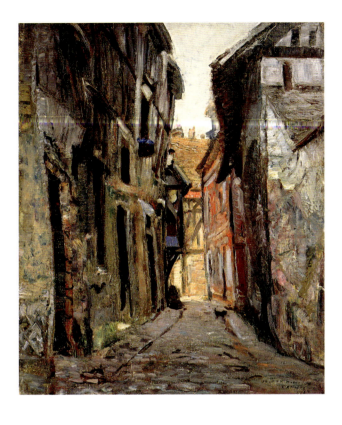

above
PLATE 173. Joseph Kleitsch, Unidentified Lane (*Ruelle Malot*), *Vernon, France*, 1927. Oil on canvas, 25 x 21". Courtesy of Edenhurst Gallery.

right
PLATE 174. Joseph Kleitsch, Unidentified Street (*Rue Bourbon-Penthièvre*), *Vernon, France*, c. 1927. Oil on canvas, 21 x 18". Private Collection.

PLATE 175. Joseph Kleitsch, *Giverny, France*, 1927.
Oil on canvas, 34 x 34". Private Collection.

Attracted by the dewy green valleys and meadows of Giverny, he painted a scene in which the sun breaks through cumulus clouds after a sudden spring rain, leaving scattered patches of blue sky and an array of vivid colors (PLATE 175). Along a bisecting, diagonal path, a lone black figure in brilliant sunlight leads the eye to the rustic farmhouses and then to green trees and the distant bluish-gray mountains hovering beneath the clouds.

Reflections recalls Édouard Manet's masterpiece *A Bar at the Folies-Bergère* (PLATE 176). In a Vernon hotel restaurant, Kleitsch posed an attractive French woman in front of a mirror (PLATE 177). The painting's visual complexity stems from the reflection in the mirror and the diffused light from the windows. The sitter, still believed by many historians and collectors to be Edna, is actually an acquaintance of the artist.

A poignant description of Kleitsch's trip to Europe was written by J. C. Bulliet: "I opine that . . . Kleitsch's happiest days were spent in the green valleys of Giverney's [*sic*] springtime, and in the brilliant streets of Seville—two absolutely divergent sketching grounds, but each perfect of its kind. . . . Highly sensitive, alertly experimental, . . . Kleitsch painted at Vernon and Giverney some beautiful

PLATE 176. Édouard Manet, *A Bar at the Folies-Bergère*, 1882. Oil on canvas, 38 x 51". Courtauld Institute of Art Gallery, London.

PLATE 177. Joseph Kleitsch, *Reflections, Vernon (Mlle at Table)*, 1927. Oil on canvas, 34 x 34". Collection of Dr. and Mrs. Edward H. Boseker.

PLATE 178. Joseph Kleitsch, Unidentified Landscape
(*The Valley of the Seine, Vernon, France*), 1926.
Oil on canvas, 23 x 23". Edenhurst Gallery.

things that may make us think of Constable." Bulliet asks, "How could [Kleitsch] . . . escape from the subtle and gentle spirit of Monet on the great Frenchman's own pleasaunce?"[247] Kleitsch's European paintings clearly show that Monet did have some influence, particularly in the case of *Ancient and Modern Normandie* (see PLATE 152) and [*The Valley of the Seine, Vernon, France*] (PLATE 178).[248]

Correspondence in June 1927 between Stendahl and Edna Kleitsch, who was living in Ohio, may have been prompted by rumors of Kleitsch's philandering in Europe. Cause for concern could well have arisen from the number of attractive women whose portraits he painted there. Edna wrote to Stendahl: "Joe is coming back a big refined dignified Kleitsch you just watch and I am absolutely out of it all—I can say I will disown him if he is not—I don't think there is a person who has better habits than Joe. I can trust him anywhere."[249] Stendahl responded to Edna "Joe is a very fine boy and on my trip through Europe with him I find that he is much better than the average man. I can see no reason why he should stay over in Europe any longer as there is much work to be done here."[250]

Kleitsch had expected Stendahl to rejoin him in Europe in 1927 to arrange a Paris exhibition, and he was extremely disappointed when Stendahl cancelled his trip at the last moment.[251] A letter from Kleitsch to Stendahl indicates the artist's anger at the lack of sales during the past year: "I don't have to sell any pictures. Have a place in the East and one in Laguna, if you please. I can stay in Chicago, paint portraits for a living and buy my own pictures. You have not sold enough pictures of mine since I am here [and] there must be about fifty of them there with you. Looking over my list, some of them [are] as good as you have seen." Kleitsch then asked Stendahl to sell $5,000 worth of paintings and send the money to his benefactor and patron, Edward B. Good, who had loaned him money as an advance against his future sales at the Stendahl Galleries.[252] Stendahl's reply was cryptic: "Out of the question is the business of 5000 dollars, business not so brisk now—European trip called off."[253]

Greatly disappointed and almost despondent, Kleitsch told Stendahl he felt as though he "had been left alone in the world," adding that it would not take much for him "to take a trip to Budapest or Bucharest and forget it." His spirits improved when he met and dined with two artists from Chicago and another from California whom he had known in the States.[254] And Kleitsch's spirits remained elevated when, in September in Paris, he met several other artists from Southern California: Norman Chamberlain (1887–1961), Haldane Douglas (1893–1980), Stanislaus Pociecha Poray (1888–1948), and Arthur Hill Gilbert (1894–1970).[255]

In November 1927 Kleitsch finally returned to America and promptly rented a large studio in the Athenaeum Building in Chicago to ready his homecoming show in Los Angeles.[256] In December, Kleitsch moved to the Hotel Mira-Mar in Chicago with his family while he was readying his paintings for the exhibition. Although he complained to Stendahl about the cold weather, he was delighted to see his friends at the Palette and Chisel Club and the Art Institute. Stendahl replied on December 10: "If you have your paintings here by January we will be able to put on a nice exhibition for you during April. We have not let down for a moment on your publicity, every week one of your paintings appears in some publication. . . . We are all going to a hard-time party at Fred Hogues house tonight, the picture would be complete if you were going to be with us."

As Stendahl had promised, the exhibition in May 1928 at the Stendahl Galleries received broad coverage from the local press (PLATE 179). A rejuvenated Joseph Kleitsch had returned after almost two years in Europe, and it seems that the press too was rejuvenated.[257] On May 6, 1928, *Los Angeles Times* critic Arthur Millier, entering the Stendahl Galleries before the opening to review "the homecoming exhibition of Joseph Kleitsch of Laguna Beach," wrote:

> I found the artist himself crowned with a little navy blue beret—not the kind with the orange tassel, but the variety that reminds one of a kewpie top-not—seated quietly at ease in the midst of chaos. Two pictures were on the wall. About him were stacks of canvases, some stretched, others unmounted, which he had evidently been attempting to fit in the frames that wouldn't . . . . Of all the painters of Southern California none is more fluent [than] Joseph Kleitsch; by the same token he is the least fluent talker in the whole United States. Paint is his life and his speech. There is a legend to the effect that he subsisted a whole week on a tube of yellow ochre . . . . Some assert that he bathes in linseed oil and applies copal varnish to his cheeks after shaving.

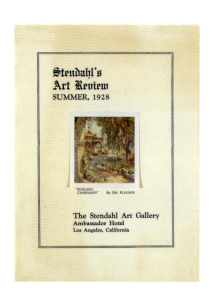

PLATE 179. "Joseph Kleitsch" in *Stendahl's Art Review*, Summer 1928. The Stendahl Art Gallery, Ambassador Hotel, Los Angeles, California, courtesy of Edenhurst Gallery.

On May 13 *Los Angeles Times* critic Antony Anderson previewed the show: "Joseph Kleitsch has successfully slowed down his pace, taken more time for thoughtful design and refinement of color and paint application. . . . This is a first reflection on his 'Homecoming' exhibition at the Stendahl Galleries."

Fred Hogue, in an article titled "A Hungarian Artist" in the *Los Angeles Times* on June 25, 1928, found Kleitsch "nesting in a square tower on the roof of the Ambassador Hotel, a secluded nook in the center of a modern city." Hogue continued:

> As I look at the canvases of Joseph Kleitsch I forget the painter. As a colorist he is not clever; he is great. If the mantle of Titian has fallen upon a modern artist, it is draped about the shoulders of this Hungarian painter. When I look at his creations I think of Titian; there is an association that I feel, but cannot express. Curiously enough, Titian is the artist that Kleitsch most admires.
>
> Joseph Kleitsch is an artist. In his breast smolder the fires of Vesuvius. When they burst forth into a flame, he transfers them to canvases and a masterpiece is born.
>
> From the windows of his eagle's nest I look down on a hundred spires. To the west rise the gray building of the studios of Hollywood, where the scenarios are filmed that encircle the

PLATE 180. Joseph Kleitsch, *The Park in Vernon, France,* 1927. Oil on canvas, 34 x 34". Private Collection.

globe. To the south, mirrored against the horizon, are the derricks of the greatest oil field known to the modern world. . . . I turned from the window to greet a landscape where the apple trees blossom in Normandy, and my ear is attuned to the chimes of Vernon village on the banks of the Seine. . . .The landscape of Vernon is not unfamiliar to me [PLATE 180].[258] I saw it last summer; but the evanescent tones and shades which have been imprisoned in the brush of a master escaped me. . . .I saw the stream; he saw only its reflection in the crystal rays of a descending sun. . . .For him the sunbeams danced, and the changing shadows of the floating clouds empurpled the wood slopes.

The last rays of the sun have disappeared. As I look from the windows I am greeted by the rosy light of a waxing moon. . . . On the wall to my right hangs a canvas of Laguna; but it is a Laguna that lives only in memory, the Laguna before the subdividers came. The palms that cast their shadows across the winding street have been uprooted; the buildings have been demolished to make way for modern progress. What the artists

PLATE 181. Joseph Kleitsch, *Portrait of Ruth Renick* (or *Jade Necklace*), 1928. Oil on canvas, 35 ½ x 39". Private Collection, courtesy of William B. Dewey.

PLATE 182. Joseph Kleitsch, *Portrait of Ruth Renick,* 1928. Unaltered version. Photograph. Laguna Art Museum Archives, Laguna Beach, California. Stendahl Art Galleries Collection.
PLATE 183. "Ruth Renick (Hollywood Silent Movie Actress)," c. 1930. Photograph. Courtesy of the Academy of Motion Picture Arts and Sciences.

call desecration the realtors call improvement; but the Laguna that is dead is dearer to me than the Laguna that has risen from its ashes.

Canvases all about me; I seem to breathe the perfume of the roses of Capistrano, to feel in my nostrils the tang of the salt spray on the rocks at Dana Point. A mist hangs over the sea and a blue haze covers with a veil of gossamer the slopes of the distant mountains. Why do I find in these canvases a harmony that I miss when I look upon the landscapes themselves. It is because the creation of the master possesses an intangible something lacking in nature itself. . . . Los Angeles is richer because the tropical bird of wonderful plumage has found a nest here.

In 1990, the author wrote in *California Light* that little information was available about Kleitsch between the time he returned from Europe until the Stendahl exhibition in May 1928. (He did not exhibit with Stendahl again until April 1931.) However several portraits painted before the 1928 exhibition were discovered recently. *Ruth Renick* (see PLATE 181), a portrait of the glamorous silent-movie actress (1890–1984), was reproduced in the Hogue article of June 1928. From this we can assume that Kleitsch painted several portraits arranged by the Stendahl Galleries, commissions that provided him with an immediate source of income. As noted earlier, in his late portraits of women such as Ruth Renick, Mrs. Marian Gould (see p. 260),[259] and Ruth E. Bach (see PLATE 135), the attitudes of his models had become more mannered and theatrical. Renick is almost subsumed in a highly decorative Hollywood interior setting in the newspaper reproduction of the original *Portrait of Ruth Renick* (PLATE 182) of 1928. With the sitter's pose varied slightly and a necklace added to the picture, the painting was retitled *Jade Necklace* (PLATE 181).[260] Renick was a prominent movie actress who appeared in a number of early silent films, among them *The Witching Hour* (1921) for Paramount (PLATE 183).

PLATE 184. Joseph Kleitsch, *Highlights*, c. 1928. Oil on canvas, 38 x 46". Collection of Joseph Ambrose, Jr., and Michael D. Feddersen.

PLATE 185. Cristoforo Munari, *Natura morta con strumenti musicali* (*Still Life with Musical Instruments*), Inv. 1890 no. 7591, 1709. Oil on canvas, 39 x 53". Uffizi Gallery, Florence, Italy.

Kleitsch's exposure to the European masters and to the visual complexity of their work began to show itself in several compositions completed after his return. In the most astounding of Kleitsch's still lifes, the autobiographical *Highlights* (PLATE 184), the artist extends his artistic skills in a complex composition that brings to mind the traditions of seventeenth-century European still-life painting (PLATE 185). *Highlights* is exuberantly baroque in its color and dazzling light. Probably one of the most freely painted of Kleitsch's works, it abounds with vigorous gestural brushstrokes, rapidly applied to sculpt both the three-dimensional forms and the decorative patterning. Using unctuous pigments, applied with brush, brush point, palette knife, and thumb, Kleitsch achieves one of his most personal statements. Amid the profusion of objects piled and strewn on the table are his violin, flute, accordion, and sheet music.[261] Painted canvases are propped against the wall, one a landscape and the other a Matisse-like subject, and there are of course his palette and pigments. Remnants of wine and fruit suggest an evening of music and conviviality among intimate friends. *Highlights* is overwhelming in its virtuosity, as compared with the simple trompe-l'oeil still lifes of Kleitsch's transitional years.

Kleitsch used the same table motif for *Sweet Peas*, a smaller and much less complicated still life (PLATE 186). The interior setting is the Kleitsch home in Laguna, with its simple furnishings of the period. The artist tilts the table forward to reveal some of the room and the simple objects on the table. The brushwork and compositional similarity indicate a date close to that of *Highlights*.

PLATE 186. Joseph Kleitsch, *Still Life with Sweet Peas*, c. 1928. Oil on canvas, 18 x 22 ¼". Collection of Joseph Ambrose, Jr., and Michael D. Feddersen.

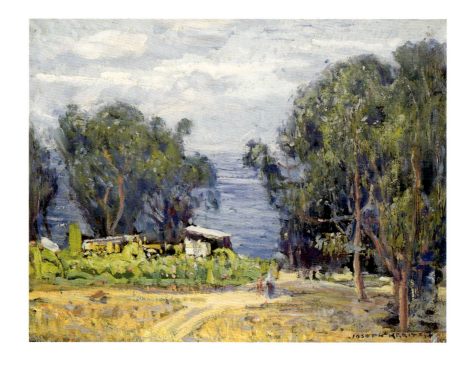

At the August 1928 meeting of the Painters and Sculptors Club, Kleitsch gave "an interesting account of his impressions found in Europe during his stay there." Minutes of the club's business meetings indicate that he never reactivated his membership. We can assume that he resumed his permanent residency in Laguna to reduce expenses and continue his quest to record scenes of the village before Old Laguna was permanently altered. During August, he went on a sketching trip with artist George Demont Otis (1879–1962) that was reported in the August 19 *Los Angeles Times:* "Otis was a good cook and Kleitsch has a good appetite, and the art of each is not likely to suffer from association with that of the other."

In January 1929, Laguna's first modern hostel, La Casa del Camino, announced a February 1 opening. Chicago and Laguna artist William W. Riddell (1877–1948), its proprietor, arranged with his friend Joseph Kleitsch to exhibit paintings of Old Laguna in the hotel lounge and dining room. The *South Coast News*, on January 11, reported that "the paintings of things that used to be in Laguna are greatly prized by Mr. Kleitsch, who attaches a sentimental value to many of them. Some are among the first paintings he made of landscapes in this State [PLATE 187], and several he has . . . repeatedly [refused] to sell."

Antony Anderson was both enthusiastic and nostalgic about the collection Kleitsch had assembled for La Casa:

> All will be scenes from Old Laguna Beach, painted . . . before our present easeful days of good roads, good water, gas and electricity. Old Laguna compelled Lagunites to wade through mud, to plow through dust, to import water, to cook with kerosene, to pant up steep hills, to fight rattlesnakes, to hang over tottering rails while waiting for their mail—
>
> But oh, how beautiful Old Laguna was, with its incomparable shoreline, its opalescent sea, its radiant hills. Nobody minded the dust and the mud, brackish water and the reluctant kerosene, for every man, woman and child was drinking in beauty every day in every pore, and all were happy. Especially the artists. They came in flocks, they painted early and late, they starved and they rejoiced. But they didn't actually die. Some of them, in fact, will live for ever because they painted Old Laguna in all its beauty. Compared from the standpoint of history their pictures are priceless. Esthetically considered, too, many of them are invaluable.
>
> . . . [Kleitsch] painted the ancient shacks [PLATE 188], gaunt hotel, the sun-bathed hills and the dreamy sea because he found them all beautiful, and he brought to his task not only great love but great understanding. . . . He is a poet—and who

PLATE 187. Joseph Kleitsch, Untitled Landscape (*Woman Seated in the Garden Sewing*), n.d. Oil on canvas. 24 x 30". Private Collection, courtesy of Julie Hopkins.

PLATE 188. Joseph Kleitsch, *Shacks, Laguna Beach* (or *Old Laguna—Foot of Anita Street*), n.d. Oil on canvas, 13 ¼ x 18". Collection of Lenoir Josey.

doubts that Laguna Beach is the true place for poets? Why, we are all poets here, whether we happen to keep shops, paint pictures, sell real estate, run newspapers, or just loaf in the sun.

Praising some of his favorite paintings in the exhibition, *Jeweled Hills* (PLATE 189), *Laguna Cove, The Lifeguard, The Old Post Office, Under the Eucalyptus Trees, Old Hotel Laguna,* and *Evening Light,* Anderson concluded, "Here, in epitome, is Old Laguna as seen and interpreted by a painter-poet."[262]

Laguna continued its transition from village to town and eventually to city. In February 1929 the Laguna Beach Art Association celebrated the opening of its new modern Art Gallery at Cliff Drive and Coast Boulevard, on a bluff overlooking the ocean, where it is still located today. It had been ten and a half years since the Laguna Beach Art Association was founded by its prime mover, artist Edgar Payne. The first gallery was in the old Town Hall, a little wooden building with limited usefulness (see PLATE 75). Kleitsch had taken part in the opening celebration,[263] donating a small painting to help raise funds for the new Laguna Beach Art Gallery, and he was now among the honored artists with paintings in this opening exhibition. To the gallery's spring show Kleitsch submitted *Jade Necklace* (*Ruth Renick*; see PLATE 181). According to Antony Anderson, the portrait received "its name from the jury of selection, for Joe consistently disdains and neglects to name his pictures. This canvas may be termed a masterpiece, and with propriety."[264]

On June 30, 1929, the *Los Angeles Times* announced that Stendahl and Kleitsch would summer in Spain, sailing for Cadiz July 16 on the liner *Magellanes.* Their intention was to visit the International Art Exhibition at the expositions in Barcelona and Seville. This report was corroborated in the monthly *California Arts and Architecture* of August 1929, which also mentioned that Kleitsch was painting and sketching in Spain that summer. The author, however, finds no corroborating evidence that Kleitsch accompanied Stendahl to Europe.[265]

During the summer and early fall, Kleitsch received further recognition at several scheduled exhibitions of his Laguna and European works. At Stendahl's

PLATE 189. Joseph Kleitsch, *Jeweled Hills*, c. 1922. Oil on canvas, 26 x 24".
Collection of Lenoir Josey, courtesy of Steven Stern.

summer show, a reporter for *Saturday Night*, July 13, 1929, remarked on Kleitsch's "old Laguna scenes in high key and full of summer sun" and on his paintings of Seville, "subdued as though veiled in the mysteries attaching to its crumbling walls." Regarding the Laguna Beach Art Association's Eleventh Anniversary Exhibit at the new Art Gallery in August, Antony Anderson wrote on August 16 in the *South Coast News,* "No doubt Joseph Kleitsch has painted his wife many times—Artist's wives are patient and long-suffering models. But I opine he never did a better thing of her than his canvas in the present show. . . . Its color scheme, delicate rose and cold blue, is an exceedingly difficult one triumphantly carried out" (see PLATE 54).

Following the stock market crash of October 1929, California's economic boom abruptly ended. The severe downturn in the economy cut across all sectors, including the arts. Kleitsch and Stendahl began to experience financial difficulties, not only with new sales of art, but with collecting debts on paintings that had already been sold.

From the dates of his pictures, we know that Kleitsch continued to paint primarily in Laguna from 1928 through 1931 in order to survive the Depression years. Although he was a prominent portraitist, he nonetheless devoted these years above all to preserving the disappearing Old Laguna.

PLATE 190. William Wendt, *There Is No Solitude Even in Nature*, 1906. Oil on canvas, 34 x 36". The Joan Irvine Smith Collection.

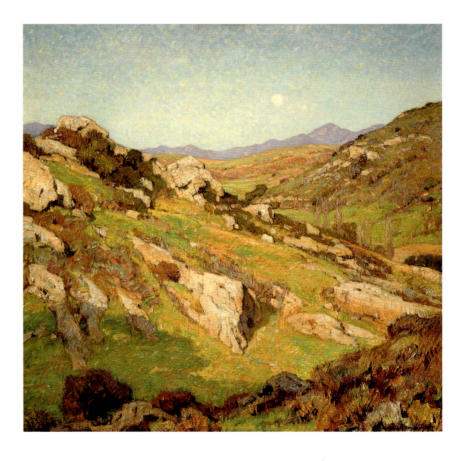

CHAPTER V

An Art of Urgency: A Sense of Time and Place, 1928–1930

Today there is both an interest in and a cultural nostalgia for the time when Joseph Kleitsch and his fellow artists created their joyous plein-air paintings—when nature was still untrammeled and an unpretentious way of life was still possible. Those were the last days of California's unspoiled, small-town character, before World War II and the defense industry changed the state forever.

Much later in the century, postmodernist landscapists like April Gornik (b. 1953), Michael Zwack (b. 1949), and John Beerman (b. 1958) would yearn for a lost paradise, the unspoiled nature that had inspired both the Hudson River School and the early twentieth-century plein-air painters of Southern California. The postmodernists, like Kleitsch and his fellow artists before them, lamented this loss, caused by humankind's adversarial relationship with nature.[266]

Contemporary plein-air painter Camille Przewodek (b. 1947) has been seduced by Laguna's South Coast Wilderness, a greenbelt saved by grass-roots efforts,[267] as she follows the paths of celebrated plein-air artist William Wendt (PLATE 190).[268] "I am interested in preserving wilderness areas," says Przewodek, a resident of Petaluma in Northern California. "If they develop everything, there will be nothing to paint other than urban scenes."[269]

The drive to save the Laguna area began in Kleitsch's time. As he noted then, "The people of Laguna Beach [today] understand better than most, living as they do in an area that almost became an unbroken urban scene. Instead, there is now a significant 17,000-acre greenbelt surrounding Laguna [known as the South Coast Wilderness]."[270]

Through his actions and paintings, Kleitsch was recognized as an early preservationist by his peers and by art critics. His recognition of Laguna's imminent transition from village to urban center prompted his efforts to record and preserve its unique lifestyle. In his quest to preserve the past, Kleitsch dedicated almost a decade to faithfully recording and interpreting the rural nature of Old Laguna. In a series of lyrical pictures, he delineated the character of its village buildings and streets, its shores and coastline, and its distant mountains (see p. 262). Critic Arthur Millier wrote of Kleitsch's nostalgic yearnings: "From his window he has a commanding view of the hills and Laguna proper, a view that moves him to romantic ruminations upon what the village might have been today had it been settled several hundred years ago by Europeans, and its hilltops crowned with Italian villas to look down upon the empurpled sea."[271]

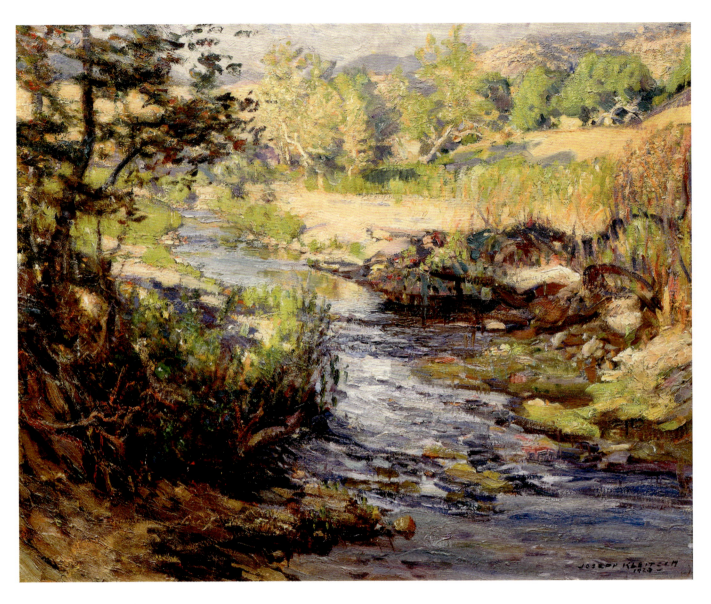

PLATE 191. Joseph Kleitsch, *Creek—Laguna Canyon,* 1923. Oil on canvas, 32 x 42". Collection of Mr. and Mrs. Thomas B. Stiles II.

PLATE 192. John Singer Sargent, *Alpine Pool*, 1907. Oil on canvas, 27 ½ x 38". The Metropolitan Museum of Art. Gift of Mrs. Francis Ormond, 1950, courtesy of Laguna Art Museum Archives, Laguna Beach, California.
PLATE 193. Christopher Bliss, "Laguna Creek," 2003. Photograph.

Today Kleitsch's art is a conduit to the past, before the spoliation of what he called Laguna's pristine environment. As early as 1922, the artist painted the general store and old post office in a rural setting, a place where local residents met to exchange views, gossip, pick up mail, and purchase basic commodities (see PLATE 96). It was an era before electricity, gas, paved streets, and potable water. In 1931 Antony Anderson called Kleitsch's early pictorial records "veritable documents, valuable as history as well as art," and really "priceless." In the same review he commented on a later group of paintings by Kleitsch of the hills, gardens, and shores of Laguna in the late 1920s, all of them "incomparably beautiful. . . . Modern progress found itself utterly unable to spoil them, though we cannot say that it didn't do its darnedest."[272]

Kleitsch's passion for producing scenes of Old Laguna also extended to the back country canyon and rustic hills. He was not unlike the American master John Singer Sargent, who late in his career indulged his insatiable curiosity and appetite for painting landscapes. Kleitsch's *Creek—Laguna Canyon* of 1923 (PLATE 191) reflects the same evocation of form through light, vibrancy of color, and force of brushstrokes that characterize Sargent's landscape painting *Alpine Pool* (PLATE 192). Kleitsch's focus on the reflective surface of the water is contrasted with the foreground shadows, while the background is illuminated by California's radiant white light.

The natural beauty of this wilderness area came from the grove of sycamore trees and the rippling waters of the blue creek threading its way through Laguna Canyon. According to Eric Jessen, Chief of the Orange County Regional Harbors, Beaches, and Parks Department for the past twenty-eight years,[273] this scene was painted near the intersection of present-day Laguna Canyon Road and El Toro Road, looking north. Jessen states that Laguna Canyon Road now occupies the creek bed depicted in the picture. (The present El Toro Road would intersect the view at the lower right corner.) The upper right quadrant of the canvas, says Jessen, depicts Sycamore Flats and Sycamore Canyon, within the James Dilley Preserve of Laguna Coast Wilderness Park. The magnificent California sycamores at the painting's top center still stand, just inland of the crossing of State Highway 73 and Laguna Canyon Road. Photographer Chris Bliss has provided a current and graphic view of a location near Kleitsch's vantage point for this painting (PLATE 193).

PLATE 194. Joseph Kleitsch, *Old Laguna*, c. 1923–24. Oil on canvas, 18 x 21". Private Collection, courtesy of Redfern Gallery.

PLATE 195. Christopher Bliss, "From Main Beach Looking up Laguna Canyon Road," 2003. Photograph.

Kleitsch painted a charming rural view of *Old Laguna* around 1923–24 (PLATE 194), before the incursion of commercial development and paved roads. The reflective surfaces of Laguna Creek Lagoon, the parched, sun-drenched meadows dotted with small houses, and a distant view of Mystic Hill provide an idyllic picture of Old Laguna. The fold in the hill at the left side of the canvas is Laguna Canyon.

As he painted this canvas, Kleitsch stood with his easel on the sand of Main Beach, his back to the crashing surf, at the foot of Broadway Street in downtown Laguna Beach (PLATE 195). In the foreground of the painting, Laguna Creek Lagoon winds its way up Laguna Canyon. Today's intersection of Broadway and Coast Boulevard (now known as Coast Highway) corresponds to the bottom center of the canvas. Old Coast Road crossed over Laguna Creek at the modest bridge near the center of the picture. Still standing are several of the houses directly above the Old Coast Bridge. The large mass of California pepper trees behind the roofs of these buildings includes the canopy of the pepper tree that still stands in front of Laguna Beach City Hall.

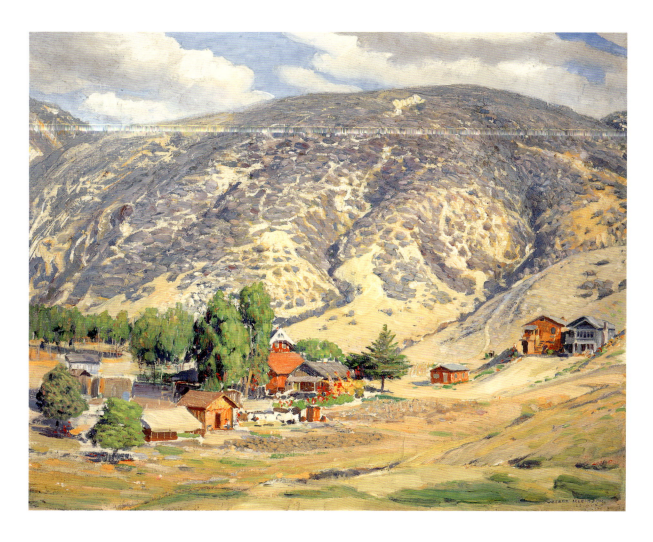

PLATE 196. Joseph Kleitsch, *Laguna Beach,* 1924. Oil on canvas, 32 x 40". Collection of the Festival of Arts.
PLATE 197. Christopher Bliss, "Mermaid and Third Streets," 2003. Photograph.

In *Laguna Beach* of 1924, Kleitsch chose to make Mystic Hill, with its reptilian surface, the dominant feature in this rural scene (PLATE 196). Standing at a spot behind present-day St. Mary's Episcopal Church, overlooking downtown Laguna (see p. 263), Kleitsch painted the cluster of houses off Mermaid and Third streets (PLATE 197). Farther up the incline (on today's Third Street), he recorded two old houses that still stand. Because of his fidelity in capturing nature, the trees in the painting are easily identifiable: the stiff evergreen near the center is a Monterey cypress, and the trees to the left are California peppers.

Kleitsch did not confine his efforts to any one part of Laguna. He painted the coastline and the shore with its ubiquitous bathers, the village and its environs, the canyons, and the surrounding hills. He shifted his easel from place to place, in the morning, at midday, in the late afternoon, and even in the evening. Driven by his longing to record the village before it became transformed, Kleitsch was almost frenetic at times. These paintings were to be housed in his own gallery as a permanent exhibition open to the public.[274]

AN ART OF URGENCY

PLATE 198. Joseph Kleitsch, *Laguna Road II*, c. 1929–30. Oil on canvas, 36 x 40". Collection of Dr. and Mrs. Edward H. Boseker.

With this objective in mind, Kleitsch felt compelled to paint another version of *Laguna Road* of 1924, since the first one had been sold to the city (see PLATE 124). The second work of 1929–30 is a close facsimile, with infinitesimal variations, a broader, more vigorous brush, and brighter hues (PLATE 198). In parts of this composition, Kleitsch was moving toward greater abstraction, compared with the tighter, more graphic rendering of the earlier painting.

PLATE 199. Christopher Bliss, "Coast Boulevard and Laguna Avenue," 2003. Photograph.

To paint the 1924 picture, Kleitsch had stood at a spot on the inland side of Coast Boulevard across from the Old Hotel Laguna (see contemporary photograph, PLATE 199). Since several of the landmarks had since been removed, he relied heavily on the earlier version to recreate the scene. In *Old Hotel Laguna* of 1924 (PLATE 200), the eucalyptus grove on his left, directly in front of the old hotel, was removed when the new Hotel Laguna was built in 1930. In both versions of *Laguna Road*, the following elements have been identified: Laguna Avenue, which crosses Coast Boulevard over the heads of the two foreground figures; the white structure known as the Isch Building at the center of the picture, immediately above the parked car; Coast Boulevard, which bends off to the left at the intersection with Forest Avenue at center right; the White House, the third building on the right with the light-colored façade and awning; and the hill in the background, now the Laguna Coast Wilderness Park.

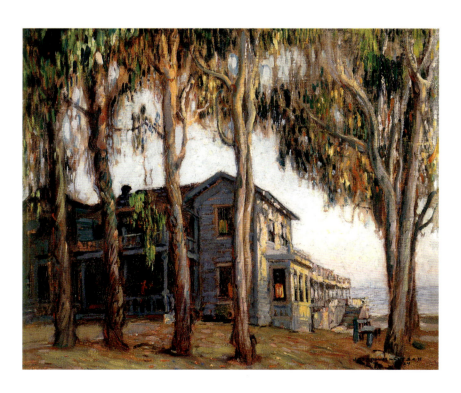

PLATE 200. Joseph Kleitsch, *Old Hotel Laguna,* 1924. Oil on canvas, 16 x 20". Private Collection.

According to Antony Anderson, in his review of Kleitsch's exhibition at the Stendahl Galleries in 1926, the most appealing paintings were those that depicted "the little houses and tangled eucalyptus trees in the village of Laguna."[275] The critic certainly had in mind *Houses among the Eucalypti* of 1925, a twilight view of Old Laguna and the Laguna Coast Wilderness Park (PLATE 202). The composition, beautifully framed by eucalyptus trees, is in subtle oranges, yellows, and reds. Kleitsch's vantage point, near the back of St. Mary's Episcopal Church and immediately in front of Mermaid Street, allowed him to record the natural beauty of the area at sundown. The white building at the center is Jahraus's Laguna Beach Lumber Company, whose owners were pioneers in the community and commissioned several portraits from Kleitsch. At the right of the red house is the ever-present and historic California pepper tree planted by the Rogers family, who first homesteaded what became downtown Laguna. In a contemporary photograph corresponding to the spot where Kleitsch painted *Houses among the Eucalypti,* the artist's view is blocked by modern development (PLATE 201).

PLATE 201. Christopher Bliss, "Mermaid Street and Park Avenue," 2003. Photograph.
PLATE 202. Joseph Kleitsch, *Houses among the Eucalypti,* 1925. Oil on canvas, 36 x 40". Private Collection.

PLATE 203. Joseph Kleitsch, *Laguna Cove* (or *Laguna Shore*), 1925. Oil on canvas, 22 x 36". Collection of Woody Stuart, courtesy of William A. Karges Fine Art.
PLATE 204. Christopher Bliss, "Panorama from Crescent Point (McKnight's Point)," 2003. Photograph.

Preservationists today applaud Kleitsch's prescience in painting what is not only a lasting record but also one of the most beautiful marinescapes of Southern California. *Laguna Cove* (or *Laguna Shore*) is a sweeping, dynamic panorama of Laguna's north coastline with its many cliffs, coves, and inlets (PLATE 203), full of movement generated by the waves and whitecaps and the scudding clouds. Highlights are achieved by the skillful blending of vivid foreground colors in contrast to the subtle atmospheric effects. Kleitsch conveys an image of the pristine, natural coastline with his random placement of houses about to be engulfed by the rolling fog that moves toward the shore. Appropriately, this beautiful, lyrical picture was selected as the frontispiece for a bound volume of poems titled *Laguna Lyrics*.[276]

Kleitsch painted *Laguna Cove* from the southeast side of McKnight's Point, now known as Crescent Bay Point Park, at the end of Crescent Bay Drive on the ocean bluff (PLATE 204). He has rendered the topography so carefully that key landforms can easily be distinguished. The bay at the center of the canvas includes Boat, Shaw's, and Diver's coves; the light-colored promontory at the center is Heisler Park, with Bird Rock extending out to sea from the tip of this promontory, where the Old Laguna Pier once reached from Heisler Park to the far extension of the rocks. In the far right distance is Mystic Hill, and beyond it Bluebird Canyon.

From a much higher elevation, Kleitsch painted a more panoramic view, *Laguna Coastline,* near Pyne Castle in north Laguna (PLATES 205 and 207). The picture's small-scale format belies the powerful impact of its sweeping view of land and sea. Here, the artist includes Dana Point Headlands at the farthest point on the horizon. He has skillfully muted the colors to convey the natural atmospheric effects of the coastal fog spreading over most of the adjacent land. The houses scattered across the light green field near Myrtle Street are summarily treated. Main Beach is to the right of the large grove of trees and buildings at the center of the canvas.

During summer, El Paseo Street, an alley by Hotel Laguna, bustled with throngs of bathers on their way to Main Beach. Kleitsch stood with his easel at the western end of the street to paint *El Paseo* sometime between 1928 and 1929 (PLATES 206 and 208). He depicted the rear of the board-and-batten-buildings fronting the old Main Beach boardwalk, and the recently graded area at the end of the street shortly after the demolition of the Old Hotel Laguna built by Joseph and Catherine Yoch (see PLATE 200). The structure was razed in order to build the new, more modern hotel in 1930. Construction of the current Hotel Laguna began on the site after this canvas was painted. The blue gum eucalyptus trees bending in the wind graphically portray the frequent offshore winds. The small figures, rich in color and painted with broad strokes, are abstractly handled, manifesting the painting style Kleitsch adopted shortly after his European trip. In this work, he portrays a more human aspect of Old Laguna, and the uncomplicated everyday life of the village.

PLATE 205. Christopher Bliss, "Coastline Panorama," 2003. Photograph.
PLATE 206. Christopher Bliss, "El Paseo," 2003. Photograph.

PLATE 207. Joseph Kleitsch, *Laguna Coastline,* n.d. Oil on canvas, 18 x 20". Collection of Joseph Ambrose, Jr., and Michael D. Feddersen.

PLATE 208. Joseph Kleitsch, *El Paseo,* 1928–29. Oil on canvas, 30 x 40". Private Collection.

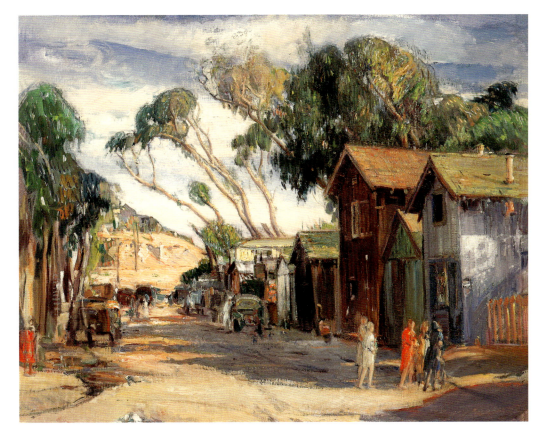

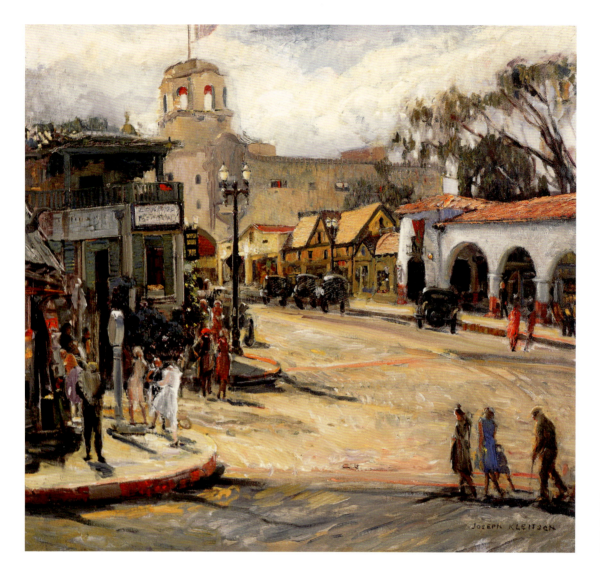

PLATE 209. Joseph Kleitsch, *Laguna Avenue and Hotel Laguna*, 1930. Oil on canvas, 36 x 40". Private Collection.

PLATE 210. Christopher Bliss, "Intersection of Forest and Park Avenues with Coast Boulevard," 2003. Photograph.

The streets, cars, and buildings of downtown Laguna held a particular fascination for Kleitsch, reflecting as they did the era he was determined to record. Several of his street scenes focused on the heavily traveled intersection of Forest and Park avenues as they merged with Coast Boulevard (PLATE 210). In the lower left quadrant of *Laguna Avenue and Hotel Laguna* (PLATE 209), the White House Café is directly behind the girl in white and to the left of the street sign. Across the street is the Isch Building, a white structure with arches that still stands. Kleitsch painted the new landmark, including the beehive of activity along its streets, shortly after the new Hotel Laguna, identifiable by its distinctive tower, opened in 1930.

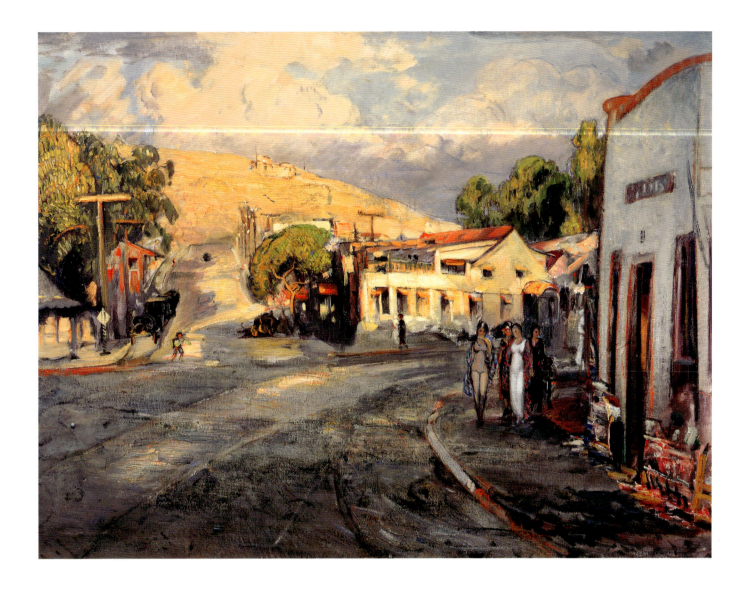

top
PLATE 211. Joseph Kleitsch, *The White House*, c. 1930. Oil on canvas, 36 x 42". City of Laguna Beach.
above
PLATE 212. Christopher Bliss, "Coast Boulevard," 2003. Photograph.

The White House of about 1930 depicts a popular local restaurant with a long, checkered past (PLATE 211; see also p. 263).[277] In painting this scene, Kleitsch set up his easel along the south side of Coast Boulevard as it curves through downtown Laguna (PLATE 212). In the picture, the restaurant is at center right, highlighted by the intense California sunlight. Mystic Hill, often seen in Kleitsch's Laguna paintings, provides the landscape's dominant background. The deep purplish-black shadows across the street contrast strongly with the sunlit yellow buildings. Foreground shadows play against the illuminated hillside with its radiant light, while the red roofs provide vivid accents of color. Abstract figures in beach apparel walk leisurely down the street toward Main Beach. In these later beach scenes, Kleitsch frequently represented bathers in a more abstract manner.

PLATE 213. "Rankin Drug Store/Pacific Coast and Forest," 1920. Photograph. First American Title Company.
PLATE 214. Christopher Bliss, "South Side of Coast Boulevard," 2003. Photograph.

From a spot on the south side of Coast Boulevard, across from the intersection of Forest and Park avenues, Kleitsch set up his easel to paint *Forest and Park Avenues* of about 1930–31 (PLATE 215; see historic photograph, PLATE 213). Focusing on Forest Avenue as it inclines, the picture follows Park Avenue as it turns to the right beyond the large tree in the middle ground. Rankin's Drugs at the far left of the composition still stands, as does the White House Café on the far right (PLATE 214). The American Catholic Cathedral on Park Avenue is identifiable by its tower and cross, visible behind the café's roofline. Mystic Hill is ablaze with color in the late afternoon sun as purple shadows complement the bright yellow sunlight. This work's greater abstraction and broader, more abbreviated brushwork indicate that Kleitsch was adopting increasingly abstract strategies just before his untimely death in November 1931.

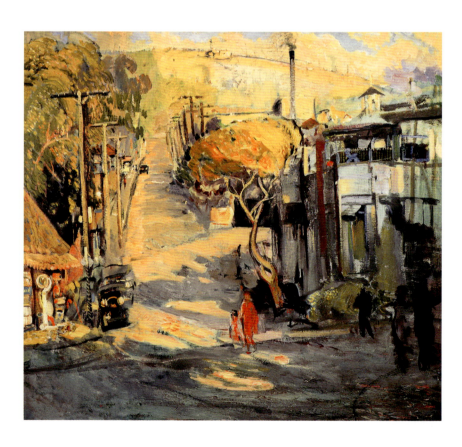

PLATE 215. Joseph Kleitsch, *Forest and Park Avenues*, c. 1930–31. Oil on canvas, 36 x 40". Private Collection.

PLATE 216. Christopher Bliss, "Looking up Laguna Avenue," 2003. Photograph.

PLATE 217. Joseph Kleitsch, *Café Las Ondas,* c. 1930. Oil on canvas, 32 x 39 ½". Private Collection, courtesy of William B. Dewey.

Café Las Ondas of about 1930 is one of Kleitsch's most captivating, ambitious compositions, with its complex choreography of figures parading and mingling along the avenue (PLATE 217). Built in Laguna Beach in the 1880s, the café was a favorite gathering place for the town's residents (see p. 263, the café in a 1950s illustration).[278] The building's façade is cast in shadow at the far left of Kleitsch's composition. Situated across from the current Hotel Laguna's dining room, the café later became Dante's Nightclub and continued to operate until the 1970s, when the old buildings on Main Beach gave way to Main Beach Park (see *El Paseo,* PLATE 208). Looking up Laguna Avenue from the old Main Beach boardwalk, Kleitsch painted a scene of everyday life in a beach city (PLATE 216, the location in a 2003 photograph). The strong sunlight reflecting off the building with blue trim marks the alignment of El Paseo—the alley between the buildings fronting on the old boardwalk (in the center, two pedestrians cross El Paseo). Old Coast Boulevard crosses the avenue in front of the three tall eucalyptus trees. Once again, Kleitsch juxtaposes the bright California light and shadows of a typical late afternoon scene with ensembles of figures in various attitudes. The abstracted, gestural figures provide the picture's movement and visual tension. Kleitsch continues his experiment with abstract strategies in this magnificent painting, but at the same time he retains solid forms and vivid, naturalistic colors. The complexity of *Café Las Ondas* sets it apart from the work of most California plein-air painters of the era, and it requires prolonged viewing to encompass the variety of beach community activities the artist has woven into his picture.

PLATE 218. Joseph Kleitsch, *Laguna on a Cloudy Day* (*Main Beach*), c. 1930. Oil on canvas, 36 x 40". Private Collection.

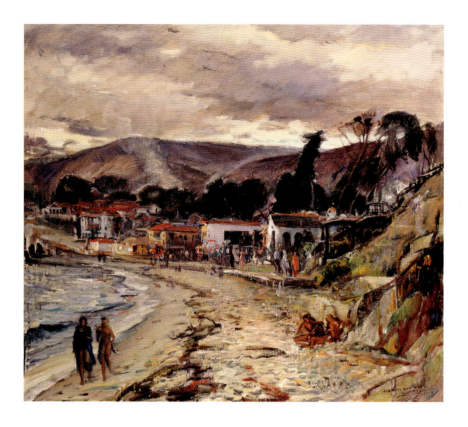

PLATE 219. "Laguna Beach," 1920s. Photograph. Laguna Art Museum Archives, Laguna Beach, California.
PLATE 220. Christopher Bliss, "Main Beach," 2003. Photograph.

In a change of subject matter, Kleitsch composed a scene at the beach on an overcast, windy day (PLATE 218 and PLATE 219, a 1920s photograph). Dark, threatening clouds and trees bent by the wind dramatize an impending rainstorm. Here again, he employs ensembles of figures participating throughout the composition, and he delineates key structures along the old Main Beach boardwalk, beginning below the white building with arched windows, the Café Las Ondas. The ochre building at center left is the Laguna bathhouse, and the three-story white building with the red tile roof and towerlike structure is an apartment building that still stands (PLATE 220).

Like East Coast Impressionists William Glackens (1870–1938) and Edward Potthast (1857–1927), Kleitsch was attracted to the liveliness of the beach scene with its throngs of bathers and sun worshippers in their motley costumes. Two late paintings of bathers, *Sunday, Laguna Beach* (*Main Beach*) of 1929 and *Ocean Front—Main Beach, Laguna* of about 1929–30 forecast a freer, more consistent, expressive approach to abstraction (PLATES 221 and 222). In *Sunday, Laguna Beach*, the abbreviated figures are summarily treated, and swirling brushwork animates the color-streaked sky, creating a sense of foreboding. To give deeper perspective to this vignette of beach life, Kleitsch steps back to a spot on South Coast Boulevard at the foot of Broadway, looking toward Main Beach boardwalk, to set up his easel. He fills his canvas with throngs of bathers, the bathhouse and old concession stand, and the lifeguard stand. To sharpen the focus, he cleverly narrows the view by using the buildings as lateral frames.

PLATE 221. Joseph Kleitsch, *Sunday, Laguna Beach,* 1929. Oil on canvas, 34 x 42". Stolen and as yet unlocated. Photograph courtesy of Redfern Gallery.

PLATE 222. Joseph Kleitsch, *Ocean Front—Main Beach, Laguna,* c. 1929–30. Oil on canvas, 36 x 40". Collection of Stephen P. Diamond, M.D.

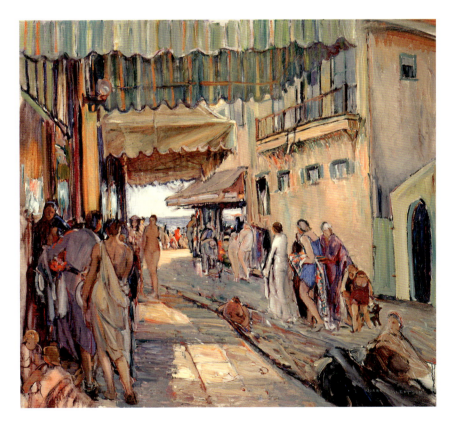

Sunday, Laguna Beach offers a more open view of the beach than *Ocean Front—Main Beach, Laguna,* which is confined to the bathhouse and adjacent human activity. To paint *Ocean Front,* Kleitsch set up his easel at the intersection of Ocean Avenue and South Coast Boulevard, looking toward Main Beach through an opening in the buildings at the foot of Ocean Avenue.[279] A historical

AN ART OF URGENCY 205

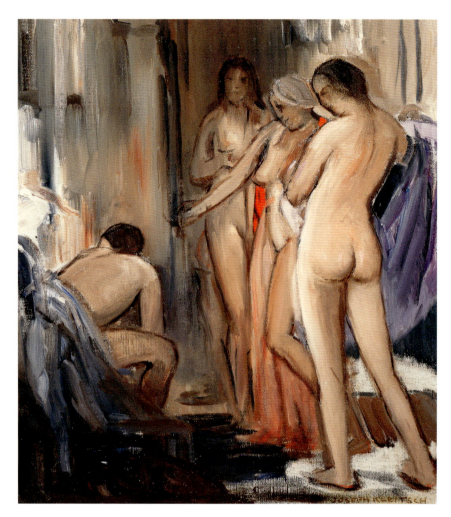

PLATE 223. "Laguna Beach Bath House," n.d. Photograph. First American Title Company.
PLATE 224. Joseph Kleitsch, *Nudes,* c. 1929–30. Oil on canvas, 20 ½ x 18". Collection of Linda and David O'Hoy.

photograph of the Laguna Beach bathhouse exterior allows us to determine how literally he represented the building (PLATE 223). On the right, adjacent to the bathhouse, is the sandy pathway to the beach, and next to it the board-and-plank sidewalk. In the painting, bathers promenade near the bathhouse with their colorful beach garb and paraphernalia, energized as they view the Pacific waters. By narrowing the pathway, Kleitsch creates a tunnel-like effect that draws the viewer's eye to the light and the blue water beyond. Moving with purpose through a bazaar-like setting, the bathers glide toward the beach and its busy concession stand. A towel-draped woman on the left in a *contrapposto* stance recalls a classical Roman figure wearing a toga.[280] Amusingly, a phantom figure seated in a car in the lower right corner reinforces the picture's diagonal forward thrust. Once again Kleitsch introduces baroque elements and compositional devices to increase the image's complexity.

In a study made during the same period, Kleitsch has humorously inserted himself in the women's bathhouse at the beach (PLATE 224). It is a rare example of the artist's sense of humor. Here, Kleitsch is clearly the center of attraction.

PLATE 225. Christopher Bliss, "Rembrandt Drive," 2003. Photograph.

In most of the Kleitsch paintings discussed here, the artist chose a recognizable location or structure, which helps us to identify the vantage point of his composition. *Scintillating* of 1930 (PLATE 226), however, has been a frustrating assignment for Eric Jessen, the author, and others who have offered suggestions and advice on identifying its location.[281] After climbing the slopes above Wendt Terrace, motoring above Summit Drive to Rembrandt Drive (PLATE 225), visiting the slopes above Catalina and Ruby Street in Woods Cove, and standing above Legion and Through streets, where the artist lived, we have finally identified the approximate location from which Kleitsch painted this view.

PLATE 226. Joseph Kleitsch, *Scintillating, California*, 1930. Oil on canvas, 36 x 40". Collection of Joseph Ambrose, Jr., and Michael D. Feddersen.

AN ART OF URGENCY

The canvas was painted at a site near the rear of the lot at 580 Park Avenue. Park Avenue is the dirt street at the lower left of the canvas. The large ochre structure on the right has now been identified as El Terrado Apartments at 487 Bent Street.[282] The tower in the distance to the left of the apartment building is the bell tower of the Laguna Presbyterian Church in downtown Laguna. Today many buildings block the view, but Kleitsch's view was unobstructed to the north coastline with its sharp curve. Cope House, with its gabled roof, is just above the spot where Park Avenue is no longer visible in the picture. One of Laguna's oldest houses, it stands proudly today at the corner of Glenneyre Street and Park Avenue. To the left of Cope House was Laguna's first church, St. Joseph's Catholic Church on Legion Street (PLATE 227). Bird Rock can be identified in the ocean waters to the left of the eucalyptus grove, which can now be seen offshore when looking directly down Park Avenue.

In the painting, the shimmering effects of late afternoon sun on the ocean offer the dazzling sight of sky meeting water. Stands of eucalyptus at the center act as a fulcrum for the other pictorial elements in Kleitsch's lyrical scene, rendered in muted, subtle colors. The artist stood at a higher elevation than the terrain he represented when he composed this picture, as the rooftops in the foreground show. The bend in the road directs the viewer's eye first to the houses on the right, then to the cluster on the left, and finally to the ocean beyond.

By 1930, it was clear that Kleitsch had redirected his efforts of the last several years toward preserving and recording the character of Old Laguna. He no longer showed an interest in painting the California missions and gardens, though he did continue to accept portrait commissions during these stressful economic times.

Even though the early Depression years of 1930–31 were becoming increasingly difficult for him financially, Kleitsch was adamant about reserving special paintings such as *Café Las Ondas, Highlights,* and *Ocean Front—Main Beach, Laguna* for the Academy of Fine Arts he hoped to open in Laguna.

Artists have always reserved paintings for themselves, whether because of a special sympathy for the subject matter, for the quality of a painting, for the development of a new direction, for use as a model for teaching, or for other, more personal reasons. But historically, artists usually sold what they painted. Kleitsch's

PLATE 227. Joseph Kleitsch, Untitled Landscape (*Laguna Coastline and Saint Joseph's Catholic Church*). Oil on canvas, 9 x 12". Private Collection, courtesy of Redfern Gallery.

insistence on keeping certain works, even in the face of grinding economic hardship, gives us insight into the obdurate, almost belligerent attitude he sometimes showed when it came to his art—and the vanishing subject matter it captured.[283]

In retrospect, the concerns of the preservation movement were largely too little, too late. Yet there have been some successes. Historical landmarks are now preserved by law, the much-maligned Coastal Commission nonetheless made a contribution, and the greenbelt that delighted Kleitsch remains.

Kleitsch would surely have been a strong supporter of the Coastal Commission, whose primary responsibility is the orderly development, preservation, and protection of California's coastline and waters.[284] Yet in the end, his instincts proved right. His depictions of a vanishing Laguna—once fiercely guarded, now scattered to collections around the world—were more successful in capturing its beauty for future generations than any preservation effort that followed.

AN ART OF URGENCY

EPILOGUE

A Tribute, 1930–1931

While the Great Depression affected all facets of the community, the indomitable spirit of the arts prevailed, although with some difficulty. Undoubtedly the climate and tranquil ambience of Old Laguna gave the village significant advantages over America's largest cities.

From 1930 until late 1931, Kleitsch continued to accept portrait commissions to relieve his financial pressures. He continued to exhibit as well. In February 1930 his work was shown at the Laguna Beach Art Gallery during the gallery's first birthday celebration.[285] In March he exhibited *Blue Thread* (see PLATE 165) at the Ebell Club in Los Angeles, and the press found it "masterly in drawing and design."[286] In April, Kleitsch showed a painting at the Catherine G. Polk Galleries in Long Beach as part of a group exhibition. That month, he worked at his Laguna Beach cottage on two important portrait commissions. One of these was of George K. Bingham, principal of the Laguna Beach grammar school, a portrait that was presented to the school by the Parent-Teacher Association at eighth-grade graduation on June 5, 1930 (PLATE 228).[287] The second portrait is unidentified and its completion unconfirmed.

Earlier that year, a few of Kleitsch's paintings were used in a statewide advertising program. The *South Coast News* reported: "Again a Laguna Beach artist has his work selected in the series of paintings used in the advertisement put out in leading magazines by the All-Year Club of Southern California." Kleitsch's *California Flowers* (also referred to as *The Flower Garden—Laguna*; see PLATE 92), the reporter wrote admiringly, has a "touch that is so characteristic of a Southern California landscape."[288]

Nor did Edna Kleitsch escape notice by the press regarding her philanthropic activity. "Mrs. Kleitsch was formerly art chairman for the Los Angeles Chamber of Commerce and Woman's Clubs and was the first to propose a series of 'art teas' for the Federation of Woman's Clubs in Los Angeles." Edna seems to have been as energetic as her spouse.[289]

On August 29, 1930, the *South Coast News* reported that Eugene Kleitsch and his mother had made a "trip from Chicago in five days, arriving . . . [in Laguna] on Wednesday, August 20." The two had left Laguna on July 6 in Edna's new Chevrolet coach and headed for Yosemite and points east. "Combining business and pleasure, Mrs. Kleitsch visited her sister and family in Chicago and then

Joseph Kleitsch, *Self-Portrait* (detail), 1909.
Oil on canvas, 54 x 38". Collection of Joseph Ambrose, Jr., and Michael D. Feddersen.

PLATE 228. Joseph Kleitsch, *Portrait of George K. Bingham*, 1930. Oil on canvas, 20 x 18". Collection of Gary Breitweiser.

anxious to get home to Laguna and Mr. Kleitsch, the two drove 500 miles a day over the 2300 mile stretch, stopping at night at hotels." For Eugene the trip was also educational, enabling him to study rock formations in Zion and Bryce canyons, "thereby satisfying his bent for geological subjects."[290]

In late fall of 1930, Kleitsch exhibited two paintings at the Laguna Art Gallery as a member of the Laguna Beach Art Association. *Miss Ketchum* (see PLATE 62) attracted the attention of a reviewer who said that he felt "a deep reverence for the painter and subject."[291] On December 12, Kleitsch's work was featured at the Stendahl Galleries under the auspices of a Laguna women's organization.

The Depression and its devastating effects on the country did not deprive Laguna's artists of a hilarious, all-out New Year's Eve bash:

> In a ballroom crowded to capacity, to the strains of Jack Gledhill's...orchestra, the artists of Laguna Beach gave...[the] most glorious party perhaps ever held within the memory of the oldest living citizen.... The walls of the Playhouse...took on a color and a quality it had never seen or even dream[ed] of. ...Thanks to Joe Kleitsch, Tom Hunt, Arthur Rider,...and others, the rather lugubrious walls of the Playhouse took on light and color and even enthusiasm.... Everything was vividness and life.... At midnight the din built up into a veritable pandemonium of noise and hilarity and Laguna took unto itself the idea of the year 1931.[292]

Three years had elapsed since Earl Stendahl had given Kleitsch a major one-person show. The exhibition in April 1931 at Stendahl Galleries led the critics to ask if the artist was now a better landscapist, portraitist, still-life, or marine artist, and whether his exquisite interiors were rivaled by his delicate depiction of atmospheric effects. Many of his patrons and loyal critics were disappointed that Kleitsch had turned his back on mission scenes and "could not be prevailed upon to paint another revered archway."[293] Sonia Wolfson wrote: "Breaking away from painting Spanish missions and flowers, Kleitsch has allowed himself to be intrigued by everything that nature can offer."[294]

On July 5 Rev. J. I. Lehane celebrated the first mass in the new St. Catherine's church on Temple Terrace in Laguna Beach. Kleitsch had promised to donate oil paintings of the fourteen Stations of the Cross and a Calvary crucifixion group, to be installed above the main altar of the new church. His untimely death precluded the completion of this major project. (There are no known sketches or studies.)[295] In late July, Kleitsch was given the opportunity to purchase the old Yoch Catholic church for his studio for $50 from Father Jeremiah Lehane. Sometime between July and September, he moved the church to his property at Legion and Through streets. The Yoch family was not pleased, because they saw it as an eyesore in the neighborhood of their company's land development. In October, Kleitsch was actively remodeling and equipping the church he had purchased as a studio and art academy. His plan was to open the Joseph Kleitsch Academy of Fine Arts, a school of higher education in art.[296]

Kleitsch's last exhibition before his death in November 1931 was held at Laguna's Community Club in August and September. A subdued critique of the exhibition by Antony Anderson appeared in the *South Coast News* on September 4, 1931, revealing a certain disappointment: "Many of Kleitsch's best pictures have been sold and the artist was unable to borrow them. However, the pictures shown are remarkably good, quite representative of Kleitsch's fine talent.... Kleitsch still remains a painter of portraits chiefly, and it is in these that his best and most individual work as an artist is to be found.... It is in these that he shows us what he can really do with his paint."

Why Kleitsch chose to exhibit a limited number of his major works is puzzling. Some of his most outstanding paintings, such as *Problematicus, The Oriental Shop, Highlights,* and *Café Las Ondas,* were still in his studio when he died. They were also among those sold at auction in 1953. Perhaps the Depression dampened his expectations of sales, and he chose not to sacrifice his important paintings, or he was keeping them in reserve for display at his studio academy.

As mentioned earlier, the stock market crash of October 1929 crippled the finances of most collectors, and Kleitsch and Stendahl experienced severe difficulties in collecting debts on paintings that had already been sold. Stendahl wrote Kleitsch on March 21, 1931: "Winston hard hit and is pitiful in spite of that he gave me a check for $100. He will also give up the painting [*Blue Thread,* 1927]

A TRIBUTE

PLATE 229. Joseph Kleitsch, *Evening (in Laguna)*, c. 1923. Oil on canvas, 16 x 20". Collection of Paul and Kathleen Bagley.

if Mr. Good will buy it for $2000—if he wants it.[297] Winston is in love with the picture still and would have paid for it long ago if he had the money. He is trying to sell an interest in his business but I don't think he will be able to sell anything right now." Not surprisingly, a rift, or at least a misunderstanding, seems to have developed between Kleitsch and Stendahl at this time. A letter to Stendahl on September 29, 1931, from D. M. Leaman, an attorney acting on the artist's behalf, supports this speculation: "Impossible to be at the opening of Stendahl's new gallery—wishes him success—business keeps him in Laguna. He desires to have all pictures and frames collected and left for him to pick up. At that time he will leave some new pictures if you care to have them. Kleitsch would like an itemized list of all sales to date and a statement."

Increasing financial pressures caused by limited sales of his work from both his European and domestic years, coupled with Kleitsch's driven personality, undoubtedly contributed to his fatal heart attack on November 16, 1931 (PLATE 229).[298]

After Kleitsch's death there was an outpouring of tributes from friends, collectors, dealers, art critics, and the news media.[299] Antony Anderson wrote of his good fortune in having known Kleitsch:

> His pictures have told us much more than the critics. These canvases told us that he was a keen and searching painter of portraits, that he rendered still-life with astonishing technical skill, that his beautiful studies of Old Laguna will be treasured by us for all time, and that his pictures from the mission church at Capistrano are among the loveliest and most subtle ever painted—for they speak of devout religious belief no less than of art's inherent rightness.... Joseph Kleitsch, artist and friend, hail and farewell! We shall miss you sorely.[300]

Another critic remarked that "to Laguna Beach 'Joe' Kleitsch was more than just one of the good painters. He was part of the old village, a part of the new city, always willing to do his share in helping the individual of the community. He was universally liked by the painters and laymen."[301] Arthur Millier, in the *Los Angeles Times* on November 22, remembered Kleitsch as "essentially a vigorous lyricist. Many of his paintings are veritable singing tapestries of color.... The qualities of sparkling color and vigor of form which characterized his painting were no more than reflections of a nature, joyous and honest, which won him a host of friends. Kleitsch combined these qualities with an independent mind and an almost naïve directness of approach to ideas and people which earned him love and respect."

A memorial exhibition of thirty paintings was held in June 1933 at Exposition Park by the Los Angeles Museum, then directed by William Alanson Bryan (PLATE 230).[302] In a *Los Angeles Times* review on June 18, 1933, Arthur Millier wrote, "Kleitsch would have nothing to do with rules. One of the most sumptuous pictures in the show, a still life called *Highlights* [see PLATE 184] was, he told me, painted after hearing a disciple of Cézanne in a Paris cafe inveigh against high lights as a form of visual superficiality which should never be reported by an artist."[303]

The International Art Exhibit of twenty-seven paintings by Kleitsch was organized by Edna Kleitsch and held at the Tower Auditorium of the Drake Hotel in Chicago February 10–24, 1934. The exhibition was extended through April, since a Memorial Concert by his friend, violinist Isador Berger, was given on April 8 with the paintings still on view.

While she was in Chicago, Edna arranged for a payment to be made on her behalf by her sister and brother-in-law, A. Paul Jones, toward a mortgage on the Laguna lot 176, a debt she had incurred on July 28, 1933. In 1934, Edna provided security for the loan with two of Kleitsch's French paintings, *Madonna and the Apples* and *Along the Seine*.[304] In March 1935, Joseph Kleitsch's estate was finally settled. To effect the closing, Edna's brother-in-law loaned her $3,000, secured by additional paintings and property.

Edna continued to live in Laguna, where she taught drawing and ceramics. For several years she was employed by the Dick Knox Ceramic Studio in Dana Point. She died in Laguna on August 4, 1950, at the age of sixty. Joseph was buried at the Angeles Abbey Memorial Park in Compton, California, and Edna was buried at the Holy Sepulcher Cemetery in Orange, California.[305] To settle Edna's estate, a public auction was held at the Kleitsch studio on Legion and Through streets on April 10 and 11, 1953. It was conducted by Oswell L. Jackson, curator of the Laguna Beach Art Gallery, who received a fee of $751.84 (15 percent). The proceeds of the sale were $5,012.25 for 124 of Kleitsch's paintings, plus books, art materials, and miscellaneous household furniture. Many of the artist's most important works were in the sale, including *Miss Ketchum, Highlights, The Oriental Shop, Café Las Ondas, The Artist's Wife*, and other paintings that had been destined for exhibition at his Academy of Art.

Kleitsch's extraordinary achievement in portraiture lies in his sensitivity to individual expression. This is especially discernible in his uncommissioned portraits, such as *The Attic Philosopher* and *Miss Ketchum*. His best portraits seem to be of sitters he knew well, whose individual visages and mannerisms were familiar to him. This acuity in representing the unique personalities of his sitters emerged again in the strong characterizations and compositions he achieved in his landscapes.

Restless in the pursuit of both his art and his life, Kleitsch frequently shifted goals and ambitions. This prevented him from fully exploiting the obvious strength of his talents. His portraits and interior scenes are masterful, and his animated California landscapes superbly convey the brilliance of the region's light and color—the elements that sparked a dramatic change in Kleitsch's art.

Another strength was Kleitsch's gestural brushstroke—the most consistent aspect of his painting. In California, as his palette lightened, his brushstroke became more vigorous, color-laden, and arbitrary, and his focus on portraiture less primary. Despite these qualities, the wealth of borrowed ideas expressed in his work gives his pictures a quality of irresolution. This sense of multiplicity and denial of resolution can also be seen in the work of today's pluralist postmodernists.

Kleitsch's independence and freedom of expression, together with his unwillingness to commit to any particular style or philosophy, led him to take his art in many directions. Revelation and discovery were part of his creative process, and he stretched his own boundaries as he paid greater attention to abstract patterning. Kleitsch followed no one. Unique among California plein-air artists in the diversity of his subjects and techniques, and in his openness to various forms of creative expression, he is an intense, vital artist whose work still holds aesthetic and historic value for us today.

PLATE 230. Joseph Kleitsch, *Green House, Laguna Beach*, 1930. Oil on canvas, 36 x 40". Private Collection.

Joseph Kleitsch, *Figure Painting*, 1923. Oil on canvas, 20 x 18". DeWitt McCall.

Joseph Kleitsch, *Portrait of Charles F. W. Nichols*. Oil on canvas, 27 x 22". DeWitt McCall.

Joseph Kleitsch, *Comrades*, c. 1928. Oil on canvas, 40 x 36". Private Collection, courtesy of Kelley Gallery.

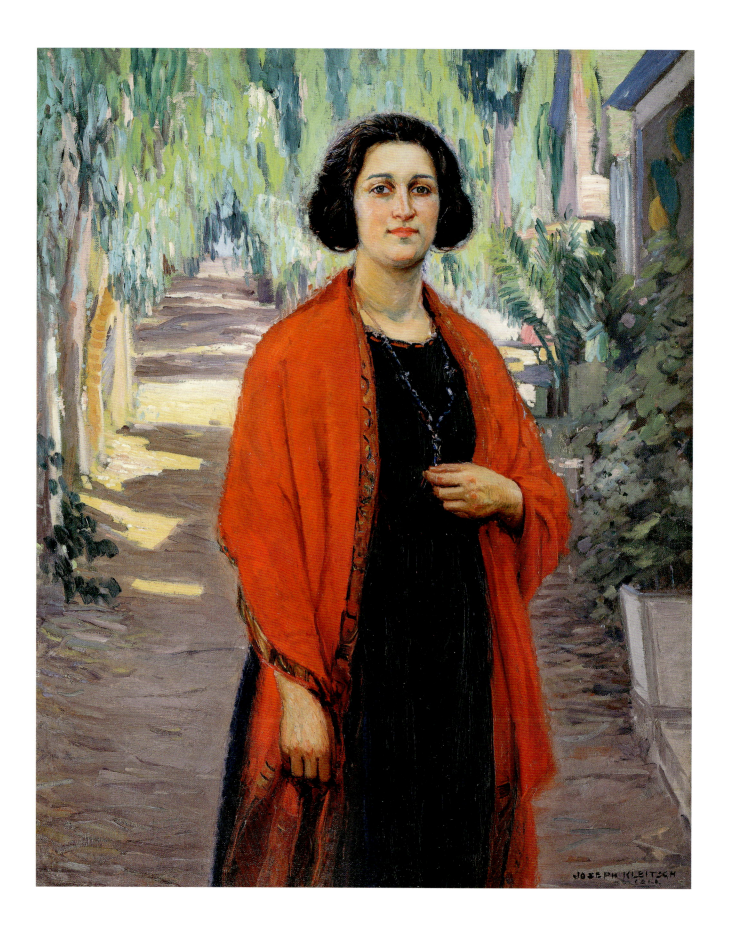

opposite
Joseph Kleitsch, *The Girl in Red*, Oil on canvas, 50 x 40".
Private Collection, courtesy of George Stern Fine Arts.

above
Joseph Kleitsch, *Children of Capistrano*, 1924. Oil on canvas,
30 x 24". Private Collection, courtesy of Redfern Gallery.

Joseph Kleitsch, *Laguna Landscape*, Oil on canvas. Private Collection.

Joseph Kleitsch, *View from the Sea*. Oil on canvas, 21 ½ x 19 ⅛".
Private Collection, courtesy of George Stern Fine Arts.

Joseph Kleitsch, *The Arch* (*Looking Toward Arch Beach*).
Oil on canvas, 18 x 19½". Estate of Pearl Martin.

Joseph Kleitsch, *Arch Beach*. Oil on canvas, 21 x 18".
Collection of Joseph Ambrose, Jr., and Michael D. Feddersen.

Joseph Kleitsch, Untitled (*Ambassador Hotel Swimming Pool*).
Oil on canvas, 24 x 24". Private Collection.

Joseph Kleitsch, *Laguna Shore Line*. Oil on canvas, 16 x 21".
Collection of Mr. and Mrs. Thomas B. Stiles II.

Joseph Kleitsch, *Laguna Beach*, 1924. Oil on canvas, 11 ¼ x 14 ¼". Collection of Ranney E. Draper.

Joseph Kleitsch, *Aliso-Laguna Overpass*. Oil on canvas, 25 x 30". Collection of Ranney Draper.

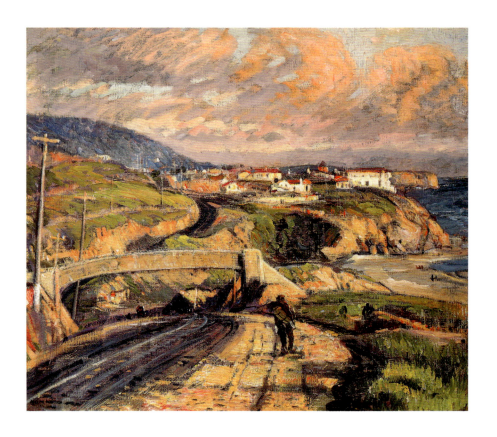

Joseph Kleitsch, *Rocky Cove, Laguna*. Oil on canvas, 21 x 22". Private Collection, courtesy of George Stern Fine Arts.

Notes

1. *Topics of the Town* (Los Angeles), April 19, 1931, Stendahl Art Galleries Records, Archives of American Art, Smithsonian Institution, Washington, D.C. Sonia Wolfson was a freelance writer who worked as a publicist at the Stendahl Galleries for several years in the early 1930s. Her first article on Kleitsch, in *California Graphic*, February 7, 1925, discussed his California mission paintings.

2. Information on Kleitsch's ancestors was provided by his second cousin Robert Kleitsch and Mrs. Lubomir Hykel. See also Steven Béla Várdy, *History of the Hungarian Nation* (Astor Park, Fla.: Danubian Press, 1969), 85–93.

3. The author appreciates the assistance of Father Robert V. Biroschak, J.C.L., J.D., Adjutant Judicial Vicar of the Archdiocese of Los Angeles, in contacting the Diocese of Timișoara, Romania, in an effort to secure Kleitsch's birth certificate. Unfortunately, baptismal records in that region were destroyed in 1896. Biographical information on Kleitsch comes from his petition for naturalization, #11831, signed January 30, 1924, Los Angeles, U.S. Court, Southern District Court, Southern District of California, and from his passport application, signed January 18, 1926, New York City, courtesy of F. J. Carmona, acting chief, Research and Liaison Branch, Office of Program Support, Passport Services, U.S. Department of State, Washington, D.C. The naturalization petition also indicates that Kleitsch had brown eyes and hair and a fair complexion, was 5'8" tall, and weighed 165 pounds. The author wishes to express her appreciation to researchers Phil and Marian Kovinick, who assisted in obtaining these documents in 1987. Published and unpublished biographical materials on the artist usually give his birth date as 1885, 1886, or 1887, and his birthplace as Banad. Kleitsch tended to give the press biographical information that presented him as being younger than he actually was. My conjecture is that because he was eight years older than his second wife, Edna, he was eager to project a virile, youthful image. On Kleitsch's death certificate, Edna gave his age as forty-six and his birth date as 1886, probably in keeping with his wishes to present himself as younger than his true age. David O'Hoy, Laguna Beach art dealer, discovered on Kleitsch's coffin plaque the true date of his birth, which suggests that Edna was aware that his birth date was 1882. Kleitsch had a limited command of English and probably misspelled the region (or province) of his birthplace, Bánát. None of his accounts includes the village in Bánát where he was born. Indeed, Kleitsch embroidered his background considerably.

4. Bánát lies near three rivers: the Danube to the south, the Maros (called Mureș in Romanian) to the north, and the Tisza (or Tisa) to the west; the Retyezat mountains to the east occupy one-third of the region, while the western two-thirds comprises fertile plains. Geographical and historical information on Temesvár and the Bánát region were provided by Athos Thiery, who was born in the same region as Kleitsch.

5. Theresa (Kleitsch) Haynel to her nephew William Kleitsch, undated (before 1984). Theresa Haynel (d. 1984) also provided a family tree for her nephew. Most of her information on Joseph Kleitsch and his ancestry is correct, except for the artist's birth date, which she gives as 1881. The author is indebted to Mrs. William (Marjorie) Kleitsch for sharing this letter.

Müller, "Joseph Kleitsch and Family," Timișoara, Hungary, c. 1886. (Joseph Kleitsch is the young boy holding a kaleidoscope.) Photograph. Hadley Marie Nagel.

6. The late Anthony Kastner, a distant cousin of the artist, to Trenton.

7. Athos Thiery to Trenton, September 29, 1989.

8. Kleitsch is not listed on the student roster of the Royal Munich Academy for 1900, 1901, or 1902. Academy records are incomplete, however, as some of them were destroyed during World War II (Dr. Cornelia Erdl, Akademie der Bildenden Künste, Munich, to Trenton, June 7, 1989).

9. Working from photographs for commissioned portraits was a popular Victorian practice in Europe and America.

10. Anthony Kastner to Trenton. Kastner stated that Kleitsch not only visited Munich but also Vienna and Paris before his departure for America. There is, however, no other evidence to support this statement.

11. According to Theresa Haynel, Kleitsch was seventeen when he painted a religious picture for his "Beppi Tante" (Aunt Barbara) to hang in the Szilas Catholic church (Német Szent Mihály was called Szilas by the local inhabitants). The painting, *Flight into Egypt*, was obviously copied from an engraving. A plaque under the picture was inscribed "Gift of Barbara Kleitsch (Beppi Tante)." Photographer Maksay Ádám reports that "the village is populated with Gypsy people and no Germans reside there today (2002). The church was devastated several times in the past by the present local people [see pp. 45 and 257]. However, the clergy removed a number of artifacts [presumably for safekeeping,] but Kleitsch's painting is unlocated at the present time."

12. The author is extremely indebted to Katherine Vollen, archives specialist, National Archives and Records Administration, Washington, D.C., who willingly and patiently searched for Kleitsch's immigration record and located the ship's manifest for the author.

13. Letter to Trenton from Walter Nugent, Andrew V. Tackes Professor Emeritus of History, University of Notre Dame, an authority on immigration.

14. "From its earliest development, Over-the-Rhine has served as a port-of-entry for [successive waves of German] immigrants to Cincinnati. In the nineteenth century the community was home to people of all economic classes and included the poorest of immigrants, working class families, shop owners, and businessmen of means. For a majority of these new residents, the unifying element was the German language and culture" (excerpt from Daniel W. Young, *Over-the-Rhine: A Description and History* [Historic Conservation Office, Cincinnati City Planning Department, 1995], http://www.irhine.com/index.jsp?page=history_history).

15. Kleitsch's destination appears on the immigration manifest. For details about Kleitsch's Over-the-Rhine residence and a general social and cultural history of the district, I owe a debt of gratitude to Prof. Robert J. Wimberg of Wilmington College, Cincinnati. The remarks on Cincinnati's Over-the-Rhine are based primarily on information he has gathered from many different archival sources. The photographs for this part of chapter two are by Prof. Wimberg.

16. An inscription on the back of a 1910 photograph of Kleitsch and his cousins in Cincinnati refers to Duveneck as Kleitsch's teacher. However, there is no other evidence to support this reference.

17. Emma's burial certificate No. 83778, August 11, 1913, Spring Grove Cemetery, Cincinnati, Ohio, authorized by her brother William Multner, cites her age as "56 yrs." This information was obtained from Spring Grove Cemetery.

18. See William H. Gerdts, "Making Arrangements: California Still Life Painting at the Time of the Impressionists," *The Not-So-Still Life: A Century of California Painting and Sculpture* (Berkeley and Los Angeles: University of California Press in association with the San Jose Museum of Art, 2003).

19. Marriage Record Report, State of Colorado, Division of Vital Statistics, No. 34530. Alan Frazer and Jourdan Houston, ardent researchers of Colorado art, were most generous in obtaining this record for the author. Before that time, it was unknown whether Joseph and Emma actually married.

20. The author expresses her gratitude to Rebecca Lintz, director of the Colorado Historical Society Library, who diligently searched the library's archival material for information on Kleitsch during his stay in Denver. The city directories reveal the following information: In 1905, Kleitsch and his wife occupied rooms at 2263 Stout; in 1906, Kleitsch's studio was listed at 509 Charles Building (at Fifteenth and the southwest corner of Curtis Street) and his residence was at 818 12th Street; in 1907, his business and residence were at 818 12th Street. These addresses indicate that his residences and studios were in downtown Denver.

21. The late Robert Kleitsch to Trenton, August 28, 1989. Robert Kleitsch's father, Joseph's first cousin William, was given a landscape (now the property of one of Robert's sons) executed by the artist during the time he was painting landscapes for the Union Pacific Railway. Unfortunately, the Union Pacific's archival records of advertising material are incomplete and for the most part uncatalogued, so this association cannot be verified (Jennifer Cook, collection manager, Union Pacific Historical Collection, Omaha, Neb., to Trenton). The author also contacted Kenton Forrest, archivist, Colorado Railroad Museum, in Golden, Colo., but he and his staff found nothing that linked Kleitsch to the Union Pacific Railway.

22. In 1917 the Artists' Club was incorporated into the Denver Art Association, which in 1923 became the Denver Art Museum.

23. During Mannheim's residence in Denver, he conducted an art school at the Women's Club and painted portraits of Dr. Wooding, Gov. Henry Buchtel, Sherman Saunders, Andrew Weingartner, and many other local people. His studio was at 14 W. 14th Avenue. Mannheim was born in Bad Kreuznach, Germany, in 1862 (Colorado Historical Society ephemera).

24. The *Denver Post* and the *Rocky Mountain News* from the years 1904–7 make no mention of Kleitsch and offer very few reports of art activity in Denver.

25. "A biographical sketch on Louis D. Riethmann indicates he was a prominent Denver merchant. He continued in the same line of business ('grocer and oyster depot') until the late 1880s. His name continued to appear thereafter in the Denver directories, with no occupation given, until at least 1911" (courtesy of Marian and Phil Kovinick, researchers, October 17, 1989). The obvious contact for this portrait commission was Emma's brother William Multner, who was a prominent grocer in Cincinnati.

26. In 1925 or 1927, Kleitsch furnished personal data for an artist's biographical form now in the archives of the Art Institute of Chicago, including mention of painting a portrait of "Senetor [*sic*] George J. Kendal of Denver" (courtesy of M. Sheryl Bailey of the Art Institute of Chicago). A George J. Kindel is listed in Percy Stanley Fritz's *Colorado: The Centennial State*, in the appendix listing of Colorado government officials (New York: Prentice-Hall, 1941), 495. Kindel served in the U.S. House of Representatives from 1913 to 1915. In 1987 an archivist of the Colorado Archives in Denver informed researcher Phil Kovinick that neither a Kendal nor a Kindel served as Senator of Colorado between 1880 and 1925. The artist probably confused the two branches of legislature.

27. Taped Recorded Interview with Conrad Buff/May 21, 1965/Interviewer Betty Hoag, pt. 2, Archives of American Art. I am most grateful to Marian Kovinick of the Archives of American Art for bringing this interview to my attention. Conrad Buff arrived in America in 1905, and on his way to California stopped off in Cheyenne, Wyo., and Denver, Colo. Disillusioned at not finding any work in his field, he continued to Los Angeles, settling there in 1907. For a biography of Buff, see Will South, "A Singular Vision," *The Art and Life of Conrad Buff* (West Hollywood, Calif.: George Stern Fine Arts, 2000).

28. The untitled still life reproduced here harkens back to his European background.

29. For further information on the Peale family, see William H. Gerdts, *Painters of the Humble Truth: Masterpieces of American Still Life 1801–1939* (Columbia, Mo., and London: University of Missouri Press with Philbrook Art Center, 1981).

30. A smaller (7 1/2 x 15 1/2") but similar still life arrangement of apples and oranges, one of them partially peeled, dated between 1905 and 1907, surfaced recently; a label on the reverse notes that it was sold through the Bowman Art Company at 526 Sixteenth Street in downtown Denver, Colo., near the artist's studio. According to the estate sale literature, the original owner was involved in a mining business in Colorado, and the family was quite prominent and wealthy (James Taylor to Trenton, December 1, 2005).

31. William Baker's papers were left to his sister and inherited by his nephew Jonathan Nardone of West Islip, N.Y. In 1903, Baker enrolled in a penmanship course at Western Art Company on Lincoln Avenue in Denver. The following year he attended Hausman's class in penmanship in Hutchinson, Kan., but returned to Denver before completing the course. A letter from L. H. Hausman to Baker, dated October 6, 1906, urges him to come back to finish the course (Baker/Nardone Collection); hence, the impetus for Baker's return to Hutchinson. He and Kleitsch undoubtedly met on the train to Denver in 1904, and they became the closest of friends (Nardone to Trenton, August 5, 1989).

32. Information from William Baker's papers. Kleitsch's first visit to Mexico City in 1907–9 is documented in these papers. Rudesill had studied at the Oberlin Conservatory of Music in Ohio. In 1890, he moved to Hutchinson with his parents and had a successful professional career as a music teacher there.

33. Baker/Nardone Collection.

34. Kleitsch presumably gave Baker the paintings and drawings, since the five works ended up in the Baker/Nardone Collection along with the photographs of Kleitsch that Baker took in Mexico City.

35. Nine art historians in Mexico were contacted to check archival records as to whether Kleitsch enrolled in the Academy of Art or in a local professional art school. Since the author failed to receive answers from these scholars and institutions, it seems that the answer is negative, as his biographical sketch in the Art Institute of Chicago archives also suggests. Nor did any of the scholars know of a medal that Kleitsch claimed he had received in one of the exhibitions of the Mexican Art Associates. Hence, the Baker papers and paintings are the only sources of information about his first trip to Mexico. Recently, another self-portrait painted in Mexico surfaced, a torso that shares a strong likeness to the full-length image of 1909.

36. Edward Maeder, chair, Curatorial Department, and curator of textiles, Historic Deerfield, Inc., to Trenton, May 13, 2002. Maeder is a specialist in men's historical clothing, and I am most grateful to him for sharing his expertise.

37. Steven Platzman, *Cézanne: The Self-Portraits* (Berkeley and Los Angeles: University of California Press, 2002), 7, 13.

38. *Los Angeles Times*, May 13, 1928.

39. Information given to the census-taker contains certain inaccuracies—in particular, the age of Kleitsch's wife. Emma is listed as "30 years old," but according to her 1913 death certificate, validated by her brother, she died at the age of fifty-six. Thus she was twenty-five years Kleitsch's senior and probably preferred not to have this fact officially recorded.

40. I am most grateful to Robert Kleitsch's son David for his support and interest in the Joseph Kleitsch Project.

41. John George Brown's paintings of urchins were illustrated in books and translated into chromolithographs. Kleitsch was probably aware of them via this medium.

42. Susan Kistler, an authority on historical costume for the film industry, provided the expertise for the boys' dress. I thank Michael Kelley for the referral to Susan.

43. Another 1910 photograph of Kleitsch and his Cincinnati relatives, Joseph Vollmer, William Kleitsch, and Philip Vollmer, was brought to my attention by Jon Nagel, a grandson of Philip Vollmer. While in Cincinnati, Kleitsch painted a portrait of Philip Vollmer (32 x 25"); the current owner is Hadley Marie Nagel. Kleitsch may have painted the portrait of William Kleitsch then or later in Chicago in 1915; the current owners are Joseph Ambrose, Jr., and Michael D. Feddersen. The 1910 photograph assisted with the identification of this unknown male portrait; the names of the sitters were inscribed on the back, along with a notation that Kleitsch had been a student of Cincinnati artist Frank Duveneck. To date there is no other evidence to support the assertion that Kleitsch studied with Duveneck.

44. Robert Kleitsch to Trenton, August 28, 1989. The connection with Schwab cannot be validated by other sources familiar with the steel magnate's life.

45. Kleitsch to Baker, Mexico City, [1912]. The letter on YMCA stationery verifies Kleitsch's residency. For information on the YMCA, see William Schell, Jr., *Integral Outsiders: The American Colony in Mexico City 1876–1911* (Wilmington, Del.: Scholarly Resources Inc. Imprints, 2001), 67–68.

46. On the manifest of the SS *Monterey*, sailing from Mexico to New York, Kleitsch lists Babcock as his friend in Mexico City.

47. Schell, *Integral Outsiders*, x.

48. Professor James Oles, Wellesley College, to Trenton, January 31, 2003.

49. Many years later, when the artist exhibited *Gypsy*, he related a story about the background of this painting to *Los Angeles Times* art critic Antony Anderson, who wrote: "It embodies an ideal held by the artist since his early childhood when he was a small boy in Hungary he and a little gypsy girl were the prize pupils in drawing, and he rather thinks the gypsy was ahead of him. She belonged to a tribe who were permitted to remain in the neighborhood because they were so peaceful and law-abiding. Joseph moved away, and when years later he saw a handsome young gypsy girl of twenty-five in Mexico City, she seemed to be the very girl he had known so long ago—and so he painted her" (June 17, 1923).

50. Art critic Fred Hogue's review of Kleitsch's European work, in the *Los Angeles Times*, May 1928.

51. In 1922 the critic Vandyke Brown related a story that Joseph Kleitsch had told him: "It seems that a few years ago . . . [Kleitsch] found himself across the border, and of course did gamble at poker, the place being Tia Juana [*sic*]. And he did lose to the tune of some hundred and fifty plunks in good American gold. And he waxed wroth with Dame Fortune, and did shake his fist in her face (a proceeding so like him,) and did cry out, 'Aha, my fickle jade, I'll get even with you yet!' So he sat him down and did paint a picture four feet square of that table and those cards and them chips. And he sallied forth into the market place of the darksome Mexicanos and sold that masterpiece for the tidy sum of three hundred plunks. Returning to the abode of Dame Fortune, he rattled the many pieces of gold in his hat under her very nose, and she hung her head, utterly confounded. For this was her first experience with a man hailing from the lost tribes of Bohemia. Rumor hath it that she has fought shy of these resourceful people ever since that memorable day when Joseph Kleitsch turned the card table on her so neatly" (*Life and Art*, July 28, 1922).

52. Quoted from Laura Caldwell, "Francisco I. Madero (1873–1913)," The Handbook of Texas Online, Texas State Historical Association, http://www.tsha.utexas.edu/handbook/online/articles/MM/fmaad.html.

53. Neither the commissioned portraits nor the gold medal have been located. On Kleitsch's biographical form for the Art Institute of Chicago, he listed paintings of Madero and his wife. Some newspaper accounts and the *Fine Arts Journal* (Chicago) of June 1919 mention only Kleitsch's portrait of Señora Madero.

54. Kleitsch to Baker, [1912].

55. A postcard addressed to Baker from Kleitsch in Mexico City mentions the artist's departure date from Veracruz to New York City and asks that Baker wait for him in New York. On the front of the card is a photograph of the steamer (formerly in the Baker/Nardone Collection). An auction of the closing of Bryden Art Galleries in Chicago on May 26, 27, and 28, 1924, lists a painting by "Josef Kleitsch" titled *Pallisades—Mexico* (50 x 72"), suggesting that the artist may have sketched the terrain while waiting for the ship in Veracruz. Unfortunately, the painting has not been located. (Pamphlet, Archives of American Art, roll D157; the author is grateful to Phil Kovinick, who brought it to her attention.)

56. The ship's manifest documents his destination as Philadelphia, where he was to meet his sisters.

57. Information obtained from Kleitsch's biographical form at the Art Institute of Chicago, and a letter written to his dealer Earl Stendahl by Kleitsch's second wife, Edna, February 14, 1926, Herald Square Hotel, New York City, Stendahl Art Galleries Records, roll 2720.

58. Quoted from Esther Sparks, "A Bibliographical Dictionary of Painters and Sculptors in Illinois, 1808–1945," 3 vols. (PhD diss., Northwestern University, 1971), 1:99. This history of Chicago's art activities is from the same source. Sue Ann Prince, ed., in *The Old Guard and the Avant-Garde: Modernism in Chicago, 1910–1940* (Washington, D.C., and Chicago: Archives of American Art, Smithsonian Institution, in association with the University of Chicago Press, 1990), xxii, writes about Chicago as a stronghold of traditionalism through the 1920s and about the ensuing struggles between traditional factions and the avant-garde. She adds, "As for local manifestations of modernism, no one particular style took root until after World War II."

59. *Fine Arts Journal* (Chicago), 26, no.1 (January 1912): 25–43. Information on art activities in Chicago in the early twentieth century is from James William Pattison's review of the Annual Exhibition of American Art at the Art Institute of Chicago.

60. Pattison gives a most favorable review of Betts' work, describing his new painterly technique in glowing terms. Ibid., 26.

61. The author is indebted to former school archivist Mary McIsaac, who kindly shared information regarding Kleitsch's enrollment at the School of the Art Institute of Chicago. No further information exists pertaining to Kleitsch's studies, as scant records were maintained for part-time students.

62. Chicago Board of Education's Employment Record Department.

63. On Emma's death certificate, Kleitsch misrepresented her age as thirty instead of fifty-six. Emma's funeral service and burial in Spring Grove Cemetery were arranged by her brother William Multner, who gave a brief obituary to the Cincinnati paper. Strangely, the only family grave without a tombstone is Emma's.

64. Kleitsch's election as an active member of the club is in the minutes of the regular meeting of December 4, 1913. The author very much appreciates the assistance provided by Palette and Chisel Club historian Frank Hensley, who checked the club's minutes for Kleitsch's admission.

65. Paraphrased from Marianne Richter, "The History of the Palette and Chisel Academy of Fine Arts," November 26, 2001 (the current name of the club). The author is most grateful to Marianne for allowing her to use material from this unpublished paper.

66. The author is indebted to Diana Haskell, Lloyd Lewis Curator of Midwest Manuscripts, Newberry Library, Chicago, for her contribution regarding Kleitsch's involvement with the Palette and Chisel Club of Chicago. Ms. Haskell searched the club's logbooks from 1909 to 1920 deposited at the library as well as all other available resources for information on the artist and constructed a brief history of the club's early years from newspaper articles of the period. Only a small portion of the club's archives are now at the Newberry.

67. Wendy Greenhouse, "Midwestern Art Organizations," *Mathias J. Alten: Journey of an American Painter* (Grand Rapids, Mich.: Grand Rapids Art Museum, 1998), 94. The author received this book courtesy of James A. Straub, one of its contributors.

68. Richter, "History of the Palette and Chisel Academy of Fine Arts," 10.

69. The spelling of Edna's maiden name varies. The alleged date and place of her birth are from her death certificate, and the date of Eugene's birth is from Joseph Kleitsch's naturalization petition, courtesy of researchers Marian and Phil Kovinick, 1987. At the author's suggestion, David O'Hoy checked the grave marker where Edna is buried and found the date of birth listed as "1888." Since Edna's mother did not arrive in America until 1892, we can assume that Edna was born in Lithuania (1910 census record provided by Janet Murphy). In 2004, Janet Murphy received a copy of Edna Gregaitis Kleitsch's Petition for Naturalization as well as the Confirmation of her Naturalization, or U.S. Citizenship, dated "February 20, 1925." These papers document that Edna was born in Lithuania, and the tombstone with 1888 confirms her year of birth.

70. Information provided by the School of the Art Institute of Chicago's former archivist Mary McIsaac.

71. Lena M. McCauley, *Chicago Evening Post*, February 7, 1914.

72. The owner, a niece of Kleitsch's living in Canada and in ill health, is unwilling to provide a photograph.

73. *Examiner*, April 22, 1915, in the Logbook, vol. 2, 1906 to 1915.

74. *The Cow Bell*, May 1, 1915, vol. 4, no. 5, courtesy of Frank Hensley, Palette and Chisel Club historian. The author is indebted to Mr. Hensley for all his research on Kleitsch's involvement with the club.

75. In John Singer Sargent's portrait of the French artist-teacher Carolus Duran, the subject sports a Légion d'Honneur pin on his lapel quite similar to the one worn by Kleitsch in his self-portrait. Costume historian Edward Maeder, curatorial chair of Historic Deerfield, Inc., writes that "today members of the Legion of Honor, in France, receive the medal and several tiny ribbon rosettes to wear on their lapel. They are usually in the form of a small cylinder, about 3/8th inch in diameter and 1/8th inch high" (letter to Trenton, May 13, 2002). Maeder also writes: "During these [pre-WWI] somewhat crazy years with their rowdy avant-gardes and scandalous 'isms,' certain artists were not content to simply contribute a personal touch (however strong) to the new dress code. Aspiring to more radical change, such artists invented utopian garb. On May 20, 1914, the Italian painter Giacomo Balla signed the first manifesto to futurist men's fashion and declared war on the old criteria of stylishness. . . . Instead, fashion involved sartorial montage, mobile volumes of material, and kaleidoscope, shimmering, ever-changing wheels of color—a dynamic street aesthetics for crowds in modern cities."

76. Susan Grace Galassi, "Whistler, Women, and Fashion," *American Art Review* 15, no. 3 (2003): 96.

77. According to David O'Hoy, a dealer in Laguna Beach, Kleitsch's painting was destroyed.

78. *The Cow Bell*, June 1, 1915, vol. 4, no. 6.

79. Richter, "History of the Palette and Chisel Academy of Fine Arts," 12.

80. Evelyn Marie Stuart, "Annual Exhibition, Palette and Chisel Club," *Fine Arts Journal* (Chicago) 36, no. 4 (April 1918): 6–7.

81. *Miss Irene Petrtyl* was exhibited in the Art Institute's Nineteenth Annual Exhibition of Works by Chicago Artists, no. 158, in March 1915.

82. Costume and hairstyle details were provided by Chief Curator Edward Maeder of Historic Deerfield, Inc., and costume historian Susan Kistler. Both gave freely of their expertise and research to help date the painting. The author is most grateful to both of them.

83. The owner of the painting remarks that the flag on the boat is Hungarian. Perhaps this may reveal the motive for Kleitsch's subject matter.

84. *The Cow Bell*, August 4, 1915.

85. Adapted from Richter, "History of the Palette and Chisel Academy of Fine Arts," 16.

86. *The Cow Bell*, October 1915. Timmins was editor of *The Cow Bell*.

87. Recently conserved by inpainting and relining, the work is in a private collection.

88. The National Association of Portrait Painters exhibition at the Reinhardt Galleries in Chicago. This tradition actually began in the Renaissance; for example, see Titian's *Man with a Glove* (c. 1520).

89. There are two versions of this portrait. The original is larger, and was exhibited in the Twenty-Third Annual Exhibition by Artists of Chicago & Vicinity at the Art Institute in March 1919. The second version (see p. 218) is in a California collection. The original, the commissioned portrait, may still be with the Nichols heirs.

90. *Los Angeles Times*, June 17, 1923.

91. See M. K. Wisehart, "'Try Giving It Up' says Wayman Adams," *American Magazine* 106 (October 1928): 26.

92. Pension records from the musician's union in Chicago verify Berger's position with the Philharmonic Orchestra. Miami newspapers and Berger's obituary and death certificate provided material for his biography. The author wishes to thank S. J. Boldrick, Florida Collection, Miami-Dade Public Library System, Miami-Dade Cultural Center, Miami, Fla., for his contribution to the research on Berger. The author also acknowledges the help of Nick Menéndez at Woodlawn Park Cemetery.

93. In the Christie's sale of Highly Important Italian Violins, Fine Watches, also Objects of Vertu, November 21, 1961, Berger sold three Stradivarius violins.

94. *Fine Arts Journal* (Chicago) 36, no. 4 (April 1918): 6.

95. Berger reproduced this painting on the cover of a concert flyer that read: "Traveling Culture: Circuit Chautauqua in the Twentieth Century."

96. Kleitsch's self-portrait, no. 127, was exhibited in the Twenty-Ninth Annual Exhibition of Water Colors, Pastels and Miniatures by American Artists at the Art Institute in May and June 1917.

97. Kleitsch's German heritage was verified by Mrs. Lubomir Hykel, whose mother was Theresa Haynel's sister-in-law.

98. Arthur K. Wheelock, Jr., *Jan Vermeer* (New York: Harry N. Abrams, 1981), 78.

99. *Ambition* (*Natsi*) and *Studio Interior* are also from this series. *Ambition* is known only from a reproduction and a description given by a reviewer for the *Fine Arts Journal* of April 1917: "Joseph Kleitsch in his 'Natsi,' suggested tantalizingly a story. Why do we feel that this sturdy little boy, so much engrossed in his palette and brushes, is a painter's boy? The sun, falling directly on the canvas on which he is working, would seem to indicate that the little fellow has set up his easel outside a regular studio and the earnestness of his young face makes one feel that this was not a posed picture, but a snapshot of 'young ambition' in an unconscious moment. Someway it seems to epitomise a thousand tales, historic and otherwise, of the poor boy who began at the bottom and climbed to the top" (*Fine Arts Journal* [Chicago] 36, pt. 1 [April 1917]: 277. The identity of the sitter is unknown, but the name "Natsi" is similar to Kleitsch's youngest brother's nickname "Matzi," for Matthew.

100. *In My Studio*, *Natsi*, and *Von M.* were exhibited in the Twenty-First Annual Exhibition of Artists of Chicago and Vicinity at the Art Institute in February and March 1917. *In My Studio* was awarded the grand prize for a figural painting at the Laguna Beach Art Association exhibition in 1923 and was exhibited at the Pennsylvania Academy of the Fine Arts in 1925. It was frequently praised by art critics of Southern California newspapers.

101. *Los Angeles Times*, June 20, 1926.

102. Lena M. McCauley, *Chicago Evening Post*, February 19, 1918. Edward Maeder writes about the costume in *Problematicus:* "It appears to be a typical dress of the period, which probably has an over-panel of embroidery that falls from the shoulders, is held in place at the waist (both front and back). The apparently transparent over-sleeves are typical of the period. One of the most interesting aspects is her hair. It is *totally* Greek! in its inspiration with the swept-back look and the modified, almost 'bun-like' knot at the back. One finds it in photographs, graphics, advertisements . . . in fact, everywhere! The tip of her shoe that protrudes looks to be a similar color to the under-sleeves. The shoe is most likely satin but metalicized leather shoes were also popular at this time. It was a revival from the 1870s" (Historic Deerfield, January 3, 2005). Once again, I am most appreciative of Maeder for sharing his expertise.

103. See "Impressions of Fall Exhibit at the Laguna Art Gallery," *South Coast News* (Laguna Beach), October 10, 1930.

104. Miss Ketchum's costume, described by textile and costume historian Edward Maeder in 1987.

105. William Pattison, "The Art of Joseph Kleitsch," *Fine Arts Journal* (Chicago) 37 (June 1919): 47–53.

106. Ibid., 47.

107. Ibid., 49.

108. The author is again grateful to Edward Maeder for his expertise on Edna's costume.

109. Interview with Michael Kelley of Kelley Gallery. The author thanks Michael for sharing this interview.

110. Trevor J. Fairbrother, *John Singer Sargent* (New York and Washington, D.C.: Harry N. Abrams in association with the National Museum of American Art, Smithsonian Institution, 1994), 57.

111. The second version is illustrated in Pattison, "The Art of Joseph Kleitsch," 48; the first is illustrated in the *Chicago Evening Post*, February 18, 1919. "The Charles F. W. Nichols Company was the second advertising agency that Kimberly-Clark hired to sell its new product they called *Cellucotton,* in 1914. After the war (1919), the company began to market the product as disposable sanitary napkins. The resulting product was first marketed as *Cellunap.* Immediately upon hire, Kimberly-Clark's first marketing agency (Charles F. W. Nichols Company) suggested changing the name to *Kotex* (short for 'cotton textile')." (Information courtesy of Janet Murphy, who researched the sitter's biography.) Kleitsch was probably commissioned by Charles F. W. Nichols to paint his portrait, which the artist exhibited in the Chicago and Vicinity show at the Art Institute in 1919. Why Kleitsch painted the second version is a mystery.

112. *Chicago Evening Post*, November 6, 1917.

113. The author is indebted to the Kovinicks for their efforts to obtain these papers.

114. Francis V. O'Connor, "The Psychodynamics of the Frontal Self-Portrait," in Mary Mathews Gedo, ed., *Psychoanalytic Perspectives on Art* (Hillsdale, N.J.: Analytic Press, 1985), 169–221.

115. The *Chicago Evening Post,* January 18, 1920, reports that Kleitsch "left for California a week ago" (January 11, 1920). That report conflicts with the date of "January 3" on Kleitsch's 1924 petition, which may mean that by 1924 he had forgotten the exact date of his arrival in California.

116. The question was raised by Anderson in the *Los Angeles Times*, June 23, 1922.

117. The commission is mentioned in Kleitsch's obituary. Kleitsch probably knew Simon William Straus, president of S. W. Straus, a powerful bonding house in New York and Chicago, and president of Franklin Trust and Savings Bank in Chicago (see *Who's Who in New York*, 1918).

118. Carey McWilliams, *The Education of Carey McWilliams* (New York: Simon and Schuster, 1979), 42.

119. Ibid.

120. *Chicago Evening Post*, January 18, 1920.

121. *Santa Ana Daily Evening Register*, February 4, 1920. The 1920 census records the Kleitsches' rental of a house in Aliso Canyon.

122. The name Ambassador was chosen because of Straus's ownership of the Ambassador Hotel Corporation in Chicago and New York. The Ambassador Hotel opened on January 1, 1921. See Margaret Tante Burk, *Are the Stars Out Tonight? The Story of the Famous Ambassador and Cocoanut Grove* (Los Angeles: Round Table West, 1980), 31.

123. *Santa Ana Daily Evening Register*, March 13, 1920.

124. The author expresses her gratitude to Janet Murphy for her research assistance in the identification of the Straus family. Madeline was married to Robert Martin, president of the Ambassador Hotel Corporation, and the couple had three sons. Her husband died in January 1930. Madeline later married Dr. Richard H. Hoffmann, a psychiatrist in New York City, and she lived there until her death in December 1974. The Straus family had a second residence in Beverly Hills, California. Harriet, the youngest sister, married Vladimir de Rachevsky, and lived in California until her death in May 1993. Louise Celestin, the middle daughter, lived in New York City.

125. Information on Madeline's costume from Edward Maeder and Susan Kistler. Elizabeth Bingham, in "Art Exhibits and Comment," *Saturday Night*, July 29, 1922, remarks that Kleitsch came to California to "paint the daughter of S. C. Strauss [sic] of the Ambassador Hotel." The portrait, however, was not included in the Stendahl show that Bingham reviewed.

126. Edee-Lou Frazee was born in 1904 and died in Pasadena in 1968. At the time she was painted by Kleitsch, she was sixteen years old. The author expresses her gratitude to Craig Walker, Edee-Lou's grand-nephew.

127. Jim Sleeper, Orange County author-historian, was most kind in sharing information from the *Santa Ana Daily Evening Register* on Hedda Nova Hurst's filming experience in Laguna Beach.

128. Hedda (Hedwiga) Nova (her screen name) was born in Odessa, Russia, on May 15, 1899, and died in Atascadero, California, on January 16, 1981. Nova worked in a number of silent movies for major Hollywood studios; her first husband, Paul Hurst, directed her in *The Gold Hunters* for Guaranteed Pictures in 1925. She later divorced him and married Lee Roberts, whose son, William Lee Roberts, identified her as the previously unknown sitter in this portrait. The author expresses her gratitude to Brian Coburn, reference librarian, Atascadero-Martin Polin Library, Atascadero, California, for his assistance in obtaining Mrs. Roberts's death certificate and probate papers.

129. *Santa Ana Daily Evening Register*, June 7, 1920. The same newspaper reported that Kleitsch had painted a number of large pictures in Laguna for the exhibition, which he had already sent to Chicago, among them the full-length portrait of Hedda Nova (as yet unlocated). Probably another of these was the large *Portrait of Mrs. Herbert Spencer Martin,* also completed in 1920. Returning to California, the Kleitsches undoubtedly stopped in Chicago to make arrangements for this large exhibition to be held in the galleries of the Fine Arts Building on Michigan Avenue in 1921.

130. "On July 27, 1918, a loosely knit organization of artists opened an exhibition in the old Town Hall. The exhibit was extremely successful and was viewed by more than 2,000 visitors. In 1920, the Laguna Beach Art Association was incorporated as a non-profit organization with Edgar Payne as President. The Association soon outgrew the Town Hall, and in 1929 after completing a successful fundraising drive, a gallery on today's Museum site was opened" as the Laguna Beach Art Museum—known today as the Laguna Art Museum ("Orange County's Oldest Cultural Institution: Laguna Art Museum," courtesy of Laguna Art Museum Archives). "The old Town Hall, which had long been abandoned to the bats, was secured and remodeled into a simple top lighted room about thirty by fifty feet in size. Gray building paper was tacked over its rough board walls and a cheesecloth ceiling stretched over its rough rafters, electric lights installed and a fine exhibition hung" ("Permanent Colony Established," courtesy of Laguna Art Museum Archives).

131. *Santa Ana Daily Evening Register,* March 13, 1920. All of these portraits presently unlocated.

132. Except for Frazee, all were connected with the Chamber of Commerce in Laguna.

133. See Robert W. Finegan, *The Barlow Story: An Illustrated History of Barlow Respiratory Hospital, 1902–1992* (Los Angeles: Barlow Respiratory Hospital, 1992). The author discovered the signed portrait hanging in the Barlow Respiratory Hospital, unidentified by hospital and administration personnel. Kleitsch's signature was particularly difficult to read on the portrait's dark background; but aware of the artist's usual practice of signing his paintings on the lower right, the author was finally able to locate it.

134. "Due to the Great Depression, the decline in art sales was devastating to many painters. Some were forced to trade their works for services. In Laguna Beach, landscape artist Robert Dudley Fullonton traded paintings for food, yet died destitute in Orange County Hospital" (courtesy of Janet Murphy).

135. *Laguna Life*, July 15, 1921.

136. Documented by the infant's birth and death certificates and the burial information obtained by Father Dennis W. Morrow (research conducted with the assistance of Janet Murphy).

137. *Los Angeles Times*, November 13, 1921.

138. *Laguna Life*, December 9, 1921, and *Los Angeles Times*, December 11, 1921.

139. *Laguna Life*, August 12, 1921.

140. Ibid., January 13, 1922.

141. Ibid., February 24, 1922.

142. Ibid., January 6, 1922.

143. Ibid., March 10, 1922.

144. Stendahl Art Galleries Records, Kleitsch correspondence, roll 2720.

145. *Impressions of the Art at the Panama-Pacific Exposition* (New York: John Lane Co., 1916), 149.

146. The author wishes to express her gratitude to Dewitt Clinton McCall of DeRu's, who has conserved many of Kleitsch's paintings, for giving insight into the artist's working methods. Kleitsch's technique allowed him to build up the physicality of his surfaces.

147. For a biographical sketch of George Turner Marsh, see *Who's Who in California,* 1928–29, 299. G. T. Marsh & Company is listed in the Los Angeles city directory and featured in an article in *Saturday Night*, November 12, 1932, 2. The House of Marsh had branches in Coronado, Los Angeles (at the Ambassador), Santa Barbara, and Monterey. Through the fine sleuthing of the Kovinicks, the location of the Oriental shop in Kleitsch's picture was identified. The author expresses her gratitude again to the Kovinicks.

148. Vandyke Brown, *Laguna Life*, August 4, 1922.

149. Illustrated in *Saturday Night*, August 12, 1922.

150. Antony Anderson, *Los Angeles Times*, June 23, 1922.

151. *Los Angeles Times*, May 14, 1922; the painting was illustrated in the same newspaper on April 30, 1922 (news clipping in scrapbooks of the Archives of the Natural History Museum, Los Angeles). The author expresses her gratitude to former archivist Gretchen Sibley for her assistance. *Portrait* was exhibited earlier in the Southwest Museum First Annual Competitive Exhibition of the Paintings of California Artists, November 1–13, 1921, #41.

152. The fields of vivid, multicolored flowers in the foreground and middle distance were somewhat disturbing to critic Antony Anderson, who was probably more accustomed to the subdued tones in the work of the region's plein-air painters (*Los Angeles Times*, May 14, 1922).

153. The painting depicts a view from the corridor outside the *sala* (now the gift shop) looking through the arcade at the worshipper in the south wing.

154. Stendahl Art Galleries Records.

155. Antony Anderson, August 27, 1922.

156. *Laguna Life*, October 13, 1922.

157. Ibid., October 20, 1922.

158. Patricia Trenton, "Joseph Kleitsch," in *75 Works/75 Years: Collecting the Art of California* (Laguna Beach, Calif.: Laguna Art Museum, 1993), 36. Information on Isch's general store and post office was provided in 1993 by Jane Janz, granddaughter of Nick Isch. For information on the post office and the Kleitsch painting, see *Laguna Life*, October 13, 1922; *South Coast News*, January 25, 1929; the Los Angeles Museum's Kleitsch Memorial Exhibition, June 1933, #3; David Iredell, "Notes from Art Gallery," (Laguna Art Museum Archives); *Laguna Life*, October 28, 1921, April 27, 1923, May 4, 1923, and June 29, 1923; Joseph S. Thurston, *Laguna Beach of Early Days* (Culver City, Calif.: Murray & Gee Press, 1947), 128, ill.; Merle Ramsey and Mabel Ramsey, *Pioneer Days of Laguna Beach* (Laguna Beach, Calif.: Merle and Mabel Ramsey, 1967), 56, ill.; Don

Meadows, "Early Laguna Beach," *Orange County Historical Volume III* (Orange County, California, 1963), 249; *South Coast News*, February 5, 1952; Stendahl Art Galleries' Exhibition Inventory for July 2, 1923, #3411.

159. "At the time of Joseph Kleitsch's death in 1931, he owned Lot 175 in Laguna, and was making mortgage payments. His studio and home were eventually located on two lots (175 and 176; Edna purchased lot 176 in July 1933), where the present-day Calvary Church now stands, on the corner of Legion and Through streets. The combined lots were 79 feet wide on the Through Street side, 99 feet deep, and 100 feet wide on the rear side. The property was sold in 1953 after Edna's death for $11,000. Also, before his death in 1931, Joseph had bought two lots in Arch Beach Heights; #9 and #10, Blk. 35. Today, Lot 9 is known as 1144 Miramar, and Lot 10 as 1140 Miramar. Each lot is 25 x 100 feet. The closest intersection is Miramar and Del Mar streets. The two lots were sold in 1953 for a combined total of $500" (information courtesy of David O'Hoy).

160. "Joseph Kleitsch at the Ebell Club," *Los Angeles Times*, January 20, 1924.

161. "Pala Mission was built as an *asistencia* to its parent, Mission San Luis Rey de Francia, to bring Catholicism to the hundreds of Indians living in that area. Located about 25 miles east of San Luis Rey, the Mission is not situated inside the Pala Indian Reservation, which is nearby" (research and statement by Janet Murphy).

162. *Laguna Life*, January 19, 1923.

163. Ibid., March 9, 1923. On March 30, *Laguna Life* reported that the artist had recently painted a woman in a black evening gown and that, amazingly, he had painted it in only "four hours" and that it was "exquisitely done." In May, Kleitsch had a show at Leonard's, a new gallery on Hollywood Boulevard, where he exhibited landscapes and figures at moderate prices.

164. *A Favorite Spot* was painted at Fisherman's Cove, Laguna Beach.

165. Most of the press coverage of this show was positive. However, the reporter for the *Laguna Life* article on June 15, 1923, found the quality of some works "uneven." He defended his remarks by saying "after all . . .the true artist . . . has no formula but comes fresh to each new attack." Sometimes they lack "the divine fire" of the "spirit of creation." Most of the press were strongly in favor of the exhibition.

166. *Laguna Life*, June 29, 1923.

167. Painters and Sculptors Club minutes of meeting July 10, 1923, Ferdinand Perret research materials on California art and artists, Smithsonian Institution Libraries, microfilmed by the Archives of American Art. The author extends her gratitude to Judy Throm, archivist at the Archives of American Art in Washington, D.C., who provided copies of the minutes.

168. Various minutes cite the names of the artists and when they were accepted into the club.

169. *Laguna Life*, August 3, 1923.

170. Kleitsch's view of Main Beach from St. Ann's Beach is identified by a 1920s photograph of the same site in the Laguna Beach Historical Society Collection.

171. Affixed to the back of *Our Garden* is the inscription: "Erin O'Brien-Moore gave away this painting in the action of the play

'The Deep Blue Sea' by Terence Rattigan, July 11–17, 1954" (courtesy of David O'Hoy).

172. *Laguna Life.*

173. Carolyn Walker, "So. Calif. Art Immortalizes Eucalyptus," *Herald Examiner* (?), June 6, 1926.

174. "In July 1931, the old church was sold to Joseph Kleitsch...as a studio....The building lasted until 1953 when it was purchased by 'The Little Church by the Sea.' It was then demolished to make way for their new church" (Rev. William F. Krekelberg, archivist, *Saint Catherine of Siena Parish: Laguna Beach, California* [Diocese of Orange, 1999], 12). See also Ramsey and Ramsey, *Pioneer Days of Laguna Beach*, 48. The exact date of purchase by Kleitsch has been established from Rev. Lehane's St. Catherine of Siena Parish account book (the author is grateful to Rev. William F. Krekelberg).

175. After Joseph Kleitsch's death in November 1931, Edna Kleitsch used the building as a memorial to her husband with a permanent exhibition of his work.

176. Walker, "So. Calif. Art Immortalizes Eucalyptus."

177. *Los Angeles Times*, October 28, 1923.

178. Joseph Kleitsch to Earl Stendahl, Carmel by the Sea, November 24, 1923. Kleitsch apologized for not contacting him before they left for Carmel and informed him that "they have visited with a good many artists and had a good time. Also met Armin Hansen, [William] Ritschel, and several others. Now am working on good compositions, the subjects are many." And as always, Kleitsch pleaded with Stendahl to send him some cash. Stendahl replied on December 4 that he had not sold any of the artist's pictures "but hope we can report something in the near future."

179. The *Los Angeles Times* covered the exhibition of thirty paintings by Kleitsch at the Biltmore Salon, Los Angeles. Among them were studies of Capistrano and Carmel.

180. *Los Angeles Times*, January 20, 1924.

181. *Laguna Life*, June 26, 1924.

182. No. 55, 26 (courtesy of the Seaver Center for Western History Research, Natural History Museum of Los Angeles County).

183. [*A Moment's Reflection*] was captured by Kleitsch in the Sacred Garden at the Mission San Juan Capistrano about 1924: this small, open-air courtyard separates the Great Stone Church from the former *sala* (reception/living room). In 1918, Father St. John O'Sullivan converted the area into a picturesque meditation garden by enclosing it with a wall and an arched entry; later, in 1920, he added a fountain. The young girl seated at the fountain is thought to be one of several local children of Native American or Hispanic descent who dressed in costume and served as tour guides for special events at the mission in the 1920s. Recently, research has disclosed the identity of the young girl as Eustalia Soto, who appears in several other mission paintings by Kleitsch (source: Don Tryon, Jerry Nieblas, and David Belardes). The photograph of "Rev. St. John O'Sullivan in the Courtyard between the Chapel and Temporary Vestry" of about 1923–24 is a view of the Sacred Garden from the arched entry, looking south at the Campanario (bell wall). When he painted the young raven-haired girl gazing raptly at her image reflected in the pool, Kleitsch stood with his back to the Campanario, looking north through the arched entry. (Information from Michael Kelley and David O'Hoy, who interviewed Mission San Juan Capistrano staff members Father William Krekelberg, Lee Goode, and Patricia March on November 24, 2003.)

184. Jean Stern, "Missions in Art, 1890–1930," *Romance of the Bells: The California Missions in Art* (Irvine, Calif.: The Irvine Museum, 1995), 114.

185. Kathleen Walker, *Mission San Juan Capistrano: A Place of Peace*, photographs by Marc Muench (Phoenix, Ariz.: Azurite Books, 2002), 79.

186. The original version is published in *Mundial* (*El Periodico Mexicano*), June 20, 1926, and *Artland*, April 1927, 14. The alternate title was also used for another painting by Kleitsch.

187. The two Hispanic girls have been identified as Lula (Dora) Avila and Eustalia Soto (viewer's right with long curls). Lula was a descendant of Don Juan Avila, an early settler of California, and Eustalia's family came from Texas to San Juan Capistrano around 1900. Both girls served as guides at Mission San Juan Capistrano during the 1920s. (Identification of the girls provided by Archivist Don Tryon, San Juan Capistrano Historical Society, Mission Archive Director Jerry Nieblas, and Native American authority David Belardes.)

188. The hotel located on Camino Capistrano (old Highway 101) was built about 1920 and operated by the Stoffel family (information courtesy of Don Tryon, archivist, San Juan Capistrano Historical Society).

189. Stern, "Missions in Art," 114. The scene is of the barracks courtyard looking north toward the central courtyard. The sheds in the background are no longer there (information courtesy of Janet Murphy, Gerald Miller, former director of the mission, and his associate Sandy Wheeler).

190. *Los Angeles Times*, August 24, 1924. William Wendt inquired of Earl Stendahl on January 15, 1924, if Kleitsch was still his portrait painter; if not, Wendt offered to recommend a woman portraitist. There is no evidence that Stendahl was disenchanted with Kleitsch or that he had inquired about other portraitists. Perhaps, a little rivalry was sparked between the artists. Stendahl undoubtedly arranged the Morgenstiern commission for Kleitsch. Russian pianist Alfred Mirovitch wrote in *California Graphic* on July 26, 1924, of Morgenstiern's impressive career in Russia: "Practically his entire life has been devoted to scientific and philanthropic endeavors and he has written many books. These deal with scientific subjects and in Russia and Europe were regarded as decidedly authoritative.... Morgenstiern is enchanted with Los Angeles ... and he really wants to remain here always."

191. On October 5, 1928, Morgenstiern was arrested in Chicago on a warrant issued in St. Louis charging him with larceny in connection with the operations of an insurance company. Apparently, he fled to St. Louis but surrendered in Chicago on October 13, posting $15,000 in bonds under a grand larceny indictment (*Chicago Tribune*, October 5 and 6, 1928). The author acknowledges the diligent and time-consuming research provided by Research Specialist Lesley Martin of the Chicago Historical Society.

192. Pamphlet courtesy of Laguna Art Museum Archives.

193. The celebrated photographer George Hurrell, who first came to Laguna with Edgar Payne from Chicago, related to the author that "Kleitsch placed his easel in the middle of the road leading back to Laguna Canyon so that the cars would have to stop, and in that way his paintings did not get full of dust from cars rushing by" (Hurrell to Trenton, 1988).

194. *Los Angeles Times*, June 20, 1926.

195. Painters and Sculptors Club Minutes, *Los Angeles Times*, December 14, 1924.

196. This version was painted in 1923. The critic failed to realize that the scattered bricks in the picture's foreground are attributes of the old man's role at the mission. Father O'Sullivan had carefully numbered each brick he found laying on the ground and elsewhere to be able to replace them correctly in restoring the mission buildings.

197. David Belardes, Chief of the Tribal Office, San Juan Capistrano, California, has raised the question that "José Juan" or "El Peón" may be José Juan Olivares, and that "Old Man Yorba" may possibly be Ramon Yorba. The two Californios were active at the mission in the 1920s. At a meeting on January 8, 2004, Belardes and the author concluded that all three portraits were of José Juan Olivares (d. March 5, 1931), based on photographic references in the Alfonso Yorba Collection. We ruled out any similarity to Ramon Yorba, who was younger than Olivares.

198. Kleitsch took out his naturalization papers in 1924, most likely in anticipation of his intended trip overseas.

199. *Los Angeles Times*, January 4, 1925.

200. Dalzell Hatfield worked briefly for Earl Stendahl in 1925, and they came together later in a short-lived partnership.

201. Gerdts, "Making Arrangements," 28.

202. Embroidered water and mountain patterns decorate this courtier's robe as well. In the center of the composition is an archaistic bronze ("Ding") cauldron used on a scholar's desk for literati taste and decoration. The small, carved wood figure represents Daikoku, one of the Shichi Fuku Jin, or Seven Gods of Luck. (Hollis Goodall, associate curator of Japanese art, and T. June Li, former associate curator of Chinese and Korean art, Los Angeles County Museum of Art, generously shared their expertise with the author.)

203. *Los Angeles Times*, February 8, 1925.

204. Good met Kleitsch in Los Angeles, where the industrialist was an investor in the Otis Elevator Company.

205. On August 21, 1925, Stendahl wrote Kleitsch that Good was in town and eager to see the artist before leaving for Lancaster, Ohio. The author believes that Good played a large role in financing Kleitsch's trip to Europe. Perhaps Good's purchases of Kleitsch's paintings from 1924 to 1928 provided the funds (Stendahl Art Galleries Records).

206. The young girl is Eustalia Soto of San Juan Capistrano, who served as a guide at the mission. She appears in several of Kleitsch's paintings (see *Going to Church* [*Sunday Morning*], p. 135).

207. The scene is in the south wing looking toward the *sala*, or dining room, now the gift shop (information courtesy of Janet Murphy, Gerald Miller, former director of the mission, and his associate Sandy Wheeler).

208. The last venue is not confirmed; it was suggested that it might be exhibited there.

209. *Laguna Beach Life*, June 5, 1925.

210. On September 25, 1925, *Laguna Beach Life* reported that the portrait of Mrs. Benjamin Frank, wife of the manager of the Ambassador Hotel, painted by Joseph Kleitsch, was on exhibition at Stendahl's Gallery. The sitter is "draped in a lovely Spanish shawl held loosely at the waist. The gown is of white satin heavily beaded, giving an opalescent look to the picture. The background is of oriental coloring, blending nicely with the brilliant hues of the shawl." (Reprinted from the *Los Angeles Times*, September 20, 1925, 30, ill.) This formal portrait was probably commissioned by Earl Stendahl for the Ambassador Hotel manager's wife. Coincidentally, Bea Frank was a close friend of the author's mother.

211. *El Peón* was reproduced in the Spanish-language periodical *Mundial* (Los Angeles) on June 20, 1926.

212. *Fine Arts Journal* (Chicago) 30 (January 1914): 17.

213. On October 2, 1925, *Laguna Beach Life* reported that the Kleitsches had left Laguna Beach on their journey, stopping first in Chicago to see family and for Kleitsch to paint a commissioned portrait in Saginaw, Michigan, before traveling to New York City to embark on their trip overseas.

214. Information on Kleitsch's European trip (1926–27) is based on correspondence between Joseph Kleitsch, Edna Kleitsch, and Earl Stendahl (Stendahl Art Galleries Records, Kleitsch correspondence).

215. Edna Kleitsch to Stendahl, Herald Square Hotel, New York, March 13, 1926. Edna writes that she will stay in the East while Kleitsch is overseas. She also mentions that "her widowed mother and sister live in Chicago, where Marcia teaches art courses in the Chicago public school" (Stendahl Art Galleries Records). Edna's father, Ambrose Gregaitis, died in 1916. Edna's relatives, the Barto family, were still living in Grand Rapids.

216. Research provided by textile and costume historian Edward Maeder.

217. Historian James A. Straub of Grand Rapids writes: "The Grand River ran through the city, and as a result of glaciers receding eons ago, dirt was thrown up on both sides of the river and thus high ridge lines ran parallel to the river valley. There have variously been many smoke stacks on both sides of the river due to the once thriving furniture industry where the Gregaitis family worked" (Straub to Trenton, May 5, 2003). The author is grateful for Mr. Straub's research and for the early 1900s photograph of Grand River Valley showing the hilly terrain in the foreground and the three smokestacks on the ridge across the river, which verified Grand Rapids as the location depicted in the self-portrait.

218. Artist Pieter van Veen (1875–1961), who Kleitsch had known in California in 1922, served as Kleitsch's witness for his passport. At this time van Veen lived in New York (Allan Kollar of A. J. Kollar Fine Paintings).

219. Correspondence in the Stendahl Art Galleries Records confirms that Edna remained in the States; we also know that she never applied for a foreign passport (Loretta A. Alfaro, chief, Research and Liaison Branch, Passport Services, U.S. Department of State, Washington, D.C., to Phil Kovinick, October 20, 1989). After Kleitsch's departure for Europe, Edna moved to Columbus, Ohio, where her efforts to sell her husband's paintings were largely unsuccessful.

220. Kleitsch to Stendahl, California Hotel, Paris, n.d. (Kleitsch correspondence). The author extends her gratitude to her friend Henri de Pierrefeu of Paris, who investigated and photographed the locations of many of Kleitsch's scenes along the Seine and at the Hotel California and Vizzavona photographic studio.

221. *Oui* does not appear in Stendahl's inventory records; *Mademoiselle M* (Stendahl Galleries exhibition list May 1928, #17/$800) may be the alternate title for the picture.

222. Edna Kleitsch to Stendahl, New York City, March 10, 1926, writes, "Joe wants you to write him in care of American Express, Madrid" (Stendahl Art Galleries Records).

223. According to a letter from Edna Kleitsch to the Stendahls, March 29, 1926, Kleitsch was already in Seville; Edna reported that he was "so enthusiastic about the place" (Stendahl Art Galleries Records).

224. The author is most grateful and indebted to Captain Alejandro Alemán, deputy director of the Regional Military Museum in Seville, for his diligent research efforts in attempting to identify the colonel. Captain Alemán and the author communicated by e-mail before finally meeting in May 2003 in Seville, where he accompanied her and her husband to sites that Kleitsch had visited and painted (the sites are identified in Stendahl's art inventory lists). Alemán was responsible for identifying the specific inner court of the Museo de Bellas Artes that Kleitsch depicted.

225. Information about Kleitsch's travels with Abel Warshawsky is from Warshawsky's draft of his autobiography, "My Brush With Life," 316 (Warshawsky Papers, Archives of American Art), and Ben L. Bassham, ed., *The Memories of an American Impressionist* (Kent, Ohio: Kent State University Press, 1980), 223–25.

226. In both versions the pavillon Bourbon-Penthièvre is visible and "belonged at the end of the 18th century to the duke of Bourbon-Penthièvre, cousin of King Louis XVI. It was some sort of 'justice's house' for the duke. From the 19th century to today, it was (and is) partly occupied by the family who controlled the circulation around the bridge (the old and the Pont Clemenceau)." (Information provided by Anne Labourdette; see n. 245 for a complete citation.)

227. The scene depicts the Vernon beach on the Seine and the île Corday. Another picture, [*Vernon Park*], shows French citizens enjoying the tranquility of being seated in a grove of trees with the promenade and beach in front and the Old Stone Bridge in the distance. This setting reappears in several of the Vernon paintings, suggesting this was a preferred site for the artist.

228. Since Vernon center was heavily destroyed in 1940 and 1944, Kleitsch's painting serves as a testament to the original buildings on Place de Paris at avenue Thiers (now avenue Pierre Mendès-France). The collegiate church and its towers (called the "Collégiale Notre-Dame") still remains. Beyond the frontal picture plane would have been the Normandie hotel, where Kleitsch probably painted this subject. Known today only through an advertising illustration, a destroyed Kleitsch painting, also dated 1926, is of Place de Paris at rue Carnot in Vernon center and depicts the town hall (still standing), the collegiate church and towers, and other buildings destroyed in World War II.

229. In the background of Kleitsch's photograph in the Parisian studio is a copy of a Velázquez portrait of King Philip IV of Spain. Kleitsch may have brought this copy home; it is at present unlocated.

230. The exhibition was held at Stendahl Galleries in the Ambassador Hotel from June 15 to July 15, 1926. In a letter to Stendahl from the Neil House in Columbus, Ohio (her new residence), on July 12, 1926, Edna expressed her delight at Kleitsch's successful show, adding that she was at work on pen-and-ink sketches that she was selling through a friend in New York; she had "settled down" and was involved in her "line of art."

231. *Los Angeles Times*, June 20, 1926. The paper also illustrated *Pacific Ripples*, painted about 1925, which depicts Fisherman's Cove in Laguna Beach.

232. *Looking thru Eucalypti* was featured on the cover of seven magazines, including *California Outdoors & In* (Christmas 1925); *California Graphic* (*Pictorial*), March 20, 1926; and *Progressive Arizona and the Great Southwest* (September 1928).

233. J. C. Bulliet (typescript, n.p.); see nn. 212 and 221.

234. Stendahl to Kleitsch, Los Angeles, November 8, 1926 (Kleitsch correspondence).

235. Highlights of Kleitsch's trip are from J. C. Bulliet, *Stendahl's Art Review*, Summer 1928, and Warshawsky's draft of his autobiography.

236. *Los Angeles Times*, May 13, 1928, a review of Kleitsch's 1928 exhibition at Stendahl Galleries.

237. Ibid.

238. Ibid.

239. Kleitsch painted two versions of *Blue Thread*, the first a larger one in 1926.

240. Jean-Baptiste-Siméon Chardin (1699–1779), *La mère laborieuse*, oil on canvas, 19 x 15", Collection of the Musée du Louvre, Paris, France, Inv. 3201 (information courtesy of Jeraldine Byrne, fine arts librarian, Beverly Hills Library, California).

241. This may be the Normandie hotel where Kleitsch stayed while in Vernon, but its interior has been renovated since 1926, making an exact identification impossible.

242. The painting attributed to Velázquez is in the collection of the National Gallery, Washington, D.C. The Frieseke painting is in a private collection.

243. See Arthur Millier, *Los Angeles Times*, May 6, 1928.

244. Bassham, ed., *Memories*, 213–14; Warshawsky Papers.

245. As he did in his renditions of Mission Capistrano, Kleitsch captured the age, solidity, texture, and beauty of Old Vernon's Norman architecture. This painting represents "ruelle [lane or alley] Malot" that exists in Vernon today near the Collégiale church. The houses are still there, and the one in the right background is still a red-pink color (I am grateful to Anne Labourdette, conservatrice du musée de Vernon, for her assistance in this subject's identification).

246. Rue Bourbon-Penthièvre was an old, picturesque street leading from the Collégiale church to the pavillon Bourbon-Penthièvre, near the Seine and the old bridge. Because the Seine used to overflow regularly, the houses were elevated, with small stairs on the exterior. At the end of the street was the harbor of Vernon, for canal boats. The sailors, forbidden to sail at night, frequented the "auberges" of the rue Bourbon-Penthièvre and caused a lot of trouble. The harbor was a district of ill-repute until World War II, when it was destroyed by bombs. It was inhabited only by poor families and lacked a proper sewer system. Ruelle Malot was part of the same district (information obtained from Anne Labourdette).

247. "Joseph Kleitsch," *Stendahl's Art Review*, Summer 1928, The Stendahl Art Gallery, Ambassador Hotel, Los Angeles, California, 10–16 (Ryerson Library Pamphlet File, Art Institute of Chicago).

248. Kleitsch appears to have painted [*The Valley of the Seine, Vernon, France*] of 1926 in the town center; the exact location has been identified by Anne Labourdette (conservatrice du musée de Vernon): "'France 1926' is a painting representing a Vernon street called 'rue du Docteur Jules Burnet' [before 1937 known as 'rue du Théâtre'], where the [hospital] now stands. The main house (typical example of late nineteenth and early twentieth century) painted by Joseph Kleitsch is still standing at an angle of the 'rue du Docteur Burnet' and the 'rue de la Gravelle.' The two other houses represented in the foreground also remain. The hills in the background are typical of the Seine Valley, particularly the bank where Giverny stands." Labourdette mentions that Vernon center was half-destroyed during World War II in 1940 and 1944. Fortunately, the subject of this painting was not touched, although the house where Kleitsch painted this scene was destroyed (Labourdette to Trenton, e-mail, November 23, 2005; I am indebted again to Ms. Labourdette for her able assistance in identifying this subject and for providing photographic backup material). (See also *Stendahl's Art Review*, Summer 1928, The Stendahl Art Gallery, Ambassador Hotel, Los Angeles, California, p.[16]). Like Claude Monet, the artist was inspired by the picturesque and historic surroundings of the Seine River Valley and recorded his immediate visual impressions by applying paint in small dabs of color. In creating an optically vibrating surface, he was able to capture the ever-changing light effects and color of the outdoors.

249. Edna Kleitsch to Stendahl, June 2, 1927.

250. Stendahl to Edna Kleitsch, June 25, 1927.

251. Edna Kleitsch was aware of Stendahl's intention to return to Europe in June and arrange a Paris show for the artist; on May 25, 1927, she wrote enthusiastically to him about the proposed show. Stendahl and Kleitsch had probably discussed this idea in Europe in 1926. Expenses and business obligations may have changed Stendahl's mind about returning to Europe.

252. Kleitsch to Stendahl, "somewhere in France," July 28, 1927.

253. Stendahl to Kleitsch, Los Angeles, August 6, 1927.

254. Kleitsch to Stendahl, "somewhere in France," July 28, 1927.

255. *Los Angeles Times*, September 25, 1927.

256. Edna Kleitsch to Stendahl, November 29, 1927. Edna was in a weakened condition, recovering from surgery; she had mentioned her hysterectomy to Stendahl, but had not told Kleitsch about it.

257. At the annual business meeting of the Painters and Sculptors Club on January 3, 1928, Kleitsch was made an absentee member for six months. The artist was fully engaged in preparations for his major exhibition in May and had to take a temporary leave from active membership.

258. *The Park in Vernon*, 1927, is near the promenade and the banks of the Seine. In the background is a glimpse of the pavillon Bourbon-Penthièvre (Labourdette to Trenton). The painting was exhibited in the Stendahl Kleitsch exhibition of 1928 as #31.

259. The portrait was loaned to the current exhibition at Stendahl Galleries by the sitter (*Los Angeles Times*, July 7, 1929, ill.). Kleitsch exhibited *Under the Eucalyptus* at the Third Annual Art Exhibit of Occidental College at Stendahl Galleries on April 19–25, 1928.

260. See *South Coast News*, August 24, 1937. A 1928 photograph of Kleitsch with the altered painting is reproduced in the newspaper cited above.

261. According to Mrs. Katherine Petty, daughter of Nicholas Isch, who lived in Laguna in the 1920s, Kleitsch played his accordion on Saturday nights, sitting along the roadside in front of his Laguna house. Her sister, Mrs. Ida Griffith Hawley, posed for Kleitsch and recalls how rapidly he worked. *Highlights* was exhibited in Kleitsch's Memorial Exhibition at the Los Angeles County Museum of Art in June 1933. The critic Arthur Millier called it "one of the most sumptuous pictures in the show" (*Los Angeles Times*, June 18, 1933). *Highlights* was first exhibited in the Laguna Beach Art Association Annual in 1930.

262. *South Coast News*, January 25, 1929.

263. See Anna A. Hills, "Past, Present, Future of Art Association," in *South Coast News*, February 15, 1929 (courtesy of Janet Blake, collections manager, Laguna Art Museum).

264. *Los Angeles Times*, April 14, 1929.

265. On October 13, 1929, the *Los Angeles Times* announced that Stendahl had just returned to California from three months spent in a half-dozen European countries; no mention was made of Kleitsch accompanying him. In fact, Kleitsch and his wife were entertaining Mr. and Mrs. Herbert Muehlenbeck of Seattle at their home in Laguna Beach after Stendahl's purported departure date for Europe (see *South Coast News*, July 26, 1929).

266. Kelli Pryor, "Back to Nature: A New Generation of Landscape Painters Scan the Postmodern Horizon," *Avenue* (February 1989): 129–37.

267. Duane Noriyuki, "One with Nature in Laguna," *Los Angeles Times*, August 7, 2003.

268. In *California Light, 1900–1930*, the late artist-writer Joachim Smith describes this painting as "depicting a hunched and craggy, withering midday in Laguna Canyon near El Toro, with Old Saddleback Mountain peaking remotely in the distance" (p. 71).

269. Camille Przewodek, quoted in Noriyuki, "One with Nature in Laguna."

270. Ibid. The area is composed of Aliso & Wood Canyons Wilderness Park, Crystal Cove State Park, Laguna Coast Wilderness Park, and the Irvine Ranch Land Reserve.

271. *Laguna Beach Life*, June 26, 1924.

272. *South Coast News*, September 4, 1931.

273. Eric Jessen's ancestors settled in Orange County in 1869. In 1915 they moved to Laguna Beach, where they founded the town's first insurance agency. Eric has lived in Laguna since 1966. His undergraduate and graduate studies were in physical geography and biogeography at Long Beach State University. These studies enabled him to develop his widely respected knowledge of Laguna's topography and the progression of human settlement and planting there. In doing so, he carefully cultivated these reflections on the works of Kleitsch, Wendt, and the other early plein-air painters. As Chief of the Orange County Regional Harbors, Beaches, and Parks Department, he has helped implement the public wilderness parks that make up the Laguna Greenbelt and the spectacular public beaches in the coves of South Laguna. Eric was supervising curator of the Irvine family's personal photographic and film archives, which span 130 years. He has also assisted various Irvine family members with their philanthropic endeavors, including the reconstruction of the original Irvine Ranch House, the establishment of the Irvine Ranch Historic Park, and the development of environmental and

historical preservation efforts. The author is grateful to him for his assistance in identifying the physical locations from which Kleitsch painted his canvases, and for his dedication to the project. I am also indebted to photographer Chris Bliss for his fine photographs and his assistance in the search for Kleitsch's vantage points.

274. *South Coast News*, August 21, 1931.

275. Antony Anderson, June 10, 1926.

276. *South Coast News*, March 14, 1930.

277. In 1917 a member of Frank Miller's family (of the Mission Inn, Riverside, Calif.) established the Waldorf-Astoria at the location of today's White House restaurant. The next owner, Claude Bronner, purchased it in 1918, made it into a pavilion-like restaurant, and probably changed the name at that time to the White House. In 1934 Richard Bird became the third owner, and the restaurant was again enlarged; it still stands at its original location (information from the present owner of the restaurant and Ramsey and Ramsey, *Pioneer Days of Laguna Beach*, 120).

278. The incorrect title for this painting first appears in the 1953 Estate Sale of Kleitsch's Inventory, cited as "Los Andes Ave." In Ruth Westphal, *Plein Air Painters of California: The Southland* (Irvine, Calif.: Westphal Publishing, 1982), 154, the same incorrect title was adopted for the illustration's caption. In the Laguna Beach 1936 Phone Book, page 21, the building is correctly identified as "Las Ondas Café at 141 Laguna Av" (courtesy of Jane Janz's research for the author in April 1996). A colored graphic illustration, "View from Hotel Laguna Terrace," depicts the façade of the café with the correct identification (courtesy of Janz).

279. "Ocean Avenue is one of several east-west streets in the center of the town . . . .Until the 1950s, its extension between the Pacific Coast Highway [then Coast Boulevard] and the shore was lined with buildings catering to beachgoers" (Nancy Moure, "Joseph Kleitsch," *A Time and Place: From the Ries Collection of California Paintings* [Oakland, Calif.: Oakland Museum of California, 1990], 120).

280. Moure first recorded the analogy in her essay on Kleitsch, ibid.

281. This was the most challenging location to find of all of Kleitsch's Laguna paintings. The driving force was the large ochre building at canvas right. There were only five large buildings in Laguna Beach at the time the canvas was painted, and the guiding assumption was that it had to be one of them. From south to north, the five large buildings were Casa del Camino Hotel, the Artist's Theater (now Laguna Beach High School Auditorium), Hotel Laguna, Laguna Presbyterian Church, and Pyne Castle. Over a period of six months, strenuous efforts were made in the field to match each of these large buildings with the topography and other visual elements in the painting. It was even speculated by Orange County historian Jim Sleeper that Kleitsch took artistic license and moved one of the large buildings (Hotel Laguna) from its actual physical location to the right. Recent evidence has refuted this assumption (Chief Eric Jessen).

282. The author and Chief Jessen are indebted to graphic designer Bill Atkins for identifying the mysterious ochre structure in this painting, which dates to the 1920s.

283. He also limited sales by posting extremely high prices for his work, evident on Stendahl's inventory sheets.

284. "The mission of the Coastal Commission is to protect, conserve, restore, and enhance environmental and human-based resources of the California coast and ocean for environmentally sustainable and prudent use by current and future generations. The California Coastal Commission was established by voter initiative in 1972 (Proposition 20) and later made permanent by the Legislature through adoption of the California Coastal Act of 1976. The Coastal Commission, in partnership with coastal cities and counties, plans and regulates the use of land and water in the coastal zone. Development activities, which are broadly defined by the Coastal Act to include (among others) construction of buildings, divisions of land, and activities that change the intensity of use of land or public access to coastal waters, generally require a coastal permit from either the Coastal Commission or the local government" ("Program Overview," California Coastal Commission, http://www.coastal.ca.gov/whoweare.html, courtesy of Jeffrey Trenton).

285. In August 1931 Kleitsch became one of the directors of the Laguna Beach Art Association board (*South Coast News*, August 14, 1931).

286. *Los Angeles Times*, March 16, 1930.

287. *South Coast News*, June 13, 1930.

288. Ibid., January 17, 1930.

289. Ibid., May 2, 1930.

290. At that time Eugene showed a decided aptitude for geology and mechanics. The trip to Chicago in August 1933 was made to enroll Eugene in the photography program of the Crane Technical School. After graduation in 1936, Eugene and his first cousin Robert Kleitsch formed a partnership in a photography business in Chicago, and they operated the company for four years, until Eugene's addiction to alcohol caused the dissolution of their partnership. Much has been written and said about Eugene's retardation, which apparently led to his commitment as a ward of the state in 1951, a year after Edna's death. Robert Kleitsch, in 1989, indicated by telephone that Eugene's condition was simply alcohol addiction. (In 1951 an individual could be committed to a state institution without his or her consent.) Eugene died of cardiac disease on May 20, 1971, at age 56, in the Metropolitan State Hospital in Norwalk, Calif. On his death certificate his occupation is listed as "laborer and ceramicist."

291. *South Coast News*, October 10, 1930.

292. "Artists and Guests See Old Year Out," *South Coast News*, January 9, 1931.

293. Sonia Wolfson, ibid.

294. *Art Digest*, April 15, 1931.

295. Information obtained from Krekelberg, *Saint Catherine of Siena Parish*, 12–15. The Mormon Schoolhouse of 1888 was purchased and remodeled by Joseph Yoch to become St. Joseph's Chapel. *The Tidings* (Archdiocese of Los Angeles), September 25, 1931, announced that Kleitsch had been engaged to paint the Stations of the Cross and a Calvary crucifixion group for the chapel (from Rev. William F. Krekelberg).

296. *South Coast News*, October 31, 1931.

297. It is the smaller of the two versions that Kleitsch painted in Paris in 1926 and 1927.

298. Kleitsch had driven his wife to the county seat in Santa Ana to pay a tax bill: "The car was parked in front of the county jail and Mr. Kleitsch had remained seated while Mrs. Kleitsch went to the court house. She returned 20 minutes later to find that he had passed away suddenly during her absence.... The funeral was held on Thursday [November 19] at Saint Catherine's Catholic Church, where a solemn requiem mass was celebrated by the Rev. Father J. I. Lehane, pastor of the church" (*South Coast News*, November 20, 1931).

299. "Friends of the late Joseph Kleitsch have started a campaign to raise funds for the community to purchase one of the noted artist's paintings as a memorial to him" (*Los Angeles Times*, November 30, 1931). *The Old Post Office* was purchased from the Estate of Joseph Kleitsch in memory of Edna Kleitsch in November 1951 for the Laguna Art Gallery's permanent memorial collection (*Los Angeles Times*, November 5, 1951).

300. *South Coast News*, November 27, 1931.

301. Ibid., November 20, 1931.

302. *Green House, Laguna Beach*, painted in 1930, was shown in the Memorial Exhibition of 1933 (no. 14).

303. Millier incorrectly directed that statement to *Highlights* when it was originally intended for *Madonna and the Apples* and Kleitsch's still life *Apples* (unlocated).

304. Mrs. Joseph Kleitsch to Mrs. Martha G. Jones and Mr. A. Paul Jones, Drake Hotel, Chicago, February 24, 1934.

305. Edna Kleitsch's obituary, *South Coast News*, August 8, 1950. Edna made all the funeral arrangements for Kleitsch's interment in the Angeles Abbey Memorial Park, then the most beautiful, regal cemetery in Southern California. Since Edna died virtually penniless, she was not buried with her husband.

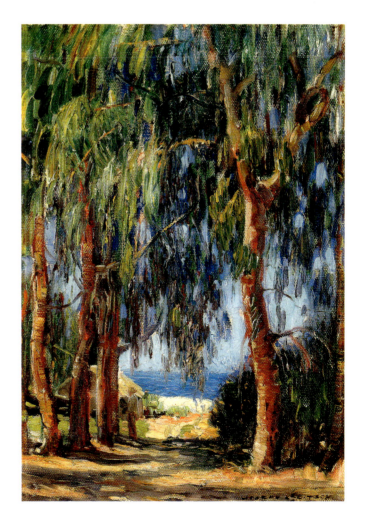

Joseph Kleitsch, *Niguel Canyon*. Oil on canvas. 15 x 11".
Collection of Ranney Draper.

Appendix

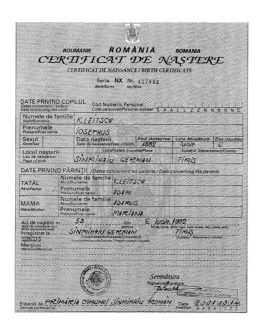

clockwise from left
Joseph Kleitsch's birth certificate, June 6, 1882. Photograph.
Maksay Ádám, "Traditional houses on the main street in Német Szent Mihály," 2002. Photograph.
Maksay Ádám, "The east view of the Roman Catholic church, Német Szent Mihály," 2002. Photograph.
Maksay Ádám, "The interior view of Roman Catholic church, Német Szent Mihály," 2002. Photograph.

opposite Joseph Kleitsch, Untitled Still Life (*Cheese, Onions, Bread, and Tankard*) (detail), c. 1905–7. Oil on canvas, 16 x 24".
Collection of Linda and Jim Freund, courtesy of Maxwell Galleries.

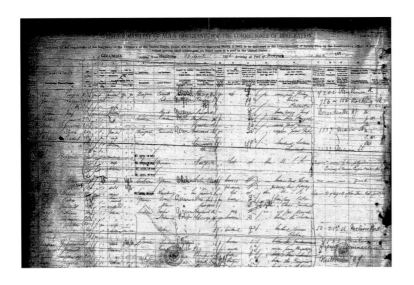

clockwise from top left
Official list or manifest of alien immigrants for the Commissioner of Immigration, dated "23 April 1902." Photograph. National Archives and Records Administration.
SS *Columbia*, built by D. & W. Henderson & Company, Glasgow, Scotland, in 1902, for Anchor Line under the British flag. Photograph.
Joseph Kleitsch and Emma Multner's marriage certificate, October 5, 1904. Photograph.
SS *Monterey* arrival log and ship manifest, March 1912. Photograph. National Archives and Records Administration.

above
Athenaeum Building, 59 E. Van Buren, Chicago. Graphic illustration from Chicago Central Business & Office Building Directory of 1912. Photograph. Palette and Chisel Club Archives, Chicago.
Joseph and Edna Kleitsch's marriage certificate, Chicago, 1914. Photograph.

right
Joseph Kleitsch, "A caricature of himself sitting on a rock drawing a nude model, Summer Camp, Fox Lake," 1915. Palette and Chisel Club, *The Cow Bell*, September 1, 1915.

far right
Joseph Kleitsch, (*A view looking south toward the town of San Juan Capistrano at Hotel Capistrano from the Soldiers' Barracks*), 1924. Photograph courtesy of Laguna Art Museum Archives, Laguna Beach, California. Stendahl Art Galleries Collection.
(*A view looking north at Mission San Juan Capistrano from the Hotel Capistrano*), 1929. Photograph. San Juan Capistrano Historical Society.

APPENDIX

clockwise from top left
Joseph Kleitsch, *Portrait of Mrs. Marian Gould,* 1928. Photograph. Ferdinand Perret research materials on California art and artists, courtesy of Smithsonian Institution Libraries, Washington, D.C. Microfilmed by Archives of American Art.
"Grand Rapids, Michigan," c. 1900s. Photograph. Grand Rapids Central Public Library. Photograph courtesy of James A. Straub.
Joseph Kleitsch, *Inner Court, Museo de Bellas Artes, Seville, Spain,* 1926. Photograph taken 1928. Ferdinand Perret research material on California art and artists, courtesy of Smithsonian Institution Libraries, Washington, D.C., micro-filmed by Archives of American Art.
"Le Pont de Pierre (The Old Stone Bridge), Vernon, France," 1900. Photograph. Archives de l'Eure, Départment de l'Eure, Evreux, France.
"Normandy-Plaisance Hôtel, Vernon, France," c. 1925. Photograph. Archives de l'Eure, Départment de l'Eure, Evreux, France.

clockwise from top left
Joseph Kleitsch, Vizzavona Studio, Paris, France, 1926. Photograph. Laguna Art Museum Archives, Laguna Beach, California. Stendahl Art Galleries Collection.
Henri de Pierrefeu, "Exterior View: Vizzavona Studio, Paris, France," 2003. Photograph.
Henri de Pierrefeu, "Exterior View: Vizzavona Studio, Paris, France," 2003. Photograph.
Edouard Vysekal, Earl Stendahl, and Joseph Kleitsch, Vizzavona Studio, Paris, France, 1926. Photograph. Laguna Art Museum Archives, Laguna Beach, California. Stendahl Art Galleries Collection.

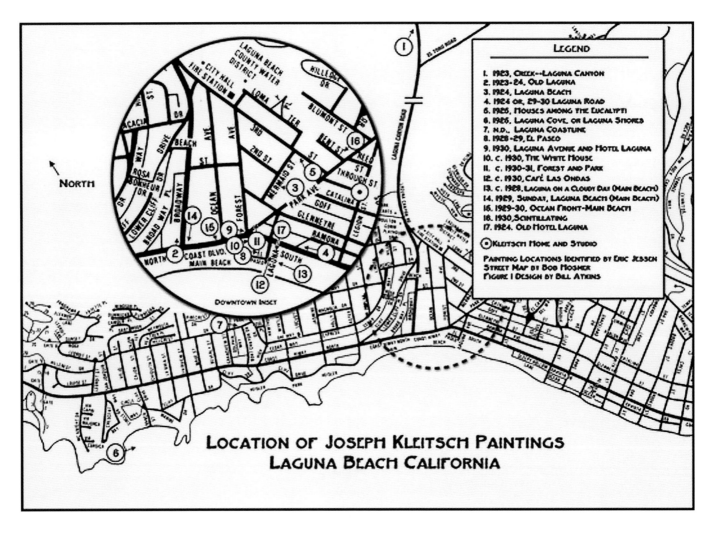

Joseph Kleitsch painting sites in Laguna Beach identified by Eric Jessen. Map by Bob Hosmer and Bill Atkins.

clockwise from top
"Looking toward the town of Laguna from upper Third Street," c. 1920. Photograph. Laguna Art Museum Archives, Laguna Beach, California.
"The White House Restaurant was a busy place in 1932. It was located at 330 South Coast Blvd., Laguna Beach." Photograph. Laguna Art Museum Archives, Laguna Beach, California.
"View from Hotel Laguna Terrace," mid-1950s. Illustration. Courtesy of Jane Janz.

Selected Bibliography

Books and Exhibition Catalogues

Anderson, Susan M., and Bolton Colburn. "Painting Paradise: A History of the Laguna Beach Art Association." In *Impressions of California: Early Currents in Art, 1850–1930*. Irvine, Calif.: The Irvine Museum, 1996.

Aufdenkamp, Lynndon. *Lynn and Thelma: It All Started in Laguna.* Laguna Beach, Calif.: Thelma Aufdenkamp, 1994.

Bach, Ira J. *Chicago on Foot: Walking Tours of Chicago's Architecture.* 3rd ed. Chicago, New York, and San Francisco: Rand McNally & Company, 1979.

Benezit, E. *Dictionnaire des Peintres, Sculpteurs, Dessinateurs, et Graveurs.* Paris: Librairie Gründ, 1984.

Brinton, Christian. *Impressions of the Art at the Panama-Pacific Exposition.* New York: John Lane Co., 1916.

Burk, Margaret Tante. *Are the Stars Out Tonight? The Story of the Famous Ambassador and Cocoanut Grove.* Los Angeles: Round Table West, 1980.

Cikovsky, Nicolai, Jr., and Franklin Kelly. *Winslow Homer.* Contributions by Judith Walsh and Charles Brock. New Haven, Conn.: Yale University Press in association with the National Gallery of Art, 1995.

Coen, Rena Neumann. *Elsie Palmer Payne: Out of the Shadow.* Minneapolis, Minn.: Payne Studios Inc., 1987.

———. *The Paynes, Edgar & Elsie: American Artists.* Minneapolis, Minn.: Payne Studios Inc., 1988.

Decker, Donald M., and Mary L. Decker. *Reflections on Elegance: Pasadena's Huntington Hotel since 1906.* Rev. ed. Laguna Niguel, Calif.: Royal Literary Publications, 1991.

Decker, Michel de. *Histoires de Vernon-sur-Seine. . . Giverny et d'alentour.* Éditions Ch. Corlet-24-26, Rue de Vire/14110 Conde-Sur-Noireau, France, 1982.

Dominik, Janet Blake. *Early Artists in Laguna Beach: The Impressionists.* Laguna Beach, Calif.: Laguna Art Museum, 1986.

Fairbrother, Trevor J. *John Singer Sargent.* New York: Harry N. Abrams in association with the National Museum of American Art, Smithsonian Institution, 1994.

———. *John Singer Sargent: The Sensualist.* New Haven, Conn.: Yale University Press in association with the Seattle Art Museum, 2000.

Falk, Peter H. *Who Was Who in American Art.* Madison, Conn.: Sound View Press, 1985.

Fehrer, Catherine. *The Julian Academy, Paris 1868–1939: Spring Exhibition.* New York: Shepherd Gallery, 1989.

Fielding, Mantle. *Dictionary of American Painters, Sculptors, and Engravers.* New York: James F. Carr, Publisher, 1965.

Joseph Kleitsch, *Vernonnet, France* (detail).
Oil on canvas, 18 x 21". Private Collection.

Finegan, Robert W. *The Barlow Story: An Illustrated History of Barlow Respiratory Hospital, 1902–1992.* Los Angeles: Barlow Respiratory Hospital, 1992.

Fried, Michael. *Manet's Modernism, or, The Face of Painting in the 1860s.* Chicago: University of Chicago Press, 1996.

Fritz, Percy Stanley. *Colorado: The Centennial State.* Appendix listing of Colorado government officials. New York: Prentice-Hall, 1941.

Gerdts, William H. *Painters of the Humble Truth: Masterpieces of American Still Life 1801–1939.* Columbia, Mo., and London: University of Missouri Press with Philbrook Art Center, 1981.

———. *Lasting Impressions: American Painters in France, 1865–1915.* Evanston, Ill.: Terra Foundation for the Arts, 1992.

———. *Monet's Giverny: An Impressionist Colony.* New York: Abbeville Press, 1993.

———. *The Friedman Collection: Artists of Chicago.* New York: Spanierman Gallery, 2002.

———. "Making Arrangements: California Still Life Painting at the Time of the Impressionists." In *The Not-So-Still Life: A Century of California Painting and Sculpture.* Berkeley and Los Angeles: University of California Press in association with the San Jose Museum of Art, 2003.

Green, Christopher. *Art in France 1900–1940.* Pelican History of Art. New Haven, Conn., and London: Yale University Press, 2000.

Greenhouse, Wendy. "Midwestern Art Organizations." In *Mathias J. Alten: Journey of an American Painter.* Grand Rapids, Mich.: Grand Rapids Art Museum, 1998.

Hartley, Lucy. *Physiognomy and the Meaning of Expression in Nineteenth-Century Culture.* Cambridge Studies in Nineteenth-Century Literature and Culture. New York: Cambridge University Press, 2001.

Hughes, Edan Milton. *Artists in California 1786–1940.* 2nd ed. San Francisco: Hughes Publishing Co., 1989.

Jones, Harvey L. Introduction to *A Time and Place: From the Ries Collection of California Painting.* Essay by Paul C. Mills and catalogue entries by Nancy Dustin Wall Moure. Oakland, Calif.: Oakland Museum, 1990.

Jones, Roger W. *The History of Villa Rockledge: A National Treasure in Laguna Beach.* Laguna Beach, Calif.: American National Research Institute, 1991.

Jordan, William B., and Peter Cherry. *Spanish Still Life from Velázquez to Goya.* London and New Haven, Conn.: National Gallery Publications, distributed by Yale University Press, 1995.

Koortbojian, Michael. *Self-Portraits.* Themes in Art. London: Scala Books, 1992.

Koszarski, Richard. *An Evening's Entertainment.* Reprint ed. Berkeley, Los Angeles, and London: University of California Press, 1994.

Krekelberg, Rev. William F. *Saint Catherine of Siena Parish.* Laguna Beach, Calif.: Diocese of Orange, 1999.

Landauer, Susan. *California Impressionists.* With essays by Donald D. Keyes and Jean Stern. Irvine, Calif.: The Irvine Museum and the Georgia Museum of Art, University of Georgia, 1996.

La Reina: Los Angeles in Three Centuries. Los Angeles: Security First National Bank, 1929.

Lochridge, Katherine, *As We See Ourselves: Artists' Self Portraits.* Huntington, N.Y.: Heckscher Museum, 1979.

MacDonald, Margaret F., Susan Grace Galassi, and Aileen Ribeiro with Patricia de Montfort. *Whistler, Women & Fashion.* New Haven, Conn.: Yale University Press in association with the Frick Collection, 2003.

McWilliams, Carey. *The Education of Carey McWilliams.* New York: Simon and Schuster, 1979.

Miller, Zane L. *Boss Cox's Cincinnati: Urban Politics in the Progressive Era.* Rev. ed. with an introduction by Howard P. Chudacoff. Columbus, Ohio: Ohio State University Press, 2000.

Miller, Zane L., and Bruce Tucker. *Changing Plans for America's Inner Cities: Cincinnati's Over-the-Rhine and Twentieth-Century Urbanism.* Columbus, Ohio: Ohio State University Press, 1998.

Moure, Nancy Dustin Wall. *Southern California Artists 1890–1940.* Laguna Beach, Calif.: Laguna Beach Museum of Art, 1979.

———. *Dictionary of Art and Artists in Southern California before 1930.* Los Angeles: Dustin Publications, 1984.

———. *Publications in Southern California Art,* 1, 2, and 3, Los Angeles: Dustin Publications, 1984.

Nunis, Doyce B., Jr., ed. *Mission San Fernando Rey de España, 1797–1997: A Bicentennial Tribute.* Los Angeles: Historical Society of Southern California, 1997.

O'Connor, Francis V. "The Psychodynamics of the Frontal Self-Portrait." In *Psychoanalytic Perspectives on Art.* Edited by Mary Mathews Gedo, Hillsdale, N.J.: Analytic Press, 1985.

Oles, James, ed. *South of the Border: Mexico in the American Imagination 1914–1947.* Essay by Karen Cordero Reiman. Washington, D.C., and London: Smithsonian Institution Press in association with the Yale Art Gallery, 1993.

Ormond, Richard, and Elaine Kilmurray, eds. *John Singer Sargent.* Princeton, N.J.: Princeton University Press, 1998.

Platzman, Steven. *Cézanne: The Self-Portraits.* Berkeley and Los Angeles: University of California Press, 2001.

Porter, Dean A. *Victor Higgins: An American Master.* Salt Lake City, Utah: Peregrine Smith Books in association with the Snite Museum of Art, University of Notre Dame, 1991.

Prince, Sue Ann, ed. *The Old Guard and the Avant-Garde: Modernism in Chicago 1910–1940,* Washington, D.C.: Archives of American Art, Smithsonian Institution, in association with the University of Chicago Press, 1990.

Ramsey, Merle, and Mabel Ramsey. *Pioneer Days of Laguna Beach.* Laguna Beach, Calif.: Merle and Mabel Ramsey, 1967.

———. *The First Hundred Years in Laguna Beach, 1876–1976.* Laguna Beach, Calif.: Hastie Printers, 1976.

Riley, Gillian. *The Dutch Table: Gastronomy in the Golden Age of the Netherlands.* San Francisco: Pomegranate Artbooks, 1994.

Rüger, Axel. *Vermeer and Painting in Delft.* London: National Gallery Co., distributed by Yale University Press, 2001.

Schell, William, Jr. *Integral Outsiders: The American Colony in Mexico City 1876–1911*. Wilmington, Del.: Scholarly Resources Inc. Imprints, 2001.

Sellin, David. *Americans in Brittany and Normandy 1860–1910*. Phoenix: Phoenix Art Museum, 1982.

Shapiro, Henry D., and Jonathan Sarna, eds. *Ethnic Diversity and Civic Identity: Patterns of Conflict and Cohesion in Cincinnati since 1820*. Greater Cincinnati Bicentennial History. Urbana, Ill., University of Illinois Press, 1992.

South, Will. *Guy Rose: American Impressionist*. Introduction by William H. Gerdts. Essay by Jean Stern. Oakland, Calif.: Oakland Museum and The Irvine Museum, 1995.

———. "A Singular Vision: The Life and Art of Conrad Buff." In *The Art and Life of Conrad Buff*. By Libby Buff and George Stern. West Hollywood, Calif.: George Stern Fine Arts, 2000.

Spike, John T. *Italian Still Life Paintings from Three Centuries*. New York: National Academy of Design, 1983.

Starr, Kevin. *Material Dreams: Southern California through the 1920s*. New York: Oxford University Press, 1990.

Stendahl, Earl. *Joseph Kleitsch*. Los Angeles: Stendahl Galleries, 1928.

Sterling, Charles. *Still Life Painting from Antiquity to the Present Time*. Translated by James Emmons. Rev. ed. New York: Universe Books, 1959.

Stern, Jean. *Masterworks of California Impressionism: The Morton H. Fleischer Collection*. Phoenix: Franchise Finance Corporation of America, 1986.

———. "Missions in Art, 1890–1930." In *Romance of the Bells: The California Missions in Art*. Irvine, Calif.: The Irvine Museum, 1995.

Stern, Jean, Janet Blake Dominik, and Harvey L. Jones. *Selections from The Irvine Museum*. Irvine, Calif.: The Irvine Museum, 1992.

Stern, Jean, and Evelyn Payne Hatcher. *Elsie Palmer Payne, 1884–1971*. Beverly Hills, Calif.: Petersen Galleries, 1990.

Sundell, Nina. *The Sense of Self: From Self-Portraiture to Autobiography*. Washington, D.C.: International Exhibitions Foundation, 1978.

Szabadi, Judit. *Rippl-Rónai*. Budapest, Hungary, 2000.

Thurston, J. S. *Laguna Beach of Early Days*. Culver City, Calif.: Murray & Gee Press, 1947.

Trenton, Patricia. *Harvey Otis Young: The Lost Genius, 1841–1901*. Denver: Denver Art Museum, 1975.

———. "Joseph Kleitsch: A Kaleidoscope of Color." In *California Light 1900–1930*. Laguna Beach, Calif.: Laguna Art Museum, 1990.

———. "Joseph Kleitsch." In *75 Works/75 Years: Collecting the Art of California*. Laguna Beach, Calif.: Laguna Art Museum, 1993.

Trenton, Patricia, and Peter Hassrick. *The Rocky Mountains: A Vision for Artists in the Nineteenth Century*. Norman, Okla.: University of Oklahoma Press, 1983.

Tufts, Eleanor. *Luis Meléndez: Eighteenth-Century Master of the Spanish Still Life;* with a Catalogue Raisonné. Columbia, Mo.: University of Missouri Press, 1985.

Várdy, Steven Béla. *History of the Hungarian Nation.* Astor Park, Fla.: Danubian Press, 1969.

Walker, Kathleen. *Mission San Juan Capistrano: A Place of Peace.* Photographs by Marc Muench. Phoenix: Azurite Books, 2002.

Warshawsky, Abel George. *The Memories of an American Impressionist.* Edited and with an introduction by Ben L. Bassham. Kent, Ohio: Kent State University Press, 1980.

Westphal, Ruth Lilly. *Plein Air Painters of California: The Southland.* Irvine, Calif.: Westphal Publishing, 1982.

Wheelock, Arthur K., Jr. *Jan Vermeer.* New York: Harry N. Abrams, 1981.

Who's Who in California 1928–29.

Who's Who in New York, 1918.

City and Business Directories

Chicago, 1912–20
Cincinnati, 1879–1904
Denver, 1904–7
Laguna Beach, California, 1920–30
Los Angeles 1920–30
Orange County, California, 1924, 1926, 1929

Articles and Reviews

Art Digest, April 15, 1931.

Artland, 1927.

Bingham, Elizabeth. "Art Exhibit and Comment." *Saturday Night,* July 29, 1922.

California Art and Architecture, August 1929 and October 1931.

California Graphic, 1923–26.

California Southland, 1918–28.

Chicago Evening Post, 1913–20.

Chicago Herald Examiner, 1914–18.

Chicago Tribune, October 1928.

Clubwoman, 1928.

Cow Bell, 1913–16, Palette and Chisel Club, Chicago.

Denver Post, 1904–7.

Fine Arts Journal (Chicago), 1912–19.

For Arts Sake, 1923 and 1925.

Galassi, Susan Grace. "Whistler, Women, and Fashion." *American Art Review* 15, no. 3 (2003).

Laguna Beach Life, 1924–25.

Laguna Life, 1921–26.

Life and Art, July 28, 1922.

Los Angeles Times, 1920–35, 1952.

Mundial (Los Angeles), June 20, 1926.

Noriyuki, Duane. "One with Nature in Laguna." *Los Angeles Times,* August 7, 2003.

Pryor, Kelli. "Back to Nature: A New Generation of Landscape Painters Scan the Postmodern Horizon." *Avenue,* February 1989.

Rocky Mountain News, 1904–7.

Santa Ana Daily Evening Register, 1920.

Saturday Night, 1922–32.

South Coast News, 1929–37, 1950.

Stendahl's Quarterly Art Review, 1927–28.

Walker, Carolyn. "Southern California Art Immortalizes Eucalyptus." *Herald Examiner* (Los Angeles), 1926?.

Weisgall, Deborah. "How Rembrandt Made His Name Painting Himself." *New York Times,* September 24, 2000.

Wisehart, M. K. "Try Giving It Up." *American Magazine* 106 (October 1928).

Archival Sources

Art Institute of Chicago Archives. Miscellaneous art exhibition records and artists' biographical records. Chicago.

Baker/Nardone Collection. Laguna Art Museum Archives, Laguna Beach, Calif.

California State Library. Index of artists. Sacramento, Calif.

Colorado Historical Society Library Archives. Miscellaneous records. Denver.

Colorado Railroad Museum Archives. Advertising records. Golden, Colo.

First American Title Insurance Company Archives. Photographic records. Santa Ana, Calif.

Laguna Beach Art Association Records. Laguna Art Museum Archives, Laguna Beach, Calif.

Los Angeles County Museum of Art Archives. Miscellaneous art exhibition records. Los Angeles.

Los Angeles County Museum of Natural History Archives. Miscellaneous exhibition records, photographs, and scrapbooks, 1920–28. Los Angeles.

National Archives and Records Administration. Census records. Laguna Niguel, Calif.

——. Immigration and naturalization records and ship manifest. Washington, D.C.

Painters and Sculptors Club of Los Angeles, California. Bylaws and minutes. Archives of American Art, Smithsonian Institution (not microfilmed).

Palette and Chisel Club Archives. Minutes and records. Chicago.

Palette and Chisel Club. Five logbooks (1895–1976), clippings, and photographs. Midwest Manuscripts Collection, Newberry Library, Chicago.

Perret, Ferdinand. Research material on California art and artists. Smithsonian Institution Libraries, microfilmed by Archives of American Art, Smithsonian Institution.

Richter, Marianne. "The History of the Palette and Chisel Academy of Fine Arts." Unpublished paper. University of Illinois at Chicago.

School of the Art Institute of Chicago Archives. Art school records. Chicago.

Sparks, Esther. "A Bibliographical Dictionary of Painters and Sculptors in Illinois, 1808–1945." PhD diss., Northwestern University, 1971.

Stendahl Art Galleries. Records. Archives of American Art, Smithsonian Institution.

Union Pacific Historical Collection Archives. Advertising records. Omaha, Neb.

Warshawsky, A. G. (Abel George). Papers, 1930–60. Archives of American Art, Smithsonian Institution.

Documentary Sources

Barto, Marianne. Interview by Michael Kelley, San Diego, Calif., n.d.

Buff, Conrad. Interview by Betty Hoag. Los Angeles, May 21, 1965. Transcript in Archives of American Art, Smithsonian Institution, Washington, D.C.

Haynel, Theresa (Kleitsch). Letter to nephew William Kleitsch containing genealogical and biographical information, n.d. (before 1984).

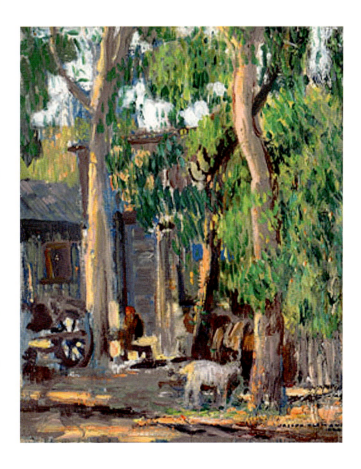

Joseph Kleitsch, *Under Eucalyptus, Laguna Beach*, 1922. Oil on canvas, 12 x 9". The Chiu Collection.

Index

Bold page numbers indicate illustrations, and italic numbers reference photographs. Numbers preceded by n or nn refer to notes.

A

Abstract Expressionism, 33, 34, 76–77
abstraction, Kleitsch's move toward, 144, 194, 198, 201–5, 217
academic-realist style, 57, 59, 64
Adams, Wayman (1883–1959), 84
    William Preston Harrison (1924), **85**
Alcázar (Seville), *154*, 155
Aliso-Laguna Overpass, **228**
Along the Seine, Paris (1927), **166**, 216
Ambassador Hotel (Los Angeles), 108, *108–9*, 112, 125, 139
Ambassador Hotel Swimming Pool, **226**
Ambition (*Natsi*), 86, 239n99, 239n100
Ancient and Modern Normandie (1926), **162**, 162, 176
Anderson, Antony, 213, 215, 235n49, 243n152
    on Kleitsch's landscapes, 130–31, 163, 185–86, 196
    on Kleitsch's still lifes, 143–46
    reviews of Kleitsch's paintings, 107, 125, 178, 191
Angora Cats (c. 1912), **68**, 70
Apples, 255n303
Apples and Strawberries, **39**
Arch Beach, **225**
The Arch (Looking Toward Arch Beach), **224**
Art Institute of Chicago, 30, 31, 53, 69–70, 86. *See also under* exhibitions
The Artist (1909), **59**
The Artist Robert Fullonton (1921), **104**, 104, 107, 108
The Artist's Dresser, Paris (1927), **170**, 170
The Artist's Wife (1919), 91, **91**, 92–93, 216
The Artist's Wife (n.d.), **133**
Asturias (Spain), 154–55
Athenaeum Building (Chicago), 71, 78, 86, 177, *259*
atmospheric effects, 80, 163, 197, 198, 212
The Attic Philosopher (1916), **84**, 84, 89, 93, 125
August Petrtyl (c. 1915), **79**, 93
Autumn Idyll (1925), **163**, 163

B

Babcock, George I., 62, 235n46
Bach, Ruth E., **149**, 181
Baker, William C., 56–57, **57**, 59–60, 67
Bánát (region of Hungary), 45, 231n4
Baptismal Font, 125
Barlow, Dr. Walter Jarvis (1868–1937), **104**, 104, 242n133
Bathers along the Seine, Vernon, France (1926), **160**, 161
Behind the Fence (c. 1910–11), 60, **61**, 62
Berger, Isador, **20**, 21, **84**, 85, 216
    music inspired by Kleitsch's art, 76, 77
Betts, Louis (1873–1961), 30, 69
    James William Pattison, **69**
Bingham, Elizabeth, 88–89
Bingham, George K., 211, **212**
Bird Rock, 112
Blue Thread (1927), 169, **169**, 211, 213, 250n239
Borg, Carl Oscar (1879–1947), 29, 129
Bougainvillea, Mission San Juan Capistrano (1924), **8**, **138**, 139
Braun, Maurice (1877–1941), 9, 29, 149
The Breakers, 125
Brookes, Mrs. C. A., 102

Joseph Kleitsch, *Curiosity* (*Mission San Juan Capistrano*) (detail), 1924. Oil on canvas, 25 x 30". Collection of Mr. and Mrs. Thomas B. Stiles II.

Brown, Helen, 75
Brown, John George (1831–1913), 60, 235n41
Brown, Vandyke, 112, 236n51
Buff, Conrad (1886–1975), 29, 53–54, 234n27
Bulliet, J. C., 154, 164, 175–76

C
Café Las Ondas (c. 1930), 203, **203**, 208, 213, 216
California, **24**
California Flowers (*Flower Garden—Laguna*) (1922), 114, **115**, 211
Cantaloupe, Paris (1927), **164**
Capistrano, 125
Capistrano Courtyard (1923), **123**
Carmel Cypress (1923–24), **131**, 131
Carmel-by-the-Sea, 97, 116–17, 131–32
Catholicism. *See* Roman Catholicism
Cézanne, Paul (1839–1906), 59, 60, 77, 215
    influence on Kleitsch, 170
Chamberlain, Norman (1887–1961), 177
Chardin, Jean-Baptiste-Siméon (1699–1779), 170, 250n240
Charles F. W. Nichols, 84, 93, **218**, 239n89, 240n111
Chemistry, 76, 85
Chicago, 30–31, 60, 67, 69
Chicago River (*Dockside in Harbor*) (1915), **80**
Children of Capistrano (1924), **221**
Cincinnati, 48–51, 49–50, 62, 67, 70
Clark, Alson Skinner (1876–1949), 30, 129, 149
Cloister, Mission San Juan Capistrano (c. 1924), **19**, 136, **137**
Coleman, Mrs. R. Clarkson, 108
Colorado, **52**, 52–56
Comrades (c. 1928), **219**
Constable, John (1776–1837), 176
Cotton, John (1869–1931), 125
Courbet, Gustave (1819–1877), 34

Creek—Laguna Canyon (1923), 109, 129, **190**, 191
Curiosity (*Mission San Juan Capistrano*) (1924), **146**, 146, 148, **273**
Curtis, Leland (1897–1989), 143

D
dealers. *See* Stendahl, Earl
Denver, **52**, 52–56
Depression. *See* Great Depression
Díaz, Porfirio (1876–1911), 64–65, 67
Diver's Cove, Laguna (1920), **23**, 112
Dockside in Harbor (1915), **80**
Douglas, Haldane (1893–1980), 33, 177
Dr. Elias Morgenstiern, 139–40, 146
Dr. Walter Jarvis Barlow (c. 1920), **104**, 104
drawings, **47**, 47, **57**, 79
The Dunes, 90
Dutch seventeenth-century painters, 48, 86
Duveneck, Frank, 50, 235n43

E
Early Morning in Laguna (1924), 140
Ebell Club of Los Angeles, 132, 211
Edee-Lou Frazee (c. 1920), **44**, 98, 100, **100**, 114
Edward B. Good (1925), 146, **146**
El Paseo (1928–29), 198, **199**, 203
El Peón (1923), 142, **142**, 148
Enchantment (1922), **11**, 117, **117**, 140
Escuela Nacional de Bellas Artes (Academy of San Marcos) (Mexico City), 64
Espagnon, Simone, 157, **157**
Eugene, 107
Evening (*in Laguna*) (c. 1923), **214**
Evening Light, Laguna (1923), 130, **130**, 186
Evening Shadows, **31**

exhibitions, 90, 107, 128, 132, 211
    Art Institute of Chicago, 74, 74–75, 86, 89, 94
    Ebell Club of Los Angeles, 132, 211
    Kleitsch's memorial, 215, 216
    Laguna Beach Art Association, 101, 117–18, 129
    Laguna Beach Art Gallery, 188, 211, 212
    Painters and Sculptors Club of Los Angeles, 142
    Painters and Sculptors of Southern California, 114, 117, 125, 140
    Palette and Chisel Club (Chicago), 72, 76–77, 82, 85
    Stendahl Galleries, 112, 125, 178, 188, 196
    Stendahl-Hatfield Galleries, 143, 146, 247n200

F
Father St. John O'Sullivan (1924), **134**, 135
A Favorite Spot (*Fisherman's Cove, Laguna Beach*) (1923), **123**
Figure Painting (1923), **218**
First Street (*now Glenneyre*) *at Legion Street* (1924), **28**, **121**
Fischer von Erlach, Emanuel, 46
Fish Market—Monterey (1923–24), 131, **132**
Fisherman's Cove, Laguna Beach (1923), **123**
The Flower Garden—Laguna (1922), 114, **115**, 211
Foothill Village (1925), **32**
Forest and Park Avenues (c. 1930–31), 202, **202**
France. *See specific towns and cities*
Frank, Mrs. Benjamin, **148**, 148, 248n210
Frazee, Edee-Lou, **44**, *100*, **100**, 100, 114
Frazee, Isaac Jenkinson, 100, *100*, 102, **103**, 107
Frieseke, Frederick (1874–1939), 75, 170
Fullonton, Robert (1876–1933), 104, **104**, 107, 108

G
The Garden Fence (1923), **140**
Gardens of the Tuileries, the Louvre, 37

Gauguin, Paul (1848–1903), 77
George K. Bingham, 211, **212**
Geraniums, **43**
Geraniums (1923), 128
Gerdts, William, 29–34, 144
Gilbert, Arthur Hill (1894–1970), 177
The Girl in Red, **220**
Giverny, 154–58, 172, 175
Giverny, France (1927), **174**, 175
Going to Church (*Sunday Morning*), *Capistrano* (1924), 135, **135**, 247n206
Golden Cliffs (c. 1922), 112, **114**
Golden Haze (1923), 130, **131**
Good, Edward B., **146**, 146, 164, 177, 214
Gould, Mrs. Marian, 181, *260*
Grace, 133, **133**
Grand Rapids, Michigan, 107, 151, 248n217, *260*
Gray Symphony, 112
Great Depression, 188, 208, 211, 213–14, 242n134
Green House, Laguna Beach (1930), **217**, 255n302
Gregaitis, Edna. *See* Kleitsch, Edna (Gregaitis) (second wife)
Gregaitis, Martha. *See* Gregg, Marcia
Gregg, Marcia, **93**, 93, 216
Griffith, Nelson, 148, **148**
Griffith, William (1866–1940), 34, 148

H
Halpert, Samuel (1884–1930), 156
Hals, Frans (c. 1581–1666), 34
Harding, June, 101
Harnett, William Michael (1848–1892), 67
    Still Life (1884), **66**
Harrison, William Preston, **85**
Hassam, Childe (1859–1935), 34, 75

Haynel, Theresa (Kleitsch). *See* Kleitsch, Theresa (half-sister)
Hedda Nova (c. 1920), **101**, 101, 107
Higgins, Victor (1884–1949), 72, 77
    Circumference (1914–19), **77**
Highlights (c. 1928), 109, 145, **182**, 183, 215
    reserved for Kleitsch's art academy, 208, 213, 216
Hogue, Fred, 178
Hotel Laguna, 195, 198, **200**, 203
Houses among the Eucalypti (1925), 163, **196**, 196
Hudson River School, 9, 189
Hungary, 45–46, 45–48, 109, 158, 257
Hurst, Mrs. Paul E. *See* Nova, Hedda
Hutchinson, Kansas, 56

I
Impressionism, 29, 33–34
    Kleitsch's move toward, 82, 89, 100, 104, 161–62
In My Studio (1917), **86**, 86, 88–89, 125, 163
    exhibited, 129, 132, 140, 148
influences
    Cézanne, 170
    Josef Israels, 149
    Manet, 175
    Matisse, 89
    Monet, 176
    Raphaelle Peale, 55, 57
    Rembrandt, 154
    Titian, 48, 154, 178
    Vermeer, 86
Inner Court, Museo de Bellas Artes (1926), 260
Interior with Woman Sewing, France (1926), 170
The Interrupted Hand (1911), 66, **66**, 236n51
Isa, 74
Isaac Jenkinson Frazee (1921), 102, **103**

Isador Berger (Rhapsody) (1917), **20**, 21, **84**, 85, 146
Israels, Josef (1824–1911), 149

J
Jade Necklace (1928), **180**, 181, 186
The Jade Shop (1925), **35**, **110**, 110, **111**
Jahraus, E. E., 102
Jardin du Carrousel, Paris (1927), **168**, 169
Jessen, Eric, 191, 207, 252n273
Jeweled Coast, 112
Jeweled Hills (c. 1922), **16**, 186, **187**
Johann Kleitsch (1901), **47**, 47
Joice Street (Nob Hill), San Francisco (1922), **105**, 117
Jones, A. Paul, 93, 216
José Juan (1925), **147**, 148
José Juan (Olivares) (1923), 142, **142**
Just before the Showers (San Juan Capistrano) (1925), **163**, 163

K
Karoline Kleitsch (1899), 47, **47**
Ketchum, Miss, 89
Kindel, George J., 53, 102, 233n26
Kleitsch, Agnes (sister), 67
Kleitsch, Bernard Joseph (son), 107, 242n136
Kleitsch, Caroline (cousin), 45
Kleitsch, Edna (Gregaitis) (second wife), 71, 79, 102, 211–12, 216
    correspondence with Stendahl, 176–77
    management of Kleitsch's career, 107, 108
    marriage to Kleitsch, 72, 259
    as model for *Enchantment*, **11**, **117**, 117–18
    as model for *In My Studio*, **86**
    as model for Kleitsch, 88, 104, 188
    as model for *The Oriental Shop* (1922), 109, **110**
    as model for *The Oriental Shop* (1925), **35**, **111**

as model for *Problematicus*, **87**

as model for *Red and Green*, **124**

portraits, **83**, **91**, 112, 126

travel with Kleitsch, 123, 132, 151

Kleitsch, Emma (Multner) (first wife), 50, 60, 62, 67, 70

marriage to Kleitsch, 52–53, *258*

in Mexico, 56, *56*

Kleitsch, Eugene (son), 101, 132, 152, 211–12, 254n290

birth of, 72

as model for Kleitsch, 82, 104

portraits of, 107, 147, **147**

Kleitsch, Johann (cousin), 47, **47**

Kleitsch, Joseph (1882–1931)

appearance and dress, 59, 86, 151

art organizations

Laguna Beach Art Association, 13, 102, 212, 254n285

Painters and Sculptors Club of Los Angeles, 125–26, 132, 142, 143, 185

Palette and Chisel Club (Chicago), 30, 71–78, 81–82, 177

awards and honors

A. H. Ullrich art medal, 75

Laguna Beach Art Association, 129, 239n100

Mexico Art Associates, 67

Painters and Sculptors Club of Los Angeles, 142

biographical sketch, 53, 70, 233n26, 234n35, 236n53

brushwork, 117, 132, 162, 202, 216

in Chicago, 60, 67, 69–96, 177

in Cincinnati, 49–51

death of, 215, 231n3, 255n298

in Denver, 52–56

early life and education, 45–48, *230*, 235n43, *257*

Art Institute of Chicago, 69–70, 237n61

finances, 116, 188, 208–9, 211, 213–14

friendships and social life, 70, 84, 107, 120, 132

Abel George Warshawsky, 156–58, 161

Edgar and Elsie Payne, 70, 96

Isador Berger, 85, 216

William C. Baker, 56–57, 59–60

in Hungary, 45–48

immigration to United States, 48, 49, *258*

in Kansas, 56

love for music, 47, 85, 107, 183

marriage to Edna Gregaitis, 72, *259*

marriage to Emma Multner, 52–53, *258*

in Mexico, 56–60, *59*, 62, 64, *64–67*

move to Laguna Beach, 96, 97, 102

naturalization, 94, 96, 231n3, 247n198

in Paris, 152–54, 156, 163–67, 171–72, 177

photographs of, *56*, *62*, *73*, *230*, *261*

preservationism, 118, 189, 197, 208, 209

productivity, 125, 143, 244n163

in Spain, 154–55

technique, 56, 59, 146, 183

atmospheric effects, 80, 163, 197, 198, 212

move toward abstraction, 144, 194, 198, 201–5, 217

move toward Impressionism, 82, 89, 100, 104, 162–62

use of color, 89, 109, 162

in Vernon and Giverny, 157–62, 175–77

See also exhibitions; influences; portraits; self-portraits; still lifes

Kleitsch, Karoline (cousin), 47, **47**

Kleitsch, Marie (cousin), *45*

Kleitsch, Matthew (brother), 239n99

Kleitsch, Theresa (half-sister), *45*, 45–46, 48, 67, *74*

Kleitsch, William, **63**

Kleitsch, William, Sr., 62

L

Laguna Avenue and Hotel Laguna (1930), **200**, 200
Laguna Beach
    art community, 13, 29, 96, 133
    bathhouse, 204–6, **205–6**
    beaches, 104, **106**, 114, **197**, **209**
    buildings and shops, **15**, 193, **194**, **199**, 200
    Diver's Cove, **23**, **197**
    historic photographs, *202*, *204*, *206*, *263*
    history of, 13
    homes, **128**, **131**, **184**
    Hotel Laguna, 195, 198, **200**, 203
    Kleitsch's move to, 96, 97, 102
    Main Beach, **204–5**
    map of, **262**
    modern photographs, *192–93*, *195–98*, *200–204*, *207*
    Old Post Office, **12**, *118*, 118, **119**
    streets, **15**, **28**, **113**, **141**, 200
    White House Café, 195, 200–202, **201**, *263*
Laguna Beach (1924) (landscape), **193**, 193
Laguna Beach (1924) (marinescape), **228**
Laguna Beach Art Association, 13, *102*, 102, 107
    Art Gallery, 101, 186, 188
    See also under exhibitions
Laguna Canyon, **140**, **191**, *191*
Laguna Coastline, 198, **199**
Laguna Cove (or *Laguna Shore*) (1925), 21, 163, 186, **197**
Laguna Landscape, **222**
Laguna on a Cloudy Day (*Main Beach*) (c. 1930), **204**, 204
Laguna Road (1924), **15**, 109, 140, **141**, 195
Laguna Road II (c. 1929–30), **194**, 194, 195
Laguna Shore (1925), **197**
Laguna Shore Line, **227**

Leren, Borghild, 102
The Lifeguard (1922), 148, **148**, 186
Looking thru Eucalypti (*Autumn Idyll*), *Laguna* (1925), **163**, 163
Los Angeles, 97, 102, 104, 112, 123
Los Angeles Museum of History, Science and Art, 114, 215
Louis D. Riethmann (1906), **53**, 53
Louvre, depictions of, **37**
Lunch Hour, Vernon, France (1926), **161**, 162
Luxembourg Gardens, Paris (1927), **168**, 169

M

Mademoiselle M, 249n221
Madero, Francisco, 67, 102, 236n53
Madonna and the Apples, Paris (1927), 170, **170**, 216
Madrid, 154–55
Maeder, Edward, 80, 92–93, 234n36, 238n75
Main Beach (1929), 204–5, **205**
Major John C. Walker, Jr., 146
Manet, Édouard (1832–1883), 34, 170, 175
    A Bar at the Folies-Bergère (1882), **175**
Mannheim, Jean (1861–1945), 29, 53, 233n23
Marsh, Florence, 109, **110**
Martin, Mrs. Herbert Spencer, 98–99, **99**, 107
Matisse, Henri (1869–1954), 89, 170, 183
McCauley, Lena M., 74, 76–77, 89
McCloskey, William (1859–1941), 53
McKnight, Lester, 120
Mexico, 56–60, 62, 64–67
Michigan, **90**
Millier, Arthur, 178, 189, 215, 252n261, 255n303
Miss Gregg (c. 1919), **93**, 93
Miss Ketchum (c. 1918), 86, **88**, 89, 125, 212
Mission Canyon (1922), **122**, 123, 140

Mission Flowers (1923), 126, **127**
Mission Poinsettias (1923), 126
Mission San Antonio de Pala, 123
Mission San Juan Capistrano, 126, 146, **221**, 245n183, *259*
    cloisters, **19**, 136, **137**
    courtyard, **116**, *123*
    El Peón (1923), **142**, *142*
    Father St. John O'Sullivan (1924), **134**, *135*
    gardens, 30, **124**, 136, **136**, *138*
    Kleitsch's interest in, 116
    ruins, 41
    south wing, **127**
    worshippers, **135**, *135*
Mission San Juan Capistrano (1924), **2**, 136, **136**
Mission San Juan Capistrano (c. 1925), 147, **147**
Mission Scribe (c. 1925), **40**
missions, depictions of, **31**, 212, 215. *See also specific missions*
M'lle 'E' (1926), **171**
Model's Throne, **27**
A Moment's Reflection (c. 1924), 245n183
Monet, Claude (1840–1926), *98*, *162*, *170*, *176*
Monterey, California, 131
Montparnasse, 154, 171–72
Morgenstiern, Dr. Elias Fedorovitch, 139–40, 146
Mrs. Benjamin Frank (1925), **148**, *148*, 248n210
Mrs. Herbert Spencer Martin (1920), 98–99, **99**, 107, 125, 242n129
Mrs. K. (*My Wife*) (1916), 82, **83**, 86
Mrs. Marian Gould (1928), **181**, *260*
Mrs. Paul Hurst (c. 1920), **101**, *101*
Mrs. R. Clarkson Coleman, 108
Multner, Emma. *See* Kleitsch, Emma (Multner) (first wife)
Munari, Cristoforo (1667–1720), *Natura morta con strumenti musicali* (*Still Life with Musical Instruments*) (1709), **183**

Munich, 47, 48, 59, 164
Munkácsy, Mihály (1844–1900), 47
Museo de Bellas Artes, 155, *155*, *260*
My Sister, *74*, *74*
My Wife (1916), 82, **83**, 86
Mystic Hill (Laguna Beach), **192–93**, *192–93*, *201*, **201**, *202*

N
Natsi, 86, 239n99, 239n100
Nebot, Fernando, 66
Nelson Griffith (*Lifeguard*) (1922), **148**, *148*, 186
Nichols, Charles F. W., 84, 93, **218**, 239n89, 240n111
Niguel Canyon, **255**
Nob Hill (1922), **105**, 117
Notre Dame cathedral, 162, **162**
Nova, Hedda, *101*, 101, **101**, 107, 241n128
Nudes (c. 1929–30), **206**, *206*

O
Ocean Front—Main Beach, Laguna (c. 1929–30), 204–6, **205**, *208*
Old Hotel Laguna (1924), 186, **195**
Old Laguna (c. 1923–24), 192, **192**
Old Laguna—Foot of Anita Street, **184**
Old Man Yorba (*José Juan Olivares*) (1929), 149, **149**
Old Man Yorba, San Juan Capistrano (1923), 142, **142**
The Old Post Office (*Laguna Beach*) (1922–23), **12**, 21, **119**, *119*, 128
    critical praise for, 186
    Laguna Art Gallery and, 255n299
Olivares, José Juan, *142*, **142**, 146, **147**, 247n197
The Oriental Shop (1922), 109, **110**, 125
The Oriental Shop (1925), **35**, 110, **110**, *111*
    reserved for Kleitsch's art academy, 213, 216
Oriental Still Life (1925), 143–44, **144**

Orientale (1925), 145, **145**
O'Sullivan, Father St. John, **134**, 135, 245n183, 247n196
Otis, George Demont (1879–1962), 185
Oui (France) (1926), 154, **154**, 249n221
Our Garden (1923), **129**, 129

P

Pacific Ripples (1925), **163**, 163, 250n231
The Paint Box (Curiosity) (1924), **146**, 146, 148
Painters and Sculptors Club of Los Angeles, 132, 142, 143, 185
    Kleitsch's role in founding, 33, 125–26
    See also under exhibitions
Painters and Sculptors of Southern California, 125, 140
    See also under exhibitions
Pala Mission, 123
Palette and Chisel Club (Chicago), 30, *81*, 81–82, 126, 259
    role in Kleitsch's early career, 71–78
    See also under exhibitions
Pallisades—Mexico, 236n55
Paris
    cafés, **172**
    Hotel California, *152*, 152, 248n220
    Jardin du Carrousel (1927), **168**
    Kleitsch's visits to, 152–54, 156, 163–67, 171–72, 177
    Luxembourg Gardens (1927), **168**
    Pont Neuf, **166**, *167*, **167**
    Tuileries (1927), **168**
Paris (1926), 152, **153**
Paris Café (1927), **172**
The Park in Vernon, France (1927), **179**
Pattison, James William, **69**, 69, 86, 90–92, 93–94
Payne, Edgar (1883–1947), 30, 70, 75, 96, 246n193
    and Laguna Beach Art Association, 13, 102, 186, 242n130
    The Restless Sea (1917), **70**
Payne, Elsie Palmer (1884–1971), 70

Peale, Raphaelle (1774–1825), 55, 57
Peonies, Paris (1927), **165**
Petrtyl, Irene, **79**, 79
Pfeiffer, Jacob (nephew), 49, 50
Pioneer Homes (1922–23), 128, **128**
Platte River in Winter, Denver (1905–7), **52**
Plaza de San Francisco (Seville), 155
plein-air painting, 21–22, 29, 118, 189, 217
Pont Neuf with Statue of Henry IV, Paris (1927), **167**
Poray, Stanislaus Pociecha (1888–1948), 177
Portrait of a Gypsy, 65, **65**, 235n49
portraits, 69–70, 82, 181, 216
    Charles F. W. Nichols, 84, 93, **218**, 239n89, 240n111
    commissions for, 123, 148
    critical praise for Kleitsch's, 90–94, 146
    Dr. Elias Fedorovitch Morgenstern, 139–40
    early, 47, 50, 53, 57–59, 67
    George J. Kindel, 53, 102
    George K. Bingham, 211, **212**
    Helen Brown, 75
    Irene Petrtyl, **79**
    John B. Woodruff, 75
    Joseph Smith, 102
    President and Mrs. Madero (1912), 67, 102, 236n53
    Simon William Straus, 96, 98
    See also self-portraits; *specific portraits*
Post-Impressionism, 162
Potthast, Edward (1857–1927), 34, 204
Prado Museum (Madrid), 154
preservationism, 189, 197, 209
    and Old Laguna, 21, 118, 189, 208
Problematicus (1918), **87**, 125, 213, 240n102
    color and decorative patterning of, 109
    and Kleitsch's figural interiors, 30, 86, 89
Puthuff, Hanson (1875–1972), 53

R

Rancho near Capistrano (1924), **139**
Red and Green (Mission San Juan Capistrano) (1923), **124**, 126
Reflections, Vernon (Mlle at Table) (1927), 170, **175**, 175
Rembrandt, 154
Renick, Ruth, 148, **180**, *181*, **181**
Reposer, Pont Neuf, Paris (1927), **166**, 167
Ressler, Josef, 46
Rhapsody (Isador Berger) (1917), **20**, 21, **84**, 85, 146
Riddell, William W. (1877–1948), 185
Riethmann, Louis D., 53, **53**, 233n25
Rocky Cliffs, Laguna (Edna and Eugene) (c. 1920–21), 104, **106**, 112
Rocky Cove, Laguna, **229**
Roman Catholicism, 45–46, 72, 132, 147, 213
Romania, 45
Romney, George (1734–1802), 92
Rose, Guy (1867–1925), 22, 29, 149
Ruins, San Juan Capistrano Mission, **41**
Ruth E. Bach (1930), 148, **149**, 181
Ruth Renick (1928), 148, **180**, 181, *181*, 186

S

San Francisco, 97, **105**, 116–17
San Juan Capistrano, 97, 125, 136, **139**, **163**
    Capistrano, 125
    Capistrano Courtyard (1923), **123**
    Rancho near Capistrano (1924), **139**
    See also Mission San Juan Capistrano
Sânmihaiu German, 45, *45*
Sargent, John Singer (1856–1925), 30, 93, 191, 238n75
    Alpine Pool (1907), **191**, 191
Sayre, Fred Grayson (1879–1939), 125, 126
Schwab, Charles, 62, 235n44
Scintillating, California (1930), **207**, 207–8
Scott, Elizabeth, 101

Seine river, 158, **159–60**, 161, **166–67**, 167
self-portraits, 59, 234n35
    1909, **58**, **59**, 59, **210**
    1915, **75**, 75, 125
    1917, **86**, 86
    1919, 94, **95**
    1925, **150**, 151
    1926, 152, **152**
Seville, *154*, *155*, 155, 175, 188
Shacks, Laguna Beach (or Old Laguna—Foot of Anita Street), **184**
Sicilian Girl (c. 1919), **91**, 91–92, 146
Simone, Vernon, France (1926), 157, **157**
Smith, Joseph, 102
Sorolla, Joaquín (1863–1923), 91, 133
Spain, 67, 154–55, 175, 188
Spanish Officer (Colonel in Infantry) (1926), 149, 155, **155**
Stendahl, Earl, 22, 151, 188, *261*
    business acumen of, 125, 143, 178
    Kleitsch's contract with, 108, 116–17, 213–14
    on Kleitsch's Europe tour, 149, 152, 163–64, 176–77, 186
Stendahl Galleries, 108, 112, 149, 178. *See also under* exhibitions
Stendahl-Hatfield Galleries, 143, 146, 247n200
Still Life with Apples and Oranges (c. 1905–7), **55**
Still Life with Fruit (c. 1905–7), **55**
Still Life with Oranges, **38**
Still Life with Raspberries (1903), **51**
still lifes, 143, 164, 183, 234n30
    early, 51, 54–56, 57
    untitled (*Cheese, Onions, Bread, and Tankard*) (c. 1905–7), **54**, **256**
    untitled (Nuts, Coconut, and Apples) (c. 1907–9), 60, **60**
The Story Teller (1925), 146, **147**, 151
Straus, Madeline, 98–99, **99**, 241n124
Straus, Simon William, 96, *96*, 98, 241n117
Stuart, Evelyn Marie, 85

Studio Interior (1915), **78**, 78, 86, 239n99, 239n100
Sunday, Laguna Beach (Main Beach) (1929), 204–5, **205**
Sunday Morning (1924), 135, **135**, 247n206
Sweet Peas (c. 1928), 183, **183**
Symons, Gardner George (1862–1930), 13, 133

T

Tangled Branches, Laguna Canyon, **140**
Temesvár, Transylvania, 45–47, 46
Through the Arches, Mission San Juan Capistrano (1922), **116**
Titian (c. 1488–1576), 239n88
    influence on Kleitsch, 48, 154, 178
tonalism, 79, 80, 86, 88, 89
Transylvania, 45, 47
trompe-l'oeil effect, 56, 66
Tuileries, Paris (1927), **168**, 169
The Turquoise Buddha, 144

U

Ufer, Walter, 76
Under the Eucalyptus Trees, 186, 251n259
Union Pacific Railway, 52, 56, 233n21
unlocated works, 236n55, 255n303
    Eugene, 107
    portrait of Hedda Nova, 101
    portrait of Simon William Straus, 98
    Sunday, Laguna Beach (Main Beach) (1929), 205
untitled works
    (*Ambassador Hotel Swimming Pool*), **226**
    (*Laguna Coastline and Saint Joseph's Catholic Church*), **209**
    portrait in Athenaeum Club Room (c. 1915), **79**
    portrait, Pala Indian Reservation (1922–23), **122**
    (*Rue Bourbon-Penthièvre*), *Vernon* (c. 1927), **173**
    (*Ruelle Malot*), *Vernon, France* (1927), **173**
    still life (*Cheese, Onions, Bread, and Tankard*) (c. 1905–7), 54, **256**
    still life with nuts, coconut, and apples (c. 1907–9), **60**, 60
    (*The Valley of the Seine, Vernon*) (1926), **176**, 176, 251n248
    (*Woman Seated in the Garden Sewing*), **184**

V

The Valley of the Seine, Vernon (1926), 176, **176**, 251n248
Velázquez, Diego Rodríguez de Silva y (1599–1660), 154, 170
    The Needlewoman (c. 1640–50), **171**
Vermeer, Jan (1632–1675), 86
Vernon, 156–63, 175, 179, 260
Vernon to Vernonnet, Vernon, France (1926), 158, *158*, **159**
Vernonnet, France, **36**, **265**
A View Across the Lake, Saugatuck, Michigan (1919), **90**
View from the Sea, **223**
View Looking North at Mission San Juan Capistrano from the Hotel Capistrano (1929), 259
The Village (1922), 112, **113**, 130
Vollmer, Philip, 62, 235n43
Von M., 86, 239n100

W

Warshawsky, Abel George (1883–1962), 156, 171–72
    Poplars near Vernon, Fall (1909), **162**
    Le Vieux Moulin (The Old Mill), Vernon, France (1912), **156**
watercolor, 86
Wendt, William (1865–1946), 29, 30, 129, 149, 246n190
    and plein-air painting, 9, 13, 34, 189
    There Is No Solitude Even in Nature (1906), **188**
White House (c. 1930), **201**, 201
White House Café (Laguna Beach), 195, 200, *202*, 202, 263
    depictions of, **200**, **201**
Whitsen, Mildred, 101

William Baker (1909), 57, **57**, 59
William C. Baker with His Parrot (1907), 57, **57**
William Kleitsch (c. 1910–15), **63**
Wolfson, Sonia, 1, 34, 212, 231n1
Woman at the Well, **42**
Woman Seated in the Garden Sewing, **184**
Woman Sewing, Paris (1926), 170, **171**
Woodruff, John B., 75

The Irvine Museum

BOARD OF TRUSTEES

Joan Irvine Smith
James Irvine Swinden
Russell S. Penniman IV
Morton Irvine Smith
Anita J. Ziebe
Mark S. Ashworth
Paul E. Mosley
Shery Grady
William Batdorf

STAFF

Mr. Jean Stern, *Executive Director*
Merika Adams Gopaul, *Assistant Director*
Christine DeWitt, *Curator of Education*
Judy Thompson, *Coordinator of Visitor Services*
Don E. Bridges, *Bookstore Manager*
Charlett Helm-Pfeiffer, *Receptionist*